TO KNOW A LIBRARY

Other Books by Daniel Gore

Advances in Understanding Approval and Gathering Plans, edited by Peter Spyers-Duran and Daniel Gore. Kalamazoo, Mich.:Western Michigan University, 1970.

Economics of Approval Plans, edited by Peter Spyers-Duran and Daniel Gore. Westport, Conn.: Greenwood Press, 1972.

Bibliography for Beginners, 2nd ed. Englewood Cliffs, N.J.: Prentice Hall, 1973.

Management Problems in Serials Work, edited by Peter Spyers-Duran and Daniel Gore. Westport, Conn.: Greenwood Press, 1974.

Farewell to Alexandria: Solutions to Space, Growth, and Performance Problems of Libraries, edited by Daniel Gore. Westport, Conn.: Greenwood Press, 1976.

TO KNOW A LIBRARY

ESSAYS AND ANNUAL REPORTS, 1970-1976

Daniel Gore _____

Library Director of Macalester College

New Directions in Librarianship, Number 1

GREENWOOD PRESS
Westport, Connecticut • London, England

Library of Congress Cataloging in Publication Data

Gore, Daniel.
   To know a library.

   (New directions in librarianship ; no. 1 ISSN 0147-
1090)
   Includes index.
   1. Library administration—Addresses, essays,
lectures. 2. Library finance—Addresses, essays,
lectures. 3. Libraries, University and college—Addresses, essays, lectures. 4. Macalester College,
St. Paul, Minn. Library. I. Title. II. Series.
Z678.G67   027.7776'581   77-84769
ISBN 0-8371-9881-X

Library of Congress Catalog Card Number: 77-84769
ISBN: 0-8371-9881-X
ISSN: 0147-1090

First published in 1978

Greenwood Press, Inc.
51 Riverside Avenue, Westport, Connecticut 06880

Printed in the United States of America
10 9 8 7 6 5 4 3 2 1

298066

To Jean Archibald and Dorothy Barnes
And all their colleagues on the Macalester Library staff

Contents

TO KNOW A LIBRARY

Introduction

How will libraries prosper—or even survive—in the long period of declining economic support that stretches before them? The question has many answers, speculative in the main and generally unproven.

This volume presents a set of answers, both theoretical and pragmatic, that were developed and tested during the seven lean years of an academic library whose financial woes by chance arrived some years earlier than those now widely experienced in libraries around the nation. The money crisis erupted at Macalester College in 1970, the year I became its library director. Some extravagant but well-meaning miscalculations by the administration (now long since departed) had burdened the college with expensive special programs causing large annual deficits even while strong measures were being taken to trim or remove the programs. The ensuing adverse publicity was commonly thought to be responsible for precipitating a steady decline in enrollment (just recently reversed) and, of course, in tuition income.

From the outset, Macalester College's economic problems appeared to me, an inexpert observer, to be both acute and chronic. If that estimation were correct, then the library would rather quickly have to find some better ways of going about its work. Oratory and exhortation would not produce the money Macalester Library needed to maintain its traditional ways of doing things.

On the other hand, there was no reason to think that the demand for library services would suddenly decline. The college was just reaching the apex of a ten-year faculty and curriculum development program designed to place this century-old institution on an equal footing with the best liberal arts colleges in the nation. The seriousness of that endeavor is demonstrated by the fact that by the late 1960s faculty pay scales at Macalester had become competitive nationally and placed a strong first in Minnesota. Most of the faculty had their doctorates, and an unusually large proportion of them were (and are) actively engaged in research and writing projects. Like themselves, the students they attracted to Macalester were (and are) diligent scholars and vigorous users of the library—even on fine spring days, raising a profound wonder why they are not all outdoors, dallying along the Mississippi River banks just down the road from the campus. In 1974-1975, 8.3 percent of the students were National Merit scholars, thereby putting Macalester in third place nationally, behind Harvard (with 8.8 percent) and Yale (with 8.5 percent). In 1975-1976, Macalester's debate teams placed first in the National Sweepstakes Award for colleges up to 9,000 enrollment, and in four of the last six years they were first among colleges with under 3,000 enrollment. A solid indicator of the students' use of the library and its services is the per capita loan rate: it remains consistent at the level of about forty items per year, or roughly double the rate reported at Macalester's six sister colleges in the Twin Cities, all of them old and substantial liberal arts colleges.

My guesses about Macalester's library problems proved correct in both respects: demand for library service remained high, and funding for the library sank low and lower. Dr. Johnson opined that the prospect of being hanged in the near future "wonderfully concentrates the mind." So does, for me, the prospect of being daily beset by clamorous calls for service that cannot be provided because the requisite funds were withdrawn—never mind by whom. People who want a book are rarely satisfied by a fiscal excuse, however plausible, for not providing it.

Equally worrisome to me was the prospect of having to dismiss staff peremptorily as the economic climate worsened. One clear route of escape from that misfortune would be routinely to leave unfilled positions that were voluntarily vacated and to make promotions from within. This was the course of action the library decided to take, long before the college-wide series of emergency layoffs began. In the first four years of the crisis, eleven library positions (of an original twenty-four) were canceled without layoffs. In the fifth year, the college administration instructed us to cancel two more positions. Here our only alternative was to lay off two people—but only two, and not the thirteen who would have been dismissed had we waited for an administrative mandate to begin carrying out staff reductions.

Having eleven people do the same job that formerly took twenty-four naturally requires many changes in the ways things are done, and in individual work assignments. Promoting from within may lead to some unusual (but highly productive) mismatches between credentials and assignments, as when, for example, an exceptionally able clerk with a high school diploma is made head of the circulation department.

Adjustments in objectives, procedures, and individual achievements abound when a staff is reduced by more than half. To keep track of them myself and keep the campus informed of the many changes in the library—and the reasons for them—I decided to write somewhat fuller annual reports than may be customary. I also sought to write them in a style that would invite rather than repel reading. The contributions of our calligrapher and illustrator, Judith Anne Duncan, to the typescript reports go far to relieve them of the dreary aspect such things ordinarily bear. So much so that, although Greenwood Press offered to have the reports set typographically here, I chose to reproduce them in their original form just to show what liveliness a touch of mature art can add to an otherwise unlovely piece of typewritten text.

Presenting the reports exactly as they first appeared will also give the careful reader a special pleasure in detecting occasional discrepancies of fact that meticulous editing would obliterate and in witnessing certain prophetic shots that in the passage of time fell wide of the mark.

Most of the essays that precede the reports have been published separately elsewhere. I bring them together here as a body of theory from which, largely, the practical results spelled out in the reports derive. Theoretical work is always—and rightly—subject to the reservation that until tested by reality its principal value may be the entertainment it provides. Macalester offered me unusually broad opportunities (or necessities) both to create theory and put it to the test instantly. As with Russian novelists, the worse things are the better they are. The situation was too dire to permit much delay or distraction by faculty or other committees, and the campus was too preoccupied with the strife and confusion spawned by the budgetary crisis to fret about the library as long as its condition was improving. Hence, we enjoyed extraordinary freedom to try out virtually anything we wished, the main restriction being that we do it within the perimeter of an ever-shrinking budget. In such a circumstance, one is not tempted to experiment with measures that would require increased budget support. Accordingly, this work says little about computers, but much about the better use of human resources, and something too about the value of thought and imagination in settling the problems of financially pressed libraries. This is not to say that the use of computers in libraries is a bad thing, but that the *experimental* use of them in a situation of diminishing support might prove a disastrous folly. And in the period covered here, nearly all use of computers in libraries was still experimental, and associated budget fiascos were commonplace.

What we attempted, we accomplished. I half wish there were at least a few minor failures to lend added verisimilitude to the reports. Having said that, I suddenly realize there was indeed one major failure, though not of accomplishment. It was a failure of strategy, brought on by my ignorance (in 1970) of Richard Trueswell's theories of collection use, of which much is said elsewhere in this volume. Despite our dwindling budget, immediately upon my arrival at Macalester we set out to reclass the 82,000 volumes still in the Dewey portion of the collections. After the reclassification was completed, I realized that at least half the effort was pure waste: since at least half of those Dewey volumes had such a low probability of ever being borrowed again, they might better have been consigned directly to a storage collection, with the Dewey call number conveniently serving as a sufficient indicator of storage status.

Our main library building (named Weyerhaeuser) was built in 1942. It was added to in 1960 in order to reach a total usable area of about 30,000 square feet, and by 1968 it was said to have reached maximum design capacity. In 1965 a small branch science library (Olin) was opened, and in 1975 it reached maximum capacity. An on-campus storage facility was provided in 1968 as a short-term emergency measure until a new main library could be provided. A full-scale building planning effort was undertaken in

MACALESTER LIBRARY FACT SHEET, 1970-1977

	1970-1971	1971-1972	1972-1973	1973-1974	1974-1975	1975-1976	1976-1977
College funds budgeted	$292,500	$255,000	$253,000	$251,900	$242,030	$195,956	$225,347
College funds spent (net)	264,259*	242,807	252,700	248,139	224,944	194,321	228,571
Staff positions (FTE)	24	17 1/2	15 3/4	14 1/2	13	11 1/6	11
Student help (in hours)	29,387	22,622	22,245	22,029	18,985	19,728	22,226
Acquisitions (value in dollars)	$108,658	$130,388	$134,469	$131,120	$104,588	$81,151	$104,370
Circulation	88,022*	88,509	77,134	80,860	76,354	73,071	73,159
Interlibrary loans received	3,399	3,442	3,041	3,335	3,287	3,126	3,467
Interlibrary loans made	438	1,017	983	1,490	1,712	2,172	2,246
Enrollment (headcount)	2,093	2,097	2,012	1,878	1,748	1,676	1,637
Loans per capita (including faculty)	41.5	41.6	37.7	42.1	43.5	42.5	41.7
Volumes cataloged	11,094	8,298	10,911	11,565	9,903	8,356	6,848
Volumes reclassified	25,923	26,778	24,891	4,303	255	73	45
Volumes in collection (at year's end)	218,000	231,000	241,300	255,600	265,000	270,000	275,200
Hours open per week	101	101	101	101	101	101	101

*Adjusted to comparable base with succeeding years.

(All data exclude the audio-visual department, which became administratively a part of the library in 1972.)

1968, involving a team of consultants, an aggressive planning committee, and numerous hearings and surveys. It yielded a 150-page planning document and nothing else—not even a formal resolve to seek funds for a new building. A second effort in 1973 produced no planning document, nor any wish to dust off and use the earlier one. The trustees did endorse a fundraising campaign for a new library building, but tne campaign was launched just as the tide of capital funding was receding nationally. Thus, once again the project was left high and dry.

The steadily worsening prospects for a new library building naturally prompted my curiosity about the feasibility of a no-growth collection. While we have not yet achieved that condition, it may be the sole option open to us five years hence. We feel no anxiety about having to exercise it when the time arrives, as the data we are gathering on collection use simply add further confirmation to the correctness of the basic no-growth theory. Operational and procedural questions associated with the no-growth model remain to be answered, of course, and only the test of experience can provide reliable answers. The advent of the COM catalog and of economical systems of computerized circulation brings us much closer to those answers today than we were several years ago, when I first began to speculate on measures for achieving a fully satisfactory no-growth library operation.

The optimistic theme that threads its way through this volume is that by vigorous pruning and much loving care a library can be made to yield better fruit, and ampler too, in its lean years than in its fat ones. As you follow the many variations on that theme in the essays and reports, you will come to know a library that has prospered through years of heavy weather. To know a library under any circumstances is ordinarily no easy thing, so numerous and various are its moving parts, and so complicated are their relationships to each other. Even when we get a general picture of *what* is going on in a library's operations, rarely do we get a glimpse of *why* it is just so and not otherwise. My aim here is to bring theory and practice together in a way that will allow the reader to see beneath the surface of things and to get to know a library as a complex but unified organism, nourished and supported by an underlying root system of ideas.

A book of this kind comes from the work of many people. That is why it is dedicated to the library staff of Macalester College, whose splendid accomplishments are celebrated in the reports. For permission to publish the library's annual reports, I extend my special thanks to Dr. John B. Davis, Jr., president of Macalester College since 1975 and, we devoutly wish, for many years to come.

Most of the essays published here have been delivered as addresses at professional meetings around the country. Although they are too numerous for personal identification, I am particularly grateful to the people who invited me to speak before their organizations, thus prodding me to do work that my native indolence would otherwise have allowed me to leave undone.

In Hot Pursuit
of FASTCAT

Let me start with a proposition we can all agree on: The availability of Library of Congress catalog copy is intolerably slow, even if we buy it in proofslip format or on magnetic tapes produced by the Machine Readable Cataloging project. The latter format—MARC tapes—appears to have carried us about as far as we can hope to go in the speedy transmission of cataloging data. But it has contributed almost nothing to solving the problem of reducing lag time between a book's publication date and the availability of LC copy. It is foolish to hope it ever will, because the problem is not, and never was, one of increasing the speed of transmitting catalog data. The problem is—or appears to be—one of increasing the speed of *creating* catalog data. And with that problem the MARC project has virtually nothing to do, any more than the Western Union Office has to do with the speedy composition of your telegram. If it takes you six months to compose your message, no technology on earth will accomplish the delivery of it in less than six months from the day you started to write it.

Now let me advance a proposition on which we will almost certainly disagree, since nothing stimulates productive thought more readily than active disagreement on matters of serious concern. My proposition is this: That the problem of cataloging delays, properly understood, is almost wholly one of our own making, much as we like to lay it on the cataloging department at the Library of Congress; and if we sincerely wish to solve that problem, we must stop casting baleful glances in the direction of Washington, and start looking for the solution in our own libraries.

For seventy years we have lamented the cataloging delays at LC, and for seventy years we have offered LC an endless stream of wonderfully good advice on how it can solve our problem for us. And at the end of seventy years, the problem is still with us. The only difference is that it is much worse than it used to be because increased accession rates have increased our cataloging backlogs.

Many of you have probably read, in recent months, Daniel Melcher's latest loading-on of good advice for the catalogers at LC. Establish strict priorities for cataloging new imprints; tighten up production schedules and put the processing operation "on daily newspaper schedules"; improve the layout of LC card order forms, and so on.[1] "Ideally," Melcher says at the outset of his thrust at LC, "a set of catalog cards should arrive with or before the book." But by the end he concludes that the ideal is hopeless of attainment, and he recommends enormously expensive temporary cataloging procedures as the only recourse for the local library. I will go one step further than Melcher and propose that the ideal is not only unattainable: it is false. For my own part, I would not care if cataloging delays at the Library of Congress were twice their present magnitude. For their cataloging schedules are already a good deal better than they need to be for my purposes. If they slow 'er down, I will not even notice it—nor will my cataloging staff at Macalester, nor the students and faculty who insist on prompt access to new books. And if they speed 'er up, they will get no special thanks from me, because, as I said, their cataloging schedules are just fine the way they are, thanks to a rather new breed of animal called the FASTCAT.

I don't know if Marvin Scilken of the Orange Public Library, New Jersey, would be flattered to hear himself identified as the father of a FASTCAT, but I think he would. In any event it won't take a paternity suit to settle the matter. Just read Scilken's delightful essay on the cataloging frontlog in LJ, September 15, 1969, and you will see that the FASTCAT (though not mentioned by name) is indeed his offspring. Without going further into the mysteries of the FASTCAT's phylogeny, I will tell you something of his features, lineaments, and prodigious prowess. Essentially, what he does is speed up your cataloging process by slowing it down; he eliminates the need for subscribing to LC proofslips or MARC tapes, or for ordering LC cards or typing your own; and the FASTCAT makes it possible to put new books in circulation the same day they arrive in the library—or the day after, if your staff prefers to move at a stately pace.

Here's how it works. At the time a new book is ordered, you assign it an order number whose first element is an alphabetic code corresponding to the broad LC classification division that the book falls into. A book ordered for the psychology department gets an order number beginning BF; for the English department, PR; for the math department, QA; and so on. Nothing very precise, of course, and no time wasted on the frills and fripperies of classification. The other element of the order number is a straightforward serial number within each subject class, so the first book ordered for psychology has the order number BF1, the second book ordered for psychology is BF2, and the twenty-fifth book ordered for math is QA25.

When the order is placed, the stiff copy of the order slip is filed in the public catalog—in the title section if you have a divided catalog, or anywhere you like if you don't, since everything gets lost in a dictionary catalog anyhow.

Then you wait for the book to arrive. When it does, your acquisitions people retrieve the order slip from their file and type the order number on a call number label with the word FASTCAT on top of it. So the first book you buy for psychology will get the call number FASTCAT BF1 labeled on its spine the day it reaches the library. On the same day, that book will be shelved in a special collection in your main reading room, prominently located where all will see it, and where all may borrow any book that lands there.

After a while, your FASTCAT will grow into a fatcat, a splendid browsing collection comprising all the new books received by the library during the past six or twelve months. The collection will be subdivided into perhaps twenty-five or thirty broad subject areas to facilitate browsing, so even a collection of 10,000 or 15,000 FASTCAT books will pose no formidable problem to the serious browser. Every new book will be available for loan to him a day or so after the library gets it, and he can see with his own eyes every new book the library acquires, instead of depending on some dreary monthly accessions list, or the whim of a librarian who chooses one book out of twenty to display briefly on a "New Book Shelf."

For purposes of catalog access to the FASTCAT collection, when a new book comes in you go to the title catalog where you filed that stiff copy order slip and attach an adhesive label to it reading "Book received; inquire at Circulation Desk." For the occasional patron who does that, your desk attendant goes to the title catalog, looks at the order slip, and copies down the order number—which he knows from the presence of the adhesive label has now become a FASTCAT call number, and so informs the patron who can now go to the FASTCAT collection and fetch the book for himself.

Consider for a moment what the FASTCAT has done for you. He swallows whole your entire cataloging backlog; turns it into a frontlog, as Scilken calls it. He makes a request for rush cataloging seem ludicrous; in fact, where the FASTCAT exists, nobody will even think of asking for rush cataloging. He creates a continuous exhibit of new books in all subject areas. He gets new books to your patrons while they're still so new that even your catalogers haven't read them. And he lets you sit back and relax for six months, a year, or longer if need be, for the catalogers at the Library of Congress to create catalog copy for your new books.

Let people like Daniel Melcher sweat and chafe about LC's tardiness, as they nervously eye their growing backlogs in the catalog workroom. Let them explain to the faculty for the thousandth time that Washington's to blame for the holdup. And let them send more and more books through rush cataloging when, for the thousandth time, the fire in the professor's eye burns no lower after he hears the Washington business again. After all, what he wants is the book—not your plausible explanation of why he and his students can't have it, even though it has been in the library for months. The FASTCAT gets the book for him, while the bluster about Washington just gets boring.

Trying to push LC around is like trying to shove a pyramid out of your path. If it gets in your way, try running around it. That's exactly what you do with the FASTCAT: run around the problem while others bang their heads against it.

And while you're running around it, the books *are* getting cataloged at LC, plenty fast for your purposes, though never fast enough to suit folks like Daniel Melcher. When the catalog copy is finally created, you don't have to use such costly devices as proofslip files, MARC tapes, or special orders for card sets to get at the data. All you need is a subscription to NUC, a Minolta Enlarger-Plus photocopier,[2] and a Xerox machine.

Here's how you go about it. Let your FASTCAT books age for six months, a year, or whatever seems right to you. Then remove from the FASTCAT collection those books that have aged the proper time. How do you tell a properly aged FASTCAT from a very recent one—one so newly received that I shall call it a FASTKITTEN? Remember what I said about the FASTCAT number being a straight serial sequence within any subject class? All right. Then the books with the lowest order number are your oldest FASTCATS, while those with the highest are the FASTKITTENS. This being so, it is a simple matter for your catalogers to determine which groups of FASTCATS have aged the requisite period, remove them from the shelves, and search them in a good fat cumulation of NUC volumes. With a little experience, the catalogers will establish aging periods calculated to yield say 80 or 90 percent LC copy on first search, so repeat searches will be negligible.

When copy is found in NUC, it is blown up directly on the Minolta Enlarger-Plus (an ordinary electrostatic photocopier with direct enlargement capability) to standard catalog card dimensions. The Minolta copy is inserted in the book at hand (no matchup problem) and forwarded to the cataloger, who then uses it almost exactly as one would use proofslip copy: adjustments are made directly on the Minolta copy as necessary; a call number is added; and the Minolta copy is then used as the master from which card sets are printed on the Xerox machine. Total production costs for a six-card set come to about eight cents, including labor and the costs of Minolta and Xerox copy (assuming you run eight-up Permec copy on the Xerox 714 or 914).

The book is ordinarily out of circulation no more than two days while going through the cataloging procedure. If catalog copy is not found in the NUC, the book is immediately returned to FASTCAT and is allowed to age quietly another six months, while catalogers and library directors around the country grow old before their time, frantically pleading for drastic improvement in production schedules at LC.

As you keep returning to the FASTCAT collection the occasional book that has no LC copy even after a year or so, you will eventually develop a small pride of hoary old patriarchs that LC just never did get around to cataloging. Let them age some more until the paper turns brittle and finally disintegrates. Then throw them out. That way you won't ever have to do any custom cataloging, and your patrons will still have the use of these old curiosities for as long as they last. Under the conventional system, they would instead disintegrate back in your catalog workroom, where your backlog becomes backsawdust if you don't keep an eye on it.

Don't worry if your acquisitions and catalog departments have to serve a dozen or more branch libraries on campus as well as the main library. The order slip will show which branch gets the book. When it comes in, send it to the FASTCAT collection in that branch. A year or so later, bring it back to the main library for a day or two, catalog it, and return it.

The FASTCAT is a particularly handy animal for libraries that receive books on an approval plan. Since those books typically reach the library months earlier than they would if conventionally ordered, the effect is to exacerbate the problem of cataloging backlogs. The sooner the book reaches the library, the longer it gets to wait in the workroom for catalog copy. With FASTCAT, the virtue of early receipt remains the virtue it was intended by the dealer to be: the book gets to the borrower much sooner than conventionally ordered books do.

Combining the virtues of approval plans with those of the FASTCAT, I find that in the Macalester College Library new books reach the borrower on an average one year sooner than they do at a neighboring college of the same size, which uses neither approval plan nor FASTCAT. And the total processing costs are substantially lower.

Patron pleasure in the FASTCAT collection has been so obvious over the last two school years that, even if catalog cards were available with every new book *at the time we acquired it*, we would still send that book for at least a six-month sojourn on the FASTCAT shelves. How else could our readers ever *see* the whole of our recent acquisitions? How ever would we have thought of offering them such a splendid service, had LC cataloging schedules not forced us—but first Marvin Scilken—to do some thinking? Sweet are the uses of adversity.

NOTES

1. Daniel Melcher, *Melcher on Acquisition* (Chicago: American Library Association, 1971), pp. 127-134.

2. Other manufacturers are beginning to market photocopiers that enlarge. Two that I know of are Olivetti and the elusive Xerox 1-2-3.

POSTSCRIPT (1977)

Macalester expects to have a COM catalog of its library collections in operation by January 1978. Although we have not yet had any experience with
feeding current cataloging data into the vendor's computer, it now appears
that the FASTCAT procedure will be as useful in that process as it has been
thus far in the production of a card catalog. The reason is that at the time
we send catalog data for an individual title to the COM vendor's computer,
we will not have available an LC call number to assign to the book—which, in
the absence of FASTCAT, would have to be held in the workroom until the
next update from the vendor arrived. Even at that time, the update might
not contain a MARC record for the title, thereby causing further delay. Thus,
at the time catalog data are sent to the vendor, we will include a FASTCAT
call number, send the book immediately to the FASTCAT shelves, and routinely wait about eighteen months (as we do now) before completing the
cataloging process. By that time, of course, the vendor's data base will predictably contain MARC data for virtually all the FASTCATs in question, just
as NUC presently does. From the patron's standpoint, the principal difference with COM/FASTCAT is that during a book's FASTCAT phase patrons will
have several points of COM catalog access to it (author, title, subject), whereas
presently we provide only title access.

   A special virtue of FASTCAT that was not fully appreciated in its early years
is the great temporal flexibility it allows in staff levels. On occasions when
temporary or even permanent redistributions of work are necessary (ma-
ternity leave, sick leave, short-notice resignations, delays in recruiting student staff, and the like), the regular cataloging process can be virtually
suspended (for many months if need be); books will simply go to the FASTCAT
shelves and stay there until the staffing situation has been comfortably
resolved. When a temporary excess of staff time is available, it can conveniently be used to trim the size of the FASTCAT collection by permanently
cataloging old FASTCATs faster than new ones arrive. FASTCAT is the functional equivalent of a water reservoir, keeping total flowage regular even
through drought or flood.

Books Versus Janitors, or Where Do You Want to Spend Library Funds in the Twenty-first Century?

Last March, I was invited to speak on the topic of what the library world will be like in the year 2000—a prophetic assignment for which I suppose I am as poorly qualified as the next person. I am no prophet, and some of my colleagues regard me as a total loss. But the invitation was too intriguing to turn down, so I accepted it. Prudently, I let six months pass before drafting my text, so that the prophetic distance to the year 2000 would not be quite so long as it was last March.

Rather than spin out some fanciful prophetic vision of what computers and information specialists may be doing at the start of the next millenium, I have decided to confine myself to a topic of much greater import to the library profession, one that has a mathematical inevitability about it that makes prophecy almost as certain as history. The topic is janitorial and other service costs, and the influence I believe they will have on library architecture by the year 2000. My approach will be somewhat round about, and I hope you will not be made uncomfortable by the suspense of waiting to hear what I will eventually get around to saying on the really astonishing subject of janitors.

This paper was presented on October 23, 1971, to the General Session of the North Dakota Library Association's Annual Convention and is published here for the first time. Although written seven years ago, the paper presents views on compact shelving with which I still agree. But its theoretical arguments against weeding I have since disavowed. I let them stand as originally presented as an illustration of one of the special charms of theory: its refutability. All cost figures should be increased by about 70 percent to allow for inflationary effects since 1971. But the ratios between building, shelving, and maintenance costs have held fairly constant, and it is those ratios that are the critical issue in the economic case for compact shelving.

There is a grandiose absurdity in all contemporary academic library architecture that usually goes unnoticed, because its extraordinary economic consequences never show up directly in a library's operating budget nor categorically in the general operating budget of a college. I am talking about the wasteful use of space in library buildings, and more specifically, about the wasteful use of space in those portions of the building where the books are kept.

Perhaps I will disappoint you in talking prophetically about books and bookstacks in the twenty-first century. I know it is the fashion among library prophets today to speak of the library of the future as a building no longer burdened with books, but chock full of other things that presumably we will like much better—things like transistors, spaghetti piles of electric circuitry, and the cool unwinking eye of cathode ray tubes.

But there was a time—and not very long ago either, several decades at the most—when the fashionable prophets proclaimed that by the 1970s most of our collections would be displaced by microfilm, the sure and certain solution for all library space problems from now until kingdom come. The prophecy remains unfulfilled, and anybody who gave ten minutes of real thought to the problem twenty years ago could have told us why.

The central reason is strictly economical and arises from the fact that most libraries serve large numbers of people who read library books in some place other than the library. Not so with microfilm. With rare exceptions, the microfilm reader reads it in the library, using costly reading equipment and taking up valuable library space while he uses it.

As an illustration, assume a collection of 200,000 volumes serving 5,000 readers. Put that collection on microfilm at today's reduction ratios of 100 to 1, and the space required to house it becomes virtually zero, instead of the 13,000 square feet of stack space required for the original format. Marvelous! At today's (1971) construction costs of about $25 per square foot, you've saved yourself a third of a million dollars.

But wait a minute. Something was overlooked, wasn't it? Yes, now that we've put the whole collection on microfilm, we're going to have to provide a lot of reading machines for people to use it. How many? Well, let's be conservative and provide one machine for every five readers, or a thousand machines for 5,000 registered borrowers. Well, a thousand first-rate machines at $500 apiece comes to half a million dollars—more than the sum you thought you had saved in construction costs. And the bills for your prophetic dream are just beginning to come in. For each of these thousand reading machines, you must also provide a thousand desks and a thousand tables, so add another $100,000 to the tab. Then you will have to provide about 30 square feet of floor space for each reading station, or 30,000 square feet in all, and that costs you another $750,000. So your bargain has already cost you a million dollars more than the obsolete model it replaced, and the big bills haven't even started to come in—bills for machine maintenance, light bulb replacements, and, yes, janitorial services.

It is small wonder then that microfilm never really caught on the way the prophets said it would. We simply can't afford it. Besides, there were still the awful problems of legibility, microfilm measles, and difficulty in using this retrograde format of the book, this throwback to the ancient scroll that was displaced in the fifth century by the infinitely superior codex form of the book.

Just within the last year (1971), however, gains have been made in microtechnology that may eliminate most and perhaps all of the difficulties I have cited. The economic problem is possibly resolved with the development of a low-cost portable microfilm reader (weighing 5 pounds) that enables borrowers to read film in their own homes, without preempting large segments of library space for reading machines. Legibility appears to be at the acceptable level; and with the new high-reduction ratios, a thousand printed pages can be placed on one 3 × 5 fiche, so a complete book can be scanned on a single sheet, almost as conveniently as in its original codex format.

Even with these vast improvements in microtechnology, I am unwilling to revive the old prophecy of replacing book collections with microfiche libraries. While the new-model microfiche holds some promise for solving a part of a library's space problems, it cannot solve the whole problem unless it displaces the codex book as the standard carrier of printed text. The likelihood of that ever happening still seems remote, for over the last 1,700 years the codex (or leaf) format has exhibited that same characteristic of unimprovable excellence which, in mechanics, we ascribe to the wheel.

Although it is highly probable that hundreds of thousands, even millions, of earlier printed books may hereafter be held by libraries only on microfiche, current publications will continue to be acquired in typographic format (trade publishers offer them in no other). Once acquired, they will remain in the library for at least fifty years, taking up a thousand times the space of microfiche equivalents.

Copyright law explains the protracted delay in future availability of microfiche replacements. For example, "The Library of American Civilization," a 20,000-volume, new-model microfiche collection currently offered by Encyclopaedia Britannica, contains only books published before 1915 and therefore in the public domain. The cost of permissions to reprint later works still under copyright protection makes microreproduction uneconomical; hence, the continuing need for libraries (all other considerations aside) to maintain very substantial collections in typographic format.

Furthermore, many useful books in the public domain may never be marketed by micropublishers. Many others, regardless of age, will be in such heavy demand that only the most legible format will be acceptable: the original typographic book.

Reading editions of Shakespeare and Sophocles may always be wanted in book form. And who will want to curl up in bed with *Wuthering Heights* tucked in a microfiche reader—even a portable one—in his lap?

Following these lines of reasoning, I conclude that the codex book will still be very much with us in the year 2,000, and that every library will have proportionately more of them to store by then than it does today. While microfiche may in fact have some braking effect on growth rates, no sign of anything like a halt is in prospect. I think, then, that we will all be compelled to turn our attention to a problem we have thus far treated only as a side issue at best: the problem of shelving more typographic books in less space.

During the 1960s, library construction flourished in this country as never before, thanks mainly to the availability of federal funding on an unprecedented scale. Thousands of new libraries, public and academic, sprang up throughout the nation, many of them architectural *tours de force,* exhibiting the most astonishing variety of design and decoration. The architectural freaks and fancies of these new libraries dazzle us with their seemingly endless diversity.

But all the new building designs have this one dismal feature in common: the problem of increasing the efficiency of book storage was systematically ignored, even though book production was expanding faster than new library space. Architects thought mainly about balconies, stairwells, and facades, while librarians thought mainly about furniture, carpeting, and ornamental plants. So all those handsome new libraries of the 1960s might just as well have been built in the 1920s, as far as the technology of housing books is concerned.

Even as far back as the 1920s, librarians had come to realize that the old cry of "more space, more space" to house growing collections could not be heeded forever. For collections that had historically doubled once every century were beginning to double every twenty years, and the prospect of doubling every decade had come clearly in view. On the day when a new and vastly enlarged library building was dedicated, some librarians found themselves in the embarrassing position of having to confide to their boards, over glasses of champagne, that the time was at hand to begin the planning and fund raising for a new and vastly enlarged library building. As the information explosion pushed them ever closer to the frontiers of absurdity, librarians began to explore ways to retreat from the frontier without in fact calling a halt to collection growth.

The solution of subtracting from the collection one book for each book added appears to be no solution at all. Philosophically, it amounts to denying that history is continuous, cumulative, and purposeful: to affirming the

Eastern vision of history as endlessly repetitive and circular. Any civilization that resorts to bronzing its babies' bootees will obviously resist any effort to discard the significant records of its past. And that, I think, is why most efforts at the wholesale weeding of library collections are doomed at the outset.

Weeding is not the answer. Neither is the commonplace solution of forming storage collections remote from the main library—"outhousing" as the English aptly call it. In the long run, both weeding and storage cost even more than new and larger buildings. (The COM catalog and automated inventory control now (1977) promise to reverse the economic relationship that existed in 1971. Development of cooperative storage facilities that can simply discard multiple copies flowing in from many libraries will substantially reduce the real estate costs of book storage.) They only buy a little time, at great expense. And microfilm, as I have explained, offers no broad-scale solution either.

What then is the answer for the twenty-first century? I will tell you as a prophet who has beheld our salvation with his own eyes, and not in a vision either. I saw it this time a year ago (i.e., 1970) in a small public library in the little town of Watertown, Wisconsin. When I saw it, I had the irresistible conviction that I was looking through a window at the library of the twenty-first century, even though what I saw had already been there (though no-where else on earth, I believe) for ten years.

What I saw was an open-access, heavily used circulating library collection, catering to all ages, shelved in compact stacks of the type we have all been led to believe are suitable only for storage of rarely used, closed-access research collections. The experience had for me the force of a mystical revelation; it made a believer of me. That is why I am willing to speak as a prophet today, prophesying the widespread use of compact shelving in all kinds of libraries in the twenty-first century. Economic pressures, if nothing else, will force us in that direction.

Most of you already know something about compact shelving, but let me tell you some of the things it can do.

First, it cuts stack space requirements in half. How? Essentially by eliminating a high percentage of the space wasted in the aisles of conventional stacks. Conventional bookstacks occupy about one-third of a stack floor, while the aisles take up two-thirds. With compact shelving the proportions are reversed: two-thirds for bookstacks and one-third for aisles, thus doubling conventional stack capacities.

How does compact shelving work? Two types are presently in general use for storage collections: rail-mounted and sliding-drawer. Rail-mounted stacks look like conventional ones but are mounted on rails so that they can be rolled together to eliminate all aisles but one between the stacks. Electric motors are used to move the stacks and open up an aisle where access is desired. Such installations are extremely costly, obviously difficult to use, and potentially dangerous (at least one fatality has been documented). Hence, they have no place in any actively used collection; they are in fact somewhat less efficient in saving storage space than the sliding-drawer compacts.

Drawer compacts of the type I saw in the Watertown Public Library resemble giant steel filing cabinets. The drawers are 4 feet deep and 2 feet wide, with the face of the drawer removed. Books are shelved along either side of the drawer and along its open face. One aisle 4 feet wide gives access to a bank of 4-foot drawers on either side, so 4 feet of aisle space is required for 8 feet of shelf depth. Hence the ratio of one-third stack area for aisles to two-thirds for shelving.

Since 1 linear shelf foot of drawer compacts naturally costs a good deal more than 1 shelf foot of conventional shelving, the economies of using it are not immediately apparent. A simple theoretical example will show where part of the economies arise. Assume a stack area of 1,000 square feet. In this area, we can install conventional stacks with a total of 2,000 lineal feet of shelving. A lineal foot of conventional shelving costs about $2.40, so we have $4,800 worth of shelving in a stack area costing $25,000 (1,000 square feet times $25 per square foot construction cost). So the *total* cost for these 2,000 lineal feet of shelving is $29,800, or $15 per lineal foot using conventional stacks.

Using drawer compacts, we can get not 2,000 but 4,000 lineal feet of shelving in the same 1,000 square foot building area. Compact shelving costs about $4.20 per lineal foot—nearly twice the cost of conventional shelving; therefore, 4,000 lineal feet of compacts will cost nearly $17,000. Add this to the building cost of $25,000, and the *total* cost for 4,000 feet of shelving is $42,000, or $10.50 per lineal foot as compared with a cost of $15 per lineal foot using conventional stacks.

It thus appears that by using compacts we can reduce capital costs (building plus shelving) by nearly 33 percent in the stack portions of the building. While this economy takes on great significance when we talk in terms of capital outlays amounting to hundreds of thousands or millions of dollars, it pales into insignificance when we place it beside the attendant savings in janitorial and utility costs.

I said at the outset that janitorial and related costs lay at the heart of my prophecy, and now you will see why. I also said something about the grandiose absurdity in contemporary library architecture going unnoticed because its economic consequences don't show up in our operating budgets, at least in academic libraries. Now you will see what I was driving at.

The average annual cost of providing janitors, heating, cooling, and lighting for a library building is about $1 per square foot. Build yourself a library of 100,000 square feet, and you can be sure of spending $100,000 every year from now on just to keep it clean, warm, and well lighted—even though the expenditure doesn't show up in your operating budget.

The other day I attended the dedication of an exquisitely beautiful new college library building, aesthetically the finest one could wish for. I covet that building, and I envy the librarians and students who will draw daily pleasure just from being in it. It is 100,000 square feet in area, and everyone is proud of its vast size and spectacular beauty. But I do not envy the president who will have to pay the service bill of $100,000 that will come in every year from now on, especially when he stops to think that at the present time—before any part of that bill falls due—he can afford to spend only $25,000 a year for books and periodicals to go in that gorgeous, costly building. Perhaps he will have to sacrifice the books altogether just to keep that building clean and warm. Perhaps if the librarians had been better informed of the true total costs of operating the library, they would have sought some way to get more books in less space. Just think: had they found a way to cut the building size by only a fourth—and I believe they could have—the president would save enough money to double the book budget, instead of having to worry, as he may be doing now, about having to cut back on the little he can now afford to spend on books.

Let's go back now and reconsider the economic benefits of compact shelving in terms of building maintenance and utility costs. Assume a stack area large enough to hold a million volumes. Using conventional stacks, you will need at least 70,000 square feet and will have to spend $70,000 every year on maintenance and utilities. Using compact shelving, you will need only 35,000 square feet and will spend $35,000 a year on maintenance and utilities. Over a fifty-year period (the usual life span of a library building), you will spend $1.7 million *more* just to maintain your collection in conventional stacks, having already spent about a third of a million dollars more in the capital costs of construction and stacks. How can you afford to spend so much money unnecessarily on janitors and utilities when you never have enough money to spend on books and librarians? The answer is that you never thought you had the opportunity to do anything else.

For while compact shelving has been rather widely used in closed-access storage collections, authorities on the subject have steadfastly maintained that compact shelving is suitable only for closed-access storage collections. In his comprehensive treatise, *The Economics of Book Storage* (Scarecrow Press, 1965), Ralph Ellsworth does not even entertain the possibility of using compact shelving in live, open collections. In Rogers' and Weber's just published *University Library Administration,* if you consult the index under "Compact Shelving," you find a cross-reference reading "See Storage collections." Like Ralph Ellsworth, they won't even think about using compacts for anything but storage collections.

Why? Well, they don't tell us. But here are two reasons given me last year on a brief tour of compact installations in Wisconsin. One librarian told me that drawer compacts are bad because when a patron opens a drawer, he blocks passage through the aisle. I tried this theory out and found that the passing maneuver is in fact easier than in a conventional stack aisle. For the aisle width is 50 percent greater than in conventional stacks, and by momentarily closing a drawer part way, one easily clears an ample passageway for another person. In conventional stacks, something like a waltz step is required to afford passage.

The other reason given was that drawer compacts present a safety hazard. A patron absentmindedly leaves a drawer open and someone else absentmindedly bumps into it. Nonsense. Properly designed compacts have a slight down slope to the drawers, so they never fail to close automatically.

The librarian of the Watertown Public Library told me that in ten years of using the compacts as the standard shelving unit, there have been no injuries nor any observable inconvenience to patrons. In very large collections, one should also take into account the specific gain in convenience of having to walk only half the usual distance to find the books one wants to see.

The case for compact shelving is certainly far from proved in the single instance of its use in Watertown, Wisconsin. If it were proved, I would, of course, be speaking as a historian, not a prophet. So in keeping to the terms of my prophetic assignment, I have deliberately taken an issue that is speculative and, in a certain measure, unpredictable in its outcome.

Should the typographic book in fact cease to be the standard carrier of art and knowledge by the twenty-first century—should it be displaced by microfiche, electronic storage, or some other technology still beyond our horizon—then the pressures presently driving us toward compact shelving techniques will be removed, and our present concern with shelving problems will appear as a very minor incident in the history of library technology.

Few of us, however, will have the luxury of waiting until the next millennium to make up our minds about the ultimate fate of the typographic book. We have to plan new library buildings on one assumption or the other. Despite the enthusiastic prophecies we have heard of the approaching demise of the book, everybody who plans a new library building plainly does so on the assumption that books are here to stay and that there will be even more of them tomorrow than there were yesterday. Since that is the only responsible assumption on which we can base our planning, I think we are bound to assume that the growing problem of housing book collections will compel us to experiment more boldly than in the past with new solutions to that ancient problem. The librarian of the Watertown Public Library has shown the way, and I for one mean to follow it whenever the opportunity arises. Not that I have any particular desire to put janitors out of work. I would just rather spend library funds to the fullest extent possible on books and librarians, and to the least extent necessary on janitors and utilities. The Watertown Public Library knows better than any of us how to do precisely that.

Adopting an Approval Plan for a College Library: The Macalaster College Experience

University libraries moving into approval-plan buying have often done so at a time when large amounts of new money were added to the book budget, permitting approval purchases to be added on top of the customary acquisitions program. Old habits were thus left largely undisturbed: retrospective collection development continued at the usual pace, and departmental allocation of book funds was modified only slightly, if at all. Even under such favorable conditions as these, transition to approval buying may arouse fierce resentments among professors and librarians who cleave to the old myth that only they are truly qualified to select books for their library.

If the transition is made, as we had to make it, at a time when virtually the entire book budget must be committed to approval buying—leaving nothing for retrospective purchases or departmental allocations—one may expect to deal with passions of epic magnitude, unless one can offer some satisfactory options when proposing a moratorium on retrospective buying and departmental allocations.

For a college library of modest size, such as Macalester's (around 200,000 volumes), the only alternative to spending heavily each year on retrospective purchases is to offer the clientele ready and convenient access to someone else's retrospective collection, preferably one that is ten or fifteen times larger, so everyone will perceive the futility of attempting to duplicate it. When that is done, the sense of urgency regarding retrospective buying largely disappears.

Long before the idea of approval buying was hinted at to the Macalester faculty, we installed a courier service to fetch from the libraries of the Uni-

---

First published in *Economics of Approval Plans,* ed. Peter Spyers-Duran and Daniel Gore (Westport, Conn.: Greenwood Press, 1972).

versity of Minnesota any book or journal article that was not available at Macalester. The courier is a staff member who makes a trip to the university libraries regularly five times a week, usually delivering requested items within about twenty-four hours. No charge is made for the service—not even for photocopies of journal articles—and, in some respects, it is even more convenient to use than our own library. Volume of requests is about 400 or 500 items per month, and the success rate appears to be leveling off at around 70 percent. The service proved so popular, and so gratifying—even to those who made no use of it—that when the time came to propose at least a temporary moratorium on retrospective buying, most of the resistance in that area had already evaporated. Where it still persisted, little argument was required to convince holdouts that the courier service in itself accomplished more than several centuries of retrospective buying at our customary levels would do. The option offered was obviously many times better than the one it replaced, while the cost of it is substantially less. Without the courier service, I doubt the faculty would ever have agreed to call a halt—even a temporary one—to retrospective purchasing. Why should they, if that is their only convenient way of access to noncurrent publications?

A solution to the problem of suspending departmental allocations was not so easily arrived at. While most of the department chairmen were willing to experiment with approval buying, and some were even eager to do so, there were several whose resistance remained intractable, since they felt that their departments might receive fewer or less suitable books than in the past if they lost control of their allocations. There was no lessening of resistance when they discovered that, in point of fact, the allocation process had been utterly meaningless in the past, since only one-fifth of the book funds was actually allocated, with the other four-fifths going into what amounted to a librarian's discretionary fund.

While the library committee had strongly endorsed approval buying in principle after hearing presentations by two competing dealers, they had done so with the understanding that no action would be taken until general consent of the department chairmen had been obtained. Given the intransigence of several chairmen, I recommended to the committee that we abandon for the present any orthodox program of approval buying and offer instead an option based on departmental allocations. The specific proposal was this:

1. That the entire book budget be allocated by departments, according to whatever formula or other method the library committee finds appropriate;
2. That a complete approval profile of the college's requirements for current imprints be drawn up;
3. That departments be notified, on the basis of their profiled needs, when books are published that are likely to be of interest to them;

4. That departments may spend all, none, or a portion of their allocated funds to purchase books that match their profiled needs;

5. That when a department's allocated funds have been fully expended, no further purchases may be made until the next fiscal year.

There being no objection to this proposal from any department chairman, the library committee adopted it with alacrity, not realizing the difficulties that lay ahead in making fair and reasonable allocations to departments. The difficulties were going to be far worse than they might have been ordinarily, since there were no legitimate precedents to follow. The only local tradition they had to guide them was the practice of allocating only a fifth of the funds and leaving the remainder to the librarian's discretion. They saw no virtue in adhering to that custom, and neither did I, since its effect was to place in the hands of one person full authority for distributing book purchases over all areas of interest. The defects of such an arrangement were too obvious for argument or even comment, and the committee found themselves in the awkward position of having to create some rational means of allocating book funds; some rational means, that is, other than a strictly controlled program of profile buying as originally proposed.

The committee's first approach to the problem was to ask me to submit a summary description of allocation methods commonly practiced in other academic libraries. There was some hope that it might be easier to start with the writing on someone else's tablet and erase what is unsuitable than to start with a *tabula rasa* and try to write something sensible of one's own devising. I gave them a list of the various methods practiced elsewhere and told them I held no personal preference for any one of them. The list I presented follows.

1. Follow percentages employed in past years, making whatever adjustments seem appropriate in the light of changing programs, etc. Impossible in our situation, since we do not know, and cannot find out, what the actual allocations were.

2. Base allocation on various enrollment statistics, e.g., number of students taking departmental offerings, number of departmental majors, honors students, independent study programs, etc. Problem here is that, e.g., five classics students may need access to more titles than five hundred physics majors. Enrollment statistics are probably meaningful only in terms of the number of multiple copies that should be bought, but allocated funds are usually spread over as many titles as possible.

3. Base allocation on circulation activity by subject. Thus, if circulation in history is twice that in literature, allocate twice as much to history. This method makes some sense, but commits library development to the past rather than the future. Subjects of no interest last year may become vitally interesting this year or next, but new books will not be available to satisfy the developing interest until circulation activity leads to their purchase. By

then, interest may have died again. A further problem is that hand-kept circulation statistics are not sufficiently detailed to be matched against departmental allocations. Thus, while we can tell how many books were circulated in the sciences this fall, and how many in literature, we cannot tell how many were circulated in the specific categories of biology, chemistry, physics, etc., or English literature, French, German, Spanish, etc.

4. Develop an elaborate mathematical formula based on some or all of the above subjective methods, announce that the formula is an objective method of allocating funds, and tell those who complain of the results that they simply cannot grasp complex, abstract formulations.

5. Ask each department chairman to indicate how much money for books he thinks his department will require, and then begin negotiations if the aggregate exceeds 100 percent of the available funds.

6. Determine allocation percentages at similar institutions, establish an average, and follow it. The blind leading the blind.

7. Determine last year's worldwide production of books, distributed by subject, and distribute book funds in the same proportion. Has same defects as point 3 above; furthermore, it is impossible to determine the total production count, let alone the distribution.

As a guide to their labors in developing a rationale for allocating funds, the committee found this summary no more helpful than a communication from the Delphic oracle. After debating the options at some length, and trying in vain to imagine some others that might be missing from the list, the committee grew visibly frustrated by the irrational results that might be expected to lie at the end of any path they followed. As the frustrations mounted, and the solution to one paradox led to the discovery of two new ones to take its place, the committee began a drift toward approval-plan buying as the only practical escape from the paradoxes of departmental allocations; and the drift soon turned into a stampede back to their earlier recommendation that the bulk of the book funds be committed to orthodox buying based on an approval-type profile. In less than an hour, they had voted to rescind their recommendation that departments be permitted to buy in or out of profile as they wished. At a subsequent meeting, they adopted a lengthy, carefully drawn set of resolutions submitted by a philosophy professor, stipulating that there would be no departmental allocations, and that, with a few necessary but minor exceptions, book funds would hereafter be expended on the basis of notification slips generated by a comprehensive profile of our current acquisition requirements. The committee left everyone with the clear impression that they had ceased to make recommendations and were now giving instructions of a kind the library was bound to follow. Opposition to the program seems to have collapsed with that development, and no further objections have since been heard, although some may well arise when full-scale implementation takes place.

This reversal of direction took me totally by surprise. I had not even speculated on such a possibility, although in retrospect it appears to be the best possible way to move into an approval program, since any residual hostility toward it may now be deflected toward the whole committee and away from the individual librarian who originally proposed the program. The outcome of these unforeseen changes of direction calls to mind Hamlet's observation that "there's a divinity that shapes our ends, rough-hew them how we will," although some of our faculty may see the devil's hand at work in it.

There is a third problem of a quite general nature, one that I did not mention earlier, that must be faced when the decision is taken to adopt an approval plan. Since a high percentage of approval purchases will reach the library before LC catalog copy is available, the advantage of early receipt of books may be largely dissipated by virtue of their simply sitting longer than usual on the processing shelves, awaiting the arrival of LC copy. Expediting the acquisition process aggravates the problem of cataloging backlogs. On top of this problem, we had the additional one of lacking any automatic system of matching books to catalog copy when both have finally reached the library. If you maintain a current proofslip file, with approval slips interfiled in it, the problem solves itself, for no matter which comes first—the proofslip or the approval slip—a match occurs automatically, without the need for systematic review either of proofslip files or approval receipts. But with acquisitions rates of about 7,000 new titles per year, the sorting and filing of about 150,000 proofslips seems an unwarranted amount of labor to achieve only 7,000 matches (or less) with approval slips. The alternative of making repeated searches of NUC supplements for catalog copy would be exceedingly cumbersome, as would the other option of ordering cards from the Library of Congress when a book is received. And the problem of extended cataloging delays would not be resolved by any of these measures. We needed a method that would at once eliminate the occasions for proofslip files, multiple searches in NUC, and protracted delays in cataloging.

The method we developed is, of course, FASTCAT. With FASTCAT's help, all approval receipts can be circulated the day they arrive, all pressures for rush cataloging are removed, and all cataloging backlogs are eliminated. For most books, a single search in NUC yields the desired copy, and, for a small remnant, a second search concludes the operation. Without such a method as this for prompt circulation and efficient cataloging of approval receipts, approval-plan buying would be far less attractive to us.

A word now about that term "approval," which somehow stirs dark passions in the hearts of some professors and some librarians. In the acquisitions program we have set up, it is a misnomer, since we are not actually buying books on an approval basis. Instead, we are receiving computer-produced notification slips from the jobber, based on a comprehensive profile of our acquisitions requirements. Books not wanted are not ordered; books ordered are kept, since further review of them on any kind of approval basis would be useless. We therefore speak of our program as a "profile plan" rather than an "approval plan," and have discovered that the shift in terminology has, in fact, removed some of the purely emotional biases against the program.

One problem of profile buying that bedevils both university librarians and their jobbers is the handling of monographs in series. University libraries feel obliged to acquire all titles in a great many series, with no exceptions tolerated; and the process of transferring their standing order files to the profile jobber is cumbersome, costly, and complicated by numerous difficulties of timing and communication. Since we regard the standing-order monographic series as an inappropriate selection device for a small college library, we simply canceled all such standing orders and instructed the jobber to notify us of titles that match our profile, without regard to any series identification they may carry. Thus, if six titles out of ten in a given monographic series fit our profile, we will acquire only those six, worrying no more about those other four than we would about any other books that lay outside the profile. The problem of identifying on receipt new monographs that should be placed in an existing series is largely settled by classing nearly all monographs separately hereafter, regardless of any series relationship that may exist. While such a Draconian solution to the problem may appear to have many theoretical defects, it is difficult to find any practical faults with it, at least in a college-library situation. Six months ago, we removed all monographic series added entries from the public catalog, and no one but the cataloger is yet aware that anything is missing.

How well is the profile program working for us now? It is too early to say, as we have been receiving slips for only a month. Our major concern at this stage is that the profile receipts not exceed the sum available for their purchase (about $70,000 per year), or, what would be equally troublesome, that they not fall substantially short of the budgeted amount. In the latter event, we might find ourselves in the allocation dilemma again, and without sufficient time to settle it before the end of the fiscal year. The jobber assures us of his keen interest in forestalling any such development. I am sure he will be able to.

Sawing Off the Horns of a Dilemma, or How to Cut Subscription Lists and Expand Access to Journal Literature

"Lord, how are they increased that trouble me!"
—*PSALM 3:1*

What I propose to speak here is damnable heresy. At least it is so regarded in Minnesota, as I discovered to my great surprise when I first broached it to an assembly of librarians there, about this time a year ago. Rumor has it that some of them are still in a state of tall indignation about that unwittingly heretical utterance, although to this day I cannot understand why.

What happened was this: The Minnesota State legislator who had been the key figure in securing appropriations for continuing the Minitex project—a statewide interloan service provided by the University of Minnesota Library—was speaking at an annual gathering of Minnesota academic librarians. At the conclusion of his talk, which had to do with the difficulties of persuading his colleagues to keep Minitex funded on a permanent basis, he asked for helpful comments from the audience on specific ways in which their individual libraries had benefited from Minitex. A good deal of predictable comment was made about how Minitex had greatly expanded their patrons' opportunities for access to library materials, and the legislator smiled blandly, as if he had heard this sort of thing before. Then, when it seemed he might go home without hearing one new thing from all those academic librarians, I got up and told him that Macalester College had been able to cut its subscription list from 1,700 down to 1,200 titles, largely as a result of the recent availability of Minitex services. Then I went on to explain that with the money saved by dropping 500 journal subscriptions,

First published in *Management Problems in Serials Work,* ed. Peter Spyers-Duran and Daniel Gore (Westport, Conn.: Greenwood Press, 1974).

we had been able to absorb the inflationary rises in the 1,200 that remained, and to keep our intake of new books at an even level despite inflation there too, and also to make certain urgent and altogether necessary inflationary adjustments in my own salary to boot. All this was possible without making any increases in our total library budget, which otherwise would have required about $15,000 in new money annually to keep the subscription list at *its* former inflated level.

Within moments after sitting back down, I discovered that the legislator and I were probably the only two people in that large assembly who took any pleasure in what I had said. Everyone else seemed to be in a state of dynamic outrage, but not at the idea of my drawing an improved salary. I'm sure they all realized I deserved it, considering what I have to suffer in consequence of speaking up in professional meetings. What infuriated them was the idea of a library's cutting back its subscription list in response to the availability of fast, reliable interloan services. They made it sound like treason, as if Macalester College had injured the whole library community in taking the simple and reasonable step of cutting from its subscription list a group of titles that were no longer needed—if indeed they ever had been. Librarians have grown so accustomed, over the last decade, to seeing everything connected with libraries growing at exponential rates, that the idea of negative growth is as anathema to them as it is to capitalist economic theorists. Although the sense of injury within this group was plain and open, nobody ventured to explain just who was injured, or how. A year later there is simply no evidence that anybody was, but the indignation, as I said, is still very much alive.

The gospel from which today's heretical text comes is found in two remarkable studies, which will be identified here in careful detail since neither of them, I believe, has yet appeared in any journal. Citations to them may also be hard to come by. The first study is by Mr. Blair Stewart and is entitled "Periodical Use in Liberal Arts College Libraries: Some Insights Based on the Experience of the Periodical Bank of The Associated Colleges of the Midwest." This study is dated December 23, 1971, and is twenty-six pages long. It was distributed to ACM librarians early in 1972. (Macalester College is a member of the ACM, but not of its Periodical Bank.) Perhaps it can still be had by writing to the author at the ACM Periodical Bank; if not, a copy of this valuable document can be obtained via interloan from Macalester College. To give you something of the flavor of this remarkable study, I quote the closing paragraph in full:

One may hazard the guess that there is little justification for maintaining most back-files for more than ten years. This conclusion and earlier statements in this report that are based on the assumption that college libraries should hold only those resources that are used, will undoubtedly increase the adrenalin secretions of many of the librarians and faculty members who read them. It is hard to shake the feeling that a college library should be a research library, or even a mausoleum, although these are both completely impractical objectives. The college library should provide the maximum service within its means to faculty members and students. It cannot maximize its services if it devotes resources to the acquisition or retention of materials that are never used. It cannot possibly provide on-site access to all the less used materials that are needed in a college that is a vital educational institution. Whenever the use of the Periodical Bank is substantially cheaper, the library should use it rather than hold the title itself. So far relatively little progress has been made at the member colleges in determining which periodicals according to this criterion should be retained and which should be eliminated from their holdings.

The other study is a grant proposal prepared by Mr. Gordon Williams, director of the Center for Research Libraries, and the Center's staff. Entitled "Background and Proposal for a National Lending Library for Journals," it runs to forty-nine pages, including appendices, and was distributed to CRL member libraries in late 1972. Carefully documented and replete with charts, cost analyses, use data, and a bibliography, Williams' proposal sets forth in luminous detail the ludicrously expensive and ultimately futile efforts of academic libraries to maintain comprehensive segments of the world's journal output under their own roof. While very few academic libraries have been able to make the sort of use studies that would reveal what portions of their journal collections receive so little demand as to be worthless to their own patrons, Williams has assembled some impressive data from the loan records of national and regional lending libraries. These data strongly suggest that we are all engaged in some monumental absurdity in maintaining gargantuan subscription lists and backfiles of journals that are likely to be called for only once in 300 years, or less, by our patrons. One example from Williams' numerous instances of the high rate of journal nonuse is from the National Library of Medicine, which found that "88% of the serial titles in its collections (including discontinued as well as currently published titles) were used less often than once a year. Put another way, 100% of the use during the twelve month period was satisfied by only 4,347 titles out of the approximately 37,000 titles in the NLM collection." The other example is from the loan records of the National Lending Library (NLL) for Science and Technology, established in 1960 by the British government to give other libraries ready access to scientific journal literature. Although the NLL serves all libraries in Great Britain, and currently maintains a subscription list of 38,000 titles, approximately half of them are used less than once a year. The number of titles that were called on at least four times a year from all the libraries in Great Britain comes to only 2,036, a meagre 5 percent of the total holdings.

What has been learned thus far from the cumulated data of regional lending libraries is exactly confirmed by citation analysis of contemporary scientific journal literature. Eugene Garfield, president of the Institute for Scientific Information (publisher of the *Science Citation Index*) reported in a recent issue of *Science* the findings of a vast and comprehensive analysis of scientific journal citations covering about a million citations appearing in 2,200 journals during the last three months of 1969. Garfield's analysis and argument, while perfectly lucid and easy to follow, and worthy of careful attention, are far too complex for summary here. What matters here is the conclusions he draws, and I cite them briefly:

This analysis gives good reason for concern about any increase in the number of scientific and technical journals. It is not merely that increased numbers of journals make coverage of the literature more difficult, but that so many journals now being published seem to play a marginal role, *if any* [italics mine], in the effective transfer of scientific information. If one accepts the contention (highly debatable in my opinion) that there are between 50,000 and 100,000 scientific and technical "journals," the data presented here indicate that only 5 to 6 percent of them are being cited.[1]

The journal reading habits of scientists, made manifest through citation analysis, are precisely reflected in the highly concentrated demands they make on the vast resources of national lending libraries.

When one considers the exceedingly low demand levels for an exceedingly high percentage of total journal collections—demand levels that are generated by a whole national population of library users, not just those on one university campus—it is difficult to escape the inference that if we actually knew the local demand levels on our own campuses, we would have trouble justifying to our administrations the enormous expenditures we make to maintain journal collections that for the most part contribute nothing whatever to our libraries except ballast. It would be cheaper in the long run, and just as productive for our users, to replace substantial blocks of our journal collections with blocks of lead having equivalent weight, if indeed we think the ballast function of journal literture to be all that important. The analytical data coming in from a variety of national and regional periodical banks will force us to think more seriously about the actual value of the huge journal collections we have developed for the alleged benefit of our local patrons, who now appear to have no interest at all in the overwhelming majority of the journal literature we have placed at their disposal.

Specifically, how many journal titles are so indispensable in a liberal arts college library that every one of the ten colleges participating in the ACM Periodical Bank should subscribe to them in order to make them always readily available to their own students and faculty? Had I been asked such a question before reading Mr. Stewart's study, I would have guessed at least 400 or 500 titles, since the ten colleges have essentially the same curricula, and the range of their current subscriptions is from a low of about 400 titles to a high of about 1,200. But the number of titles currently subscribed to by all ten college libraries is in fact an astonishingly low figure: 74, to be exact. Based on this and certain other data of like tendency, Stewart makes the flat but disquieting assertion that "the number of titles that every self-respecting liberal arts college library must hold is less than 100."

Macalester College, as noted earlier, currently maintains a subscription list of 1,200 titles—down by 500 over the last three years. If Stewart's claim is correct, and I am inclined to think it may be, then there is reason to think that even after having cut 500 titles from our list, we still have 1,100 more that have only casual value—or less—to our readers. What is the cost to us in dollars of providing this extravagant surplus to the patron? In the grant proposal referred to earlier, Williams estimates that the annual cost of maintaining a $10 per year journal subscription (plus processing and binding costs) comes to about $40. Scaling this down to an annual cost of only $30, to stay on the conservative side, we may fairly estimate that Macalester College is spending about $33,000 per year to maintain those 1,100 subscriptions that Stewart contends we probably do not need. With sums of that magnitude at stake, we can no longer postpone our responsibility to find out whether we cannot in fact get along very well indeed without some or all of those 1,100 potentially useless titles.

How does one go about such a task? An obvious approach is to collect definitive use data on the existing collection, and then cancel those subscriptions that show little or no evidence of current use. Collecting such data is a tricky, arduous, and costly business; and even if it were done you might still be left with the formidable problem of the professor who perversely demands that a title be retained, even if the data irrefutably show that it has not been used once by anybody in the course of a year. "How do you know," he will ask you, "there may not be a great demand for this journal ten years hence? Then if you have done what you propose to do, it will not be here when I and my students need it." Some professors, like some librarians, still think we are operating under conditions that existed in the 1940s, when not to own a particular journal meant literally and unconditionally not to have any convenient means of access to it. As always, times have changed faster than attitudes.

So what was done at Macalester College to accomplish the Phase I reduction of 500 titles was to force the professor into a Hobson's choice, by letting him know that if he did not give up some journal subscriptions then he would have to give up some book purchases instead. The acquisitions budget was going to stay constant, while the cost of journals was rising magnificently, and the price of books was going up too. To make sure his choice would be the right one, we let him know that while we could procure for him a photocopy of almost any journal article he wanted within seventy-two hours or less—and at no direct cost to him personally—we would never be able to borrow a new book for him from another library *while it was still new,* since all the libraries to which we had ready access were always a year or more behind us in buying new books and making them ready for loan. Faced with this disagreeable but inescapable choice, the professors abstained from the "But what of ten years hence?" argument, and got on with the business of recommending individual journal titles for cancellation. Titles were extracted on a one-by-one basis, just like teeth, and in two years' time 500 of them were gone. After that painful procedure was completed we were all feeling the need of a rest, so in the third year we suspended our efforts to accomplish the additional withdrawals that still seemed possible and necessary. In the third year, we focused our energies instead on persuading the Chemistry department to give up its subscription to *Chemical Abstracts*; after several months of delicate negotiations, that effort succeeded too.

Another reason for taking a year-long intermission was to give the faculty more time to become convinced of the efficacy of interloan in procuring journal articles when wanted. In the course of three years, we have developed an interloan system that yields some 90 percent of all journal articles requested by either students or faculty, and nearly always delivers them in a maximum of three days following request. The system involves a consortium of seven college libraries and the Hill Reference Library, plus the University of Minnesota's, and there is a union list of the periodical holdings of all nine libraries. The list includes more than 20,000 titles, and nondelivery of a request results mainly from the nonavailability of an issue (at the bindery, etc.) rather than from its not being owned by any of the libraries. Prompt transmission of requests, and delivery of photocopies, are accomplished by means of a courier service operated and paid for by the consortium.

Now that the faculty have had ample opportunity to see what the interloan service can do for them, the time has come to enter Phase II of the subscription cancellation process: the removal of a substantial number of those 1,100 titles which Stewart believes we do not need. Our immediate goal will be to cancel 500 of them and get the subscription list down to about 700 titles. If that is accomplished, then the subscription list will be right back where it was just ten years ago—when it was more than double what it had been just ten years before that time. Patrons will still have ready access to more than ten times as much journal literature as they did just three years ago, when the reduction process began and when the interloan service now provided was barely a dream. At the same time, Macalester College will have released some $30,000 each year for more productive uses than the acquisition of a thousand journals for which it appears to have had very little use even when it subscribed to them.

When one speaks among librarians about cutting subscription lists and supplying wanted articles from dropped journals via interloan, the question inevitably arises, "But how will you be able to make up for lost browsing capability when the journals are no longer on your shelves?"

The answer, of course, is that you can't. But a more interesting question to ask at this point is, "Why the sudden concern for lost browsing capability, when most academic libraries thwart it anyhow by placing journals on the shelves in alphabetical rather than classified order?" The impossibility of browsing an alphabetically arranged journal collection is self-evident, and in itself accounts for the virtual nonexistence of serious browsing in such a collection. No need to worry ourselves at this point about losing something we never wanted badly enough to have, even when it was within our financial means.

The disturbing spectre of adverse copyright restriction always looms large when one takes the long-range decision to rely upon photocopying rather than ownership to provide access to journal literature. What indeed will Macalester College do five years hence should unforeseen developments in copyright law foreclose absolutely, or even partially, access via photocopy? Would we then be able to go back and buy a five-year run of those thousand canceled subscriptions? Since the cost would come to at least $100,000, we could not pay the bill. Are we not then making a dangerous and irresponsible gamble on the future course of copyright law?

I think not, for the reason that the journal literature will *still* be abundantly available from other libraries, even if not so much as one article from it can be had in photocopy format. How can that possibly be? The solution is so easy and obvious I was startled by it myself when I first read it in Gordon Williams' grant proposal: the lending library, instead of sending a photocopy, sends out the original volume of the journal itself. This is seemingly out of the question, for if there is one universally applicable truism of interlibrary loan operations, it is that one library never, under *any* circumstances, lends a bound journal to any other library. The Dewey Decimal system will perish from the face of the earth, and librarians will cease to worry about their image, before ever a library will lend to another its precious bound periodical.

And why should that be so? Obviously because journals are in such high demand, and irreplaceable if lost. Well, after looking at the data that have been pouring in from the national lending libraries, we can hardly keep a straight face any longer about not lending a bound journal because of the hot demand for it locally. And in the era of microfilm and Xerox, the argument of irreplaceability won't bear scanning either.

Why not lend the bound volume rather than sending a photocopy? The British National Lending Library has been doing just that for years, simply because it is both cheaper and faster to do so—and the problem of competing demand for the same volume just never amounted to anything. Why should it, when the evidence is in (from the University of Chicago Library) that nearly half the serial volumes in a major research library will be used, on the average, less than once in 300 years? The Center for Research Libraries has from the beginning supplied bound volumes rather than photocopies, and may continue to do so regardless of copyright developments.

This reasonable practice will assuredly become widespread as more librarians begin to realize that the average demand on their journal collection is exactly the opposite of what they always imagined. And should copyright restriction ever actually foreclose the photocopy approach, one may confidently forecast that the lending of bound volumes will become universally routine overnight, since that will be our only mode of access—and a perfectly convenient and economical one too, as the long experience of the NLL and the CRL has proved. Let us then worry ourselves with something other than fantasies of calamity by copyright.

NOTE

1. Eugene Garfield, "Citation Analysis as a Tool in Journal Evaluation," *Science* 178, no. 4060 (November 3, 1972): 475.

The Destruction of the Book by Oversewn Binding - and How to Prevent It

"Oh, the havoc I have seen committed by binders."

—WILLIAM BLADES

Several years ago Matt Roberts published a jeremiad on oversewn binding that deserves much wider attention from librarians than it ever got.[1] His theme is lucid, convincing, and utterly dismaying: Oversewing (the machine process universally employed for library binding), far from accomplishing the traditional and honorable aim of preserving books, in the end achieves the opposite result—it guarantees their destruction. "The shortcomings of oversewing," Roberts states, "while few in number, are decisive:

1. An oversewn book does not open easily and will not lie flat.
2. Oversewing presumes the destruction of the original sections [i.e., the folds that form the sections are shaved away by the binder], thus making further rebinding all but impossible.
3. The oversewn book has a greatly diminished inner margin. Aside from the obvious loss of proportion, lessening the inner margin may result in damage to, or partial concealment of, plates and illustrations.
4. A book that is tightly sewn and has little inner margin is difficult to photocopy and is frequently damaged in the attempt.
5. Paper that is even a little brittle will break due to the unyielding grip of oversewing.[2]

Roberts speaks bluntly of binders as "executioners of the book," and of librarians as judges who pass the sentence that sends the book off to its execution—not a flattering estimate of a profession whose central and oldest tradition has been the preservation of the book. Refuting Roberts is no easy

First published in *Management Problems in Serials Work,* ed. Peter Spyers-Duran and Daniel Gore (Westport, Conn.: Greenwood Press, 1974).

task, since the destructive effect of oversewing is indisputable, and virtually all libraries specify oversewing for virtually all the books they send to the binder.

How did librarians ever get themselves in the awkward position of prescribing destruction for the books they are committed to preserve? It is largely a matter of economics, as Roberts argues the case—although one is inclined to think that mere ignorance of the facts may have some bearing on the matter too. Oversewing, which is done on machines, is simply a much cheaper method of binding books than handsewing, which, while it does in fact preserve books (and has done so for hundreds of years), puts a strain on library budgets that administrators have decided it is not possible to bear. By putting the strain on the book itself, *through oversewing,* they have relieved the strain on their budgets—but only in the short run since eventually someone will have to bear the very high cumulative costs of the mass destruction wreaked on literally millions of books through the process of oversewn binding. The real burden of binding costs is casually (and irresponsibly) being passed on for a later generation of librarians to bear.

What can be done to end the present destruction of books? Roberts argues that we must either face up to the facts of the situation and pay the high price of preserving books by flexible handsewing, or develop economical machine techniques that will duplicate the methods and results of handsewing. The virtues of handsewing (setting aside the question of cost) are thus enumerated by Roberts:

1. A book sewn on tapes or cords opens easily and lies flat.
2. The sewing is strong and durable.
3. Since most of the strain is carried by the cords or tapes, there is much less danger of the paper breaking. This is very important in the rebinding of books with brittle paper.
4. The sections are preserved, thus retaining the full inner margin of the book.
5. Because the cords or tapes can be continued beyond the limits of the book proper, and extended between boards and board paper, the book is less likely to lose its covers.
6. In the event a second rebinding becomes necessary, it is easily accomplished, because the book is not at all diminished by the first rebinding.[3]

While no one yet seems disposed to bear the costs of handsewing, as Roberts advocates, a machine binding technique has been developed in the last decade, by the Japanese, which appears to possess the virtues of handsewing cited by Roberts, although in fact no sewing of any kind is used. The machine, marketed in this country by the Bro-Dart Company as the "Bro-Dart 800," has unfortunately been touted by the seller as a device for temporary binding only, when in fact its product is far more permanent than oversewing (and not in the least destructive) and is probably as durable as flexible handsewing, though only the test of time will conclusively establish the fact.

The process is simple and inexpensive (about *one-fifth* the cost of oversewing), and it can be performed in-house by student assistants with minimal training and experience. There can be no question of its being the method of choice for binding journals, on economic as well as technical grounds, but our experience (between 1973 and 1977) shows it to have little application in the binding of books.

Issues forming a binding unit are stacked in order, with a cover board top and bottom, aligned, and locked securely in a clamp. A drill press is then used to drill (usually) three holes along the inner margin, 1/8'' to 3/16'' in from the folds of the paper. (Note well that nothing is shaved away; the original structure of the sections is never altered.) Flexible plastic rivets with a head on one end are then inserted through the whole sandwich, and the headless ends are clipped to extend about 1/4'' beyond the outer board. A heat-fusing device is applied to each extended end, converting it to a flat head so the rivet then has a head on either end, locking the sandwich together securely between the two outer boards. (An adhesive spine tape, with lightweight manila board backing, may be wrapped around the issues, extending slightly inside the outer boards, before the unit is clamped together preparatory to drilling.) A title and volume number label is applied to the spine strip, and the bound volume is ready for shelving. The binding operation (excluding labeling) requires about fifteen minutes' labor per volume.

Compare the virtues of this binding with those Roberts cites for handsewing:

1. A volume bound with flexible plastic rivets opens easily and lies flatter than an oversewn volume.
2. The rivets are strong and durable. (Under extreme pressure a rivet may—though it rarely does—break off. It can be replaced at a cost of two cents, plus the cost of several minutes' labor.)
3. Since most of the strain is carried by the rivets, there is much less danger (as compared with oversewing) of the paper breaking.
4. The sections are preserved, thus retaining the full inner margin (and original structure) of the journal.
5. Because the rivets continue beyond the limits of the journal proper and lock the covers to it, it is unlikely ever to lose its covers, except from abnormally heavy use.
6. In the event a second rebinding becomes necessary, it is easily accomplished, because the margin is not at all diminished (except for the three inconsequential drilled holes) by the first binding. (Should one ever wish to apply a flexible-sewn binding to a rivet-bound volume, there would be not the slightest difficulty in doing so, since the original structure of the sections is never altered.)

Handsewing, as noted, is far more expensive than machine oversewing; hence, the nearly universal preference for the latter, even though it ultimately destroys the book. Rivet binding, which appears to have the technical virtues of handsewing (aesthetic considerations aside), is far cheaper even than oversewing.

Cost data for binding at the Macalester College Library, using the Bro-Dart 800 over the past two years (to bind about 1,000 volumes per year), indicate an average cost per bound volume of $1.10 (40 cents labor and 70 cents materials), excluding amortization of the binding equipment (cost around $800), which appears to be negligible. In 1973, the average cost for a commercially oversewn binding in the Twin Cities area was about $5.00 per volume—not including preparation and recordkeeping costs to the library (eliminated by the in-house procedure), conservatively estimated at $1.00 per volume. In summary, it appears that the Macalester Library has reduced its binding costs on the order of $5.00 per volume, or $5,000 per year aggregate at current levels. Reductions in journal binding costs of this magnitude obviously release far more budget dollars than will ever be needed to pay for flexible handsewing of all books whose value as artifacts justifies the high cost of aesthetically (as well as technically) superior bindings. The cost equation is such that there is no longer any reason to submit any volume to the ruinous treatment of oversewn binding.

Using rivet binding for journals, one feels no hesitation in binding a unit *even if an issue happens to be missing.* If the missing issue is later secured, the volume can be unbound in seconds and rebound in minutes to include the missing issue. The routine (and often interminable) delays posed by the commonplace missing issue problem are thus eliminated, and patron access to current journal literature is accordingly improved.

Off-shelf time for a journal being treated to in-house binding averages about three days, in contrast to the five- or six-week turnaround time routinely required for commercial binding. The measure of improved access to current journal literature is self-evident.

Photocopying from a rivet-bound journal poses no hazard whatever to the journal itself, although it will eventually destroy (and that rather soon) any oversewn volume. Since the flexible rivet-bound volume will ordinarily open flat with moderate pressure, the problem of losing photocopied text along the gutters seldom arises. If it does, and one feels obliged nonetheless to secure acceptable photocopies, it is simple to clip the rivets, copy the resulting unbound issue and then rebind the volume at negligible cost. The worst damage that can possibly be inflicted on a rivet-bound journal through photocopying—or any other form of abuse—is the popping of a rivet head. As noted above, this damage can be repaired for pennies, whereas the characteristic damage to an oversewn volume, namely the separation of pages from the binding (which is bound to occur even in the process of repeated normal use), can never be repaired, and the damaged volume must eventually be discarded as a total loss.

The economic benefits to be derived from rivet binding should be decisive for any library binding more than a hundred volumes a year, both in terms of short-range costs (the price of the binding itself), and the longer range (and far more substantial) costs of collection preservation. For academic, research, and large public libraries, the potential economic benefits of rivet binding are magnificent.

It is an interesting question why so few libraries have to date made any substantial use of rivet binding. Part of the answer is that so few librarians yet understand the havoc wrought upon their collections by oversewn binding—Matt Roberts' clarion warning notwithstanding. The oversewn binding *looks* so handsome and seems, and feels—and is—so very strong. It is so strong, in fact, that it destroys the relatively weak paper sheets it is imagined to preserve.

The rest of the answer must lie in the fact that the Bro-Dart Company does not yet understand the remarkable capacities of its unprepossessing little binding device, and so has been modest to the point of reticence in proclaiming its virtues. Bro-Dart salesmen (and, for that matter, sales managers) understand so little of the purely technical virtues of their device that they have been content to market it, almost apologetically, as an instrument suitable only for "temporary" binding—whatever that may mean. To make matters worse, no one in the company (salesmen included) seems to have an adequate grasp of the simple procedural steps to be followed in producing a sturdy and craftsmanlike rivet-bound volume; nor has the company produced, to date, even the most rudimentary sort of operation manual for using the equipment. The customer is thus being offered, in what must be a soft sell of unprecedented softness, a machine whose almost magical virtues he does not understand, and whose operating procedures neither he nor the seller has been able to learn nearly as much about as they should. (In the years since this was written, Bro-Dart has of course remedied these deficiencies.)

Under the circumstances, it may be remarkable that the device is still being marketed in this country. Perhaps the failings of the Bro-Dart Company will be viewed more charitably against the darker background of the library profession's widespread ignorance of, or, worse, indifference to, the nightmarish problem of wholesale book destruction occasioned by the broadscale use of oversewn binding as a technique of book preservation. "If gold rust," as Chaucer said, "What shall iren do?"

Librarians who know nothing about the history and technology of bookbinding (their numbers are legion) are quietly creating a scandal of the dimensions we might expect from a body of physicians who understand nothing of the circulation of the blood, or of physicists who have not yet heard about the law of gravity. A close and concerned reading of Matt Roberts' anatomy of oversewn binding should persuade any librarian that the scandal is both real and epidemic. A careful consideration of the capabilities of rivet binding as a more-than-economical alternative may show him the way to call an immediate halt to the systematic, universal destruction of the book, in the name of false economy.

NOTES

1. Matt Roberts, "Oversewing and the Problem of Book Preservation in the Research Library," *College and Research Libraries* 28 (January 1967): 17-24. This paper is dutifully cited in the bibliographical appendix to the 1972 edition of the *Library Binding Manual,* edited by Maurice Tauber for the Library Binding Institute. But its grim message is passed over in discreet silence. I note without comment that the Library Binding Institute is a trade association of binders who depend heavily on library orders for oversewn binding for their livelihood.

2. Ibid., p. 18.
3. Ibid., p. 20.

Let Them Eat Cake While Reading Catalog Cards: An Essay on the Availability Problem

I have long cherished the neat reason Will Cuppy gave for not reading Thomas Carlyle's *Sartor Resartus*.

"*Sartor Resartus* is simply unreadable," says Cuppy, "and for me that always sort of spoils a book."

Anyone who has worked in cataloging or acquisitions will instantly perceive what Cuppy is getting at.

Some books are simply unreadable, and it is a waste of critical effort to explain why. I used to see so many thousands of them in my years as a cataloger, I thought it might be helpful if I compiled a bibliography of unreadable books, with current supplements, of course, as a caution to the innocent bibliographical voyager—a kind of buoy to steer you away from shoal waters.

The task was immense, but I was prepared to undertake it, for humanitarian reasons, until I realized someone had beat me to it. I refer of course to *The National Union Catalog,* which, with a few scattered exceptions here and there, accomplishes very nicely what I had in mind.

Don't get me wrong. I have nothing personally against unreadable books, so long as I don't have to read them myself. I haven't had to read *Sartor Resartus* since I escaped from graduate school fifteen years ago, and even the resentment I feel towards it is fading away. In fact, when I look at all the unreadable new books on my FASTCAT shelves, I get a certain sense of subversive pleasure in knowing that I will never have to read any of them, while my friends on the faculty will.

Not only do I harbor no personal antagonism towards unreadable books, I don't even object to them from the professional standpoint, so long as

Reprinted from *Library Journal* January 15, 1975. Published by R. R. Bowker Co., a Xerox company. Copyright © 1975.

the acquisition and maintenance of them does not seriously interfere with the provision of sufficient numbers of readable books for people who want to read them.

A readable book I define simply as one that *people* read—not implying in that definition any absolute exclusion of college faculties. As a corollary to that definition, I might characterize a readable book as one that you have a very poor chance of finding on a library's shelves, even if you found it entered in the catalog, as you nearly always will. Most of us do a really splendid job of providing catalog entries for readable books.

Consider, for example, the amazing findings of the catalog-use study done at Yale several years ago and reported on by Ben-Ami Lipetz.[1] Of the 50 million titles published since Gutenberg's time, the Yale catalog records some two and a half million, or roughly 5 percent. Yet, the catalog-use study shows that nearly 90 percent of the books that people want to read are entered in the catalog. That result is exactly eighteen times better than you would expect from a completely random book selection program, and it demolishes the pessimistic claim that nobody really knows anything about book selection. If that argument were true, then the Yale Library would have to buy 42 million more books to achieve in a random unknowing way, the 90 percent catalog-entry finding rate that a rational selection policy made possible.

Not that book selection is all that difficult a business. It is one of those blessed enterprises that nearly always turn out well when conducted by responsible people in a reasonably systematic fashion. I have good reason to believe that a catalog-use study at Macalester College, which owns about 0.4 percent of all published books, would yield the same 90 percent finding rate reported at Yale, and I suspect that most other academic libraries above the 200,000 volume mark would do about as well for *their* clientele, or better.[2]

What the Yale study does not tell us, to my considerable regret, is what happens after people leave the catalog, call-numbers in hand, and go to the shelves to fetch the books. Will they find all of them? 90 percent? 80 percent? Less?

If they go in quest of *Sartor Resartus,* I'll bet they find it—and leave it there too, for the next man's benefit.

But if it's *Watership Down* they're after, I'll give high odds they'll not find it this year, nor next year either, unless they resort to heroic measures.

Before I started looking into the literature on the subject, I would have guessed the average rate of availability, among books actually owned by a college library, to be at least at the 75 percent level, and perhaps better. That is to say, I would guess that three times out of four you would find on the shelves a book you found entered in the catalog. That guess would rest on two considerations:

1. In an academic library of any size, only 5 percent or so of the total collection is likely to be on loan at any one time, leaving 95 percent on the shelves waiting to be borrowed; and

2. I wouldn't think students would tolerate a failure rate in excess of 25 percent. Why should we expect them to when you and I would not endure the same frustration rate in a drug store or supermarket?

To my considerable astonishment, I found studies done in four different university libraries, all purporting to show the average failure rate to lie in the range of 40 to 50 percent.[3] "If this is indeed generally true," I thought, "then the rebelliousness of college students has been much exaggerated." Either that, or they don't greatly care whether they find a book on the shelves, as long as they have a chance to read its catalog card.

Now though the latter proposition is plainly absurd, neither has the volatility of Macalester students been doubted in recent years—so I concluded that the failure rate in the Macalester Library must be a good deal lower than reported elsewhere. Either the 40 + percent failure rate is not the rule, or if it is, we are, for reasons not easily guessed at, an exception to it. For there have been no riots in the Macalester Library.

But in a 1974 survey, we discovered, through reports on the outcome of a thousand efforts by students to find books that we owned, that the average failure rate in the Macalester Library is about 42 percent—this in a library of a quarter million volumes, serving only 1,800 readers! And with never more than 3 percent of the collection on loan at any time. Given data like those, I believe something is seriously amiss with our management policies, specifically as they relate to acquisitions and loan periods, and that dramatic improvement in performance is both necessary and possible within existing budget limits. I marvel that we have gotten by so long with so scandalous a rate of failure as 42 percent.

What has spared us, I suspect, is widespread student belief that the library is being systematically robbed. Assuming they were the victims of their own malfeasance, the students have indulged our shortcomings in a wonderfully high-minded way.

But a year ago we took a complete census of holdings and found 10 percent more volumes on the shelves than the inventory records showed we owned. While that put to rest all fears of theft, it did nothing to explain why students perceived us to be a thieves' paradise.

That's when I started looking seriously into the literature on availability rates.

Perhaps, as members of a profession that nowadays promotes the service aspects of its mission, with diminished emphasis on its more traditional curatorial functions, you will share my surprise in discovering that *Library Literature* has no subject heading whatever for availability rates, performance rates, success rates, satisfaction rates, or whatever language you care to cast the concept in.

The subject heading is lacking, of course, because the literature itself is almost nonexistent. Over a fifty-year period, I find only a dozen or so pieces directly concerned with this subject (entered under the heading "Duplicates"), most of them published in the last few years, and coming mainly from England and Canada, where the problem appears to be well understood and vigorously dealt with—at least among the new universities.

Arthur Hamlin raised a bright battle standard on this field in 1966 for American librarians, but no one rallied around;[4] and there is a remarkable series of statistical inquiries into the general question of library inventory control, published in recent years by the industrial engineer R. W. Trueswell.[5] But, like Hamlin's paper, these too have been ignored.

Eric Moon, in an LJ editorial of May 15, 1968,[6] lambasted public librarians for their inattention to the availability problem; and the redoubtable Marvin Scilken addressed a pungent note to the same audience in the *Wilson Library Bulletin* of September 1971,[7] wryly observing that "Purchasing multiple copies violates Scilken's First Empirical Law of Librarians' Science, 'that librarians much prefer buying books that no one wants to buying books that they know everyone wants,' or, 'It's better to serve a possible reader later than to serve an actual reader now.'" Scilken protests that "librarians use much verbage, effort, and even some money, on so-called public relations trying to convince patrons that they should think well of an institution that rarely seems to have what they want until the desire for it has disappeared. As things are now . . . it is good business and not very expensive to have the best kind of public relations—the books!" Except for these few sallies, the rest is silence on an issue which appears, at least from the patron's standpoint, to dwarf all others in the field of library service.

Let me underscore the paradoxical indifference to the availability problem in two related propositions regarding library services.

1. Through vigorous attention to the availability-rate phenomenon, one can theoretically *double* the per capita loan rate of an academic library.

2. By exploiting interlibrary loan services to the fullest degree, in a geographical setting ideally suited to maximizing interloan services, one can theoretically increase the per capita loan rate of books by about 5 percent.

The first proposition, while stated theoretically, is based on actual results obtained at the University of Lancaster Library, as reported on by Michael K. Buckland,[8] who has written extensively on the subject. When measures were taken at Lancaster to raise the availability rate from 60 percent to 86 percent, the *per capita* circulation rate more than doubled. While one swallow may not make a summer, it does attest to summer's possibility and to a possible end of "this winter of our discontent." And what has actually happened in one library is at least theoretically possible at another.

The second proposition, relating to interloan services, derives from actual experience at Macalester College over the last four years, where with swift reliable access to some 2 million titles in Twin Cities libraries, we have been able to add through interloan something like 5 percent to the per capita borrowing rate. Without detailing my reasons here, I believe that is the saturation rate for us, and I suspect it would be for most other libraries too, since our geographical and certain other circumstances are ideal for maximizing interloan service. Incidentally, our failure rate on interloan is only 17 percent, or less than half the failure rate in finding on our shelves, on demand, books we actually own.

To recapitulate: By improving availability rates in your own holdings, you may improve use rates 100 percent. By maximizing interloan services, under ideal conditions, you may improve use rates 5 percent.

How then do you account for the fact that over the past fifty years hundreds of articles have been written on the interloan question, while only a dozen have dealt with the availability problem?

Is it because we assume that availability is so routine a problem it should and must take care of itself, whereas interloan situations are sporadic, individualistic, and often rather interesting? Public health work goes on unnoticed and keeps the nation healthy, whereas heart transplants are glamorous and heavily publicized, and contribute absolutely nothing to the health of the masses. Interloan service is highly visible and plainly gratifying to the rare patron who requests it. But making books available from your own collection is a task that goes on behind the scenes, and the patron never knows just whom to praise or blame on any occasion of success, or failure. The process is invisible, and our concern with it slight—beyond the one visible step of ensuring that we have cards *in the catalog* for all the right books. After that, who cares? Let them eat cake while reading catalog cards.

In giving such elaborate attention to the process of borrowing books that we don't own, while largely ignoring the enormous problem of delivering the books that we do own, have we not been straining out gnats and swallowing camels?

What we have *learned* recently from interloan networks may be more valuable than the loan service itself. Data from the ACM Periodical Bank, the British National Lending Library, and the National Library of Medicine illuminate an extraordinary imbalance in patron demand for journal literature: most journals are read by practically no one, while a very few journals seem to be read by everyone.[9] Of all the journals available through the ACM Bank, those that receive the heaviest use turn out to be the very ones that are *owned* by the libraries making a request for them. Those that receive the least use are those that are owned by none of the ten libraries belonging to the Bank. As far as journal literature is concerned, what the overwhelming majority of readers appear to want is not access to an infinite variety of journal titles, but prompt availability of articles in an exceedingly small percentage (say 5 percent or less) of the journals that are available from a lending center.

One may suppose a similar pattern of reader interest obtains with respect to monographs as well. Certainly the Yale catalog study reveals an extremely narrow concentration of reader interest in books, when 5 percent of the world's publications satisfy 90 percent of the catalog searches. The range of titles readers want to see may be far smaller than we imagine. Though I have no extensive interloan data to bear this out, I have some general facts that do. Seven college libraries in the Twin Cities, owning an aggregate 250,000 unique titles, form an interloan network which calls upon the University of Minnesota Library as a source of last resort. Although the University of Minnesota holds nearly ten times as many titles as the college network, it supplies only 25 percent of the filled requests, while 75 percent of them are filled within the network. Given the extraordinary fact that the collection that is ten times larger fills only a quarter of the interloan requests, it is hard to escape the inference that the interloan program really satisfies a need not for esoteric or even uncommon publications, but for rather obvious, commonplace titles that *should* be available in the requesting library, but for some reason are not. At Macalester, for example, some 25 percent of book requests through interloan are for books that we own ourselves, but for whatever reason cannot supply when the patron wants them. I estimate that another 25 percent of the requests are for books that we should own but don't, leaving some 50 percent as normal candidates for interloan activity. I suspect that we have been using interloan as a very poor substitute for effective inventory control, just as a profligate spender will go in debt to finance his food and shelter, having exhausted his resources on baubles and trinkets.

The reason I consider even a highly effective interloan service to be a poor substitute for effective inventory management is this: The finding-rate survey I mentioned earlier indicates that students fail to find books we own *when they want them* on the order of 35,000 times per year. Yet, the interloan data indicate that students will ask for only 500 of these books via interloan in the course of a year. That is to say, interloan makes up for only 1.5 percent of the failures, and therefore seems hardly worth the candle.

One may well retort that if a student's interest in an unavailable book is so slight that he will request interloan backup only 1.5 percent of the time, why strain yourself to accommodate so fleeting and flimsy an interest? I would answer such a question in two ways.

First, what we are seeing may not be a feeble interest on the student's part at all, but rather an overwhelming capacity on our part to convince him of the hopelessness of his quest. The 1.5 percent we don't convince are just incorrigibly stubborn.

Second, I would again cite the results observed at the University of Lancaster Library when steps were taken to improve in-house availability of high-demand books: the per capita circulation rate more than doubled.

While none of this absolutely proves anything, I find it powerfully suggestive, and that is about as close to certainty as we ever come with any of the fundamental issues in library management. Indeed, I am so convinced by the little that has been said by others on the matter of availability, and by the appalling magnitude of the problem we have discovered in the Macalester Library, I regard the solving of this problem as our top action priority over the next few years.

There are several ways to tackle the problem, each involving so many imponderables that it is impossible to say exactly what the costs, or effectiveness, of any one of them will be.

Very briefly, the approaches are these: (1) shorten the general loan period; (2) shorten the loan period for high-demand titles only; (3) buy multiple copies of high-demand titles; and (4) some combination of the above.

The University of Lancaster reduced to one week the loan period of high-demand titles, with the result, as mentioned, of doubling the per capita circulation rate. This decision was based upon computer simulation of the problem, but the definition of what is a "high-demand title" appears to have been rather intuitively determined as covering the 10 percent of the collection that exhibited the greatest recorded use. To identify that 10 percent required the manual inspection of all 70,000 volumes then in the library, which has since grown to several times that size. I do not know whether Lancaster still takes that approach. I doubt it. With computerized circulation, which I assume Lancaster did not then have, identification of popular titles would be no problem. Reprocessing them for shortened loan periods probably would be in any case.

At the University of Windsor (in Canada), a computer was used to identify popular titles and to predict the number of multiple copies required of each to achieve a 95 percent satisfaction rate.[10] Out of a circulating collection of 200,000 volumes, only 40,000 different titles circulated at least once in the course of the academic year. And of those 40,000 the computer analysis indicated that 3,257 titles needed more than one copy to assure a 95 percent availability rate. Of those 3,257 titles, only 570 needed more copies than the library already held, so there was no dramatic "before and after" result to report as there was at Lancaster. Presumably, Windsor was already close to the 95 percent satisfaction level before the study began (the general loan period for all books, incidentally, is one week), and that is indeed a very fine performance rate. The Windsor study, while extremely valuable for the rest of us, amounted to an inquiry into a problem that didn't exist at Windsor.

The least elegant approach to the problem is simply to shorten the loan period for all books and do nothing else but that. The ultimate in that direction is to reduce the loan period to zero and then you have what used to be called a reference library. Maximizing availability in that way will also reduce your circulation rate to zero, which is not the goal at Macalester.

The other routes appear to require either computerized circulation, or tedious inspection of every volume in your library, to identify those that will either get an extra copy, or a shorter loan period, or perhaps both.

Macalester has neither computerized circulation, nor any disposition to make a wholesale inspection of the loan records in each of its quarter of a million volumes. That seemed to leave us with the sole inelegant option of simply reducing the loan period for all books to one week, or less.

Then we began to think about Richard Trueswell's remarkable discovery that 70 percent or more of the books you lend on a given day will have circulated *at least once* in the previous year. Since the average circulation rate at Macalester Library is once every four years, it appears that 70 percent of the books that are actually borrowed will exhibit a demand rate *at least* four times greater than the average. The majority of books returning from loan are *ipso facto* relatively high-demand titles and potential candidates for duplication. By examining only those books that are being discharged from circulation, a student assistant can conveniently identify for you all books that meet any level-of-use criterion you may specify for high-demand titles. The criterion we are presently using, arrived at through highly sophisticated intuitive methods, is this:

Any book that has circulated at least four times within the last twelve months will be set aside and considered as a candidate for duplication, simply because it exhibits a demand rate at least sixteen times greater than the average.

About 6 percent of the books returning from loan meet this criterion, or roughly seventy books per week. These books are then submitted to a review process that is far more sensitive, responsive, and complex than anything a computer could do. The Library's associate director, Jean Archibald, looks at these books, and relying upon her vast knowledge of student reading habits, and of all the anomalies and idiosyncrasies of class assignments and individual tastes, and of the levels of transitoriness and durability of the various types and fields of literature, she makes an expert judgment as to which of those seventy books per week shall be duplicated. During the first six months of this undertaking, it turns out that roughly half the books considered for duplication are in fact being duplicated, or about 3 percent of total general circulation. At this rate, the acquisitions costs for the first full project year will run about $10,000, a figure that will presumably decline in succeeding years as the saturation point is approached.

Data from the interloan operation are also being continuously reviewed to identify titles in need of either duplication or first purchase. The circulation survey obviously gives no clue about popular titles you never bought, or those you bought only to have them immediately and permanently sequestered on some professor's office shelves. Information from interloan therefore makes a convenient hook for catching the relatively few titles you will never dip out of the circulation pool.

Selective reduction of loan periods for popular titles appears too cumbersome to be practical in our situation, although Lancaster obtained excellent results through that approach, in a collection of 70,000 volumes.

We are considering, however, a modest blanket reduction in the general loan period, from five weeks to three, as a means of multiplying the effects of systematic duplication. Before any such reduction is made, we will, of course, let the students know what we propose to do and why. And if the reduction is strongly resisted, and the present level of duplication is not bringing the availability rate up to the desired 80 or 90 percent range, then we will seek additional funding for duplicate purchases, either through new moneys for the book budget or reallocation of ordinary funds.

Funding for our current duplication project came mainly from reallocation, and with the blessings of the library committee, bestowed before either they or I knew exactly how bad the failure rate is in the Macalester Library. Now that we all know the shocking magnitude of that rate, the prospects for continued and perhaps increased reallocation in subsequent years are good.

Here is where the issue of spending money on unreadable books becomes a lively professional concern to me, since budgets are always finite, and what is spent in one place cannot be spent in another. Too many unreadable books may mean too few copies of those that are read. In libraries as in life, the essential thing is balance, and compromises must be made to achieve it. Much has been said in the past about "balanced" collections, but that meant only balancing titles in one area against those in another, not weighing the demonstrable need for multiple copies of certain titles against the imagined need to maximize the number of different titles by eliminating duplication altogether.

What sort of balance exists in the Macalester Library when 6 percent of our loans exhibit demand rates sixteen times greater than the average, yet supply of copies is not balanced against measurable demand upon that fraction of the collection? That degree of imbalance in an auto parts inventory would put you out of business in a week. But we get away with it in libraries because there is rarely a competitor to whom our frustrated clientele can turn.

Still we pay a price of sorts for our indifference to the inventory problems caused by sharp differences in demand rates from one title to the next. When I think of those 35,000 searches in the Macalester Library that end in failure every year, even though we own the books that are being sought, I begin to understand for the first time how there can be so many people who love books, and so few who love librarians. With all that frustration, I think we're lucky just to be tolerated.

Now that the shock of discovery is wearing off, and I'm beginning to see how a well-stocked, well-supported, and allegedly well-balanced library can routinely thwart its patrons on nearly half their quests, it occurs to me that we librarians have not an image problem, but a performance problem.

For rarely does an academic library show the slightest concern for the availability problem, beyond the token acknowledgment of its existence which the traditional reserve operation provides. But the human condition that creates the problem must be widespread, since most people want to read readable books, and most aren't. So a lot of people are always pursuing a very few books, and numerous disappointments are bound to ensue. And since so very few librarians have undertaken to solve the problem, the problem itself must be as widespread as the human condition that begets it. No wonder our public clings so tenaciously to the image of the librarian as a forbidding, frustrating, and virginal figure. Why should they think of us in images of helpfulness, and generosity, and availability, when half the time we send them away empty-handed? The extraordinary persistence of the sour spinster image, decades after it lost all external relevance, must carry some rather special message. I think it does. I think it says that the pleasures we presume to offer aren't nearly so available as our callers would like them to be.

NOTES

1. Ben-Ami Lipetz, "Catalog Use in a Large Research Library," in *Operations Research: Implications for Libraries,* ed. by Don R. Swanson and Abraham Bookstein ("University of Chicago Studies in Library Science"; Chicago: University of Chicago Press, 1972), pp. 129-39.

2. A survey done recently in several English university libraries indicates substantially poorer results (Carol A. Seymour and J. L. Schofield, "Measuring Reader Failure at the Catalogue," *LRTS,* Winter 1973: 6-24). The methodology employed, however, raises serious questions about the accuracy of the findings.

3. Three of these studies are cited in Richard W. Trueswell's *Analysis of Library User Circulation Requirements: Final Report* (N.S.F. Grant GN0435, January 1968), p. 1. The fourth is Michael Buckland's paper, cited below. A fifth study, done at Cambridge University, yielded results quite different from the other four: the failure rate was in the 10 to 15 percent range, rather than 40 to 50 percent. Cf. J. A. Urquhart and J. L. Schofield, "Measuring Reader Failure at the Shelves," *Journal of Documentation* (December 1971): 281.

4. Arthur T. Hamlin, "The Impact of College Enrollments on Library Acquisitions Policy," *Liberal Education* (May 1966): 204-210.

5. Richard W. Trueswell, "Two Characteristics of Circulation and Their Effect on the Implementation of Mechanized Circulation Control Systems," *College & Research Libraries* (July 1964): 285-91; "Determining the Optimal Number of Volumes for a Library's Core Collection," *Libri* 16 (1966): 49-60; "Some Circulation Data from a Reserch Library," *College & Research Libraries* (November 1968): 493-495; "User Circulation Satisfaction vs. Size of Holdings at Three Academic Libraries," *College & Research Libraries* (May 1969): 204-213; "Article Use and Its Relationship

to Individual User Satisfaction," *College & Research Libraries* (July 1970): 239-245.

6. Eric Moon, "Satisfaction Point," *LJ* (May 15, 1968): 1947.

7. Marvin H. Scilken, "The Read and Return Collection," *Wilson Library Bulletin* (September 1971): 104-105.

8. Michael K. Buckland, "An Operations Research Study of a Variable Loan and Duplication Policy at the University of Lancaster," in *Operations Research* (University of Chicago Press, 1972), pp. 97-106.

9. Daniel Gore, "Sawing Off the Horns of a Dilemma, or, How to Cut Subscription Lists and Expand Access to Journal Literature," in *Management Problems in Serials Work,* ed. by Peter Spyers-Duran and Daniel Gore. (Westport, Conn.: Greenwood Press, 1974), pp. 104-114. (Reprinted in this volume, pp. 28-35.)

10. Robert S. Grant, "Predicting the Need for Multiple Copies of Books," *Journal of Library Automation* (June 1971): 64-71.

The View from the Tower of Babel

> *"And they said, Go to, let us build us a city, and a tower,*
> *whose top may reach unto heaven; and let us make us a name,*
> *lest we be scattered abroad upon the face of the whole earth."*
>
> —*GENESIS 11:4*

You might imagine that what I am seeing, from my lookout post on the Tower of Babel, is some glorious spectacle on the far horizon, a bright vision of libraries with stacks mounting heavenward, their numbers multiplying to reach from one end of the horizon's arc to the other, an endless replication of Babel Towers.

But I am seeing no such thing.

For I am looking not far out but down deep, straight down to the foundations of the Tower of Babel. And what I see going on down there, dim but certain, is something that concerns me mightily, situated as I am—along with the rest of you—at the tiptop of this cloudshouldering Tower.

I see some people carefully removing the foundation stones one by one. And already the mildest zephyr sends tremors through this ancient word-house.

The pioneer who is leading that quiet undermining expedition is unknown to most of us in the Tower, working mainly out of sight beneath the walls. But soon that work will receive the clamorous attention it calls for, when the Tower begins to tilt.

For those pioneers look capable and determined to me, and what I'm thinking is, I'd better climb down from this perilous height while there is still time, and see up close what they are doing with our foundation stones.

It feels to me now like this old building is about to come tumbling down. And the place I want to be before it falls is on the ground, scouting sites for a new building that will have more of reason and restraint in its design, and

---

less of pride than that old Tower did. Something to make us not a name, but a mission more modestly fitted to human needs, and human capacities, than the storming of heaven this Tower was built for.

Here endeth the Prologue.

A funny thing happened on the way to the biggest building boom in library history. Book collections grew faster than the new space to hold them, so when the boom was over the aggregate space problem of academic libraries was a little worse than it was at the beginning.

During the roughly eight-year span of the rise and fall of the boom, some 570 new or expanded library buildings sprang up on the campuses of four-year and graduate institutions around the nation. It was, in the exuberant words of Jerrold Orne, "the greatest flowering of academic library building experience this country has ever known or is likely to see."[1]

From its beginning in 1967 to its tag end in 1974, the boom generated new building space to accommodate 163 million more volumes. But while it was boom times for buildings, it was flush times for acquisitions, and aggregate collection growth over the same time span came to 166 million volumes: 3 million more than the frenzied builders of Babel were able to provide new space for.[2]

So even in the best of times, our celebrated capacity to achieve a bricks-and-mortar solution to geometric collection growth could not quite measure up to our traditional ability to achieve a problem.

Are we not facing here a dilemma like the one that formerly baffled the traffic engineers in Manhattan? They believed that widening the streets would ease traffic congestion. So they tried it, and found that the traffic jams continued unabated—but they occurred on a grander scale than before, because two automobiles in Jersey or Long Island were always poised, waiting to fill up each new space created by trimming the sidewalks of New York.

I am reminded here of the obnoxious metaphor used several decades ago by the Spanish philosopher José Ortega y Gasset, in his essay entitled "The Mission of the Librarian."[3] Ortega declares that the modern librarian's mission, something "incomparably higher" than the missions of the past, is to "become a policeman, master of the raging book." "Is it too Utopian," Ortega asks, "to imagine in a not too distant future librarians held responsible by society for the regulation of the production of books, in order to avoid the publication of superfluous ones and, on the other hand, to guard against the lack of those demanded by the complex of vital problems in every age? . . . And let no one offer me the foolish objection that such an organization would be an attack upon liberty. The collective organization of book production has nothing to do with the subject of liberty, no more nor less than the need which has demanded the regulation of traffic in great cities of today."

Ortega wrote those words forty years ago, worrying not about the space problems of libraries, but the bibliographical burdens of scholars. "There are already too many books," says he. "Even when we drastically reduce the number of subjects to which man must direct his attention, the quantity of books that he must absorb is so enormous that it exceeds the limits of his time and his capacity of assimilation. . . . At the same time, it also happens that in all disciplines one often regrets the absence of certain books, the lack of which holds up research." Too many books and too few.

Nothing is so resistible as an idea whose time is past. Ortega's invitation to librarians to become traffic cops, censors of the press, found no takers, at least in the free world; but the dilemma that prompted him to extend it— the existence of both too many books and too few—deserves close attention, for it lies at the heart of the most urgent problem facing academic librarians today, though not in exactly the way Ortega imagined.

In a very few years, the majority of academic libraries will own more books than they can shelve; yet, half the time they are unable to deliver the books they already own to a patron who wants them. Too many books and too few.

Too many books! The very thought is so heretical to an academic librarian, I never allowed myself to think it until I realized, about a year ago, that the library I direct at Macalester College was swiftly running out of space, while the prospects for a new building were running away with rampant inflation and a receding economy. In that limited, accidental sense, we would soon know the spatial reality of too many books.

And so, it seems, will a great many other academic libraries. In the last two waning years of the building boom—1973 and 1974—newly created shelving capacity came to only 25 million volumes nationwide, while collections grew by 41 million. And with capital funds for new construction at the vanishing point, while acquisition budgets remain fairly stable, since they account for only 1 percent or so of a college or university's total budget, the majority of American academic libraries must infallibly run completely out of space over the next few years.

Too many books! Not just for my library, but for yours and practically everyone else's as well. And at the same time too few books to meet the ordinary needs of our readers.

As I pondered that paradox and envisioned the mounting frustration of our patrons when no more books could be added to a collection that already seemed too small, I began to ask myself whether there might not in fact be such a thing as "enough" books, and, if so, whether such a quantity would turn out to be a fixed and unchanging sum, or only a temporal baseline from which further growth would always be necessary.

Oddly enough, even if you generously construe "enough" books to be one copy of all the books in the world, you will discover that it is "too few" books for your readers, for they would still fail half the time to find the book they want when they want it.

Thinking of such a total library, and its unexpected disappointments, I remember the haunting words in Jorge Luis Borges' surrealist story "The Library of Babel."[4] Borges, you will recall, was for some years director of the National Library of Argentina. Here is his fantastical account of the total library:

Everything is there: the minute history of the future, the autobiographies of the archangels, the faithful catalogue of the Library, thousands and thousands of false catalogues, a demonstration of the fallacy of the true catalogue, the Gnostic gospel of Basilides, the commentary on this gospel, the commentary on the commentary on this gospel, the veridical account of your death, a version of each book in all languages, the interpolations of every book in all books.

When it was proclaimed that the Library comprised all books, the first impression was one of extravagant joy. All men felt themselves lords of a secret, intact treasure. There was no personal or universal problem whose eloquent solution did not exist—in some hexagon. The universe was justified, the universe suddenly expanded to the limitless dimensions of hope. . . .

But the searchers did not remember that the calculable possibility of a man's finding his own book, or some perfidious variation of his own book, is close to zero. . . .

The uncommon hope was followed, naturally enough, by deep depression. The certainty that some shelf in some hexagon contained precious books and that these books were inaccessible seemed almost intolerable.

Who but a librarian could have written such a pungent corrective to the vain notion that a vast library must yield unbounded joy? Who but a librarian could so exactly prefigure the melancholy outcome of research library expansion in the twentieth century? Depressed scholars tell puzzled administrators that the Harvard Library of today, with its 9 million volumes, is less adequate to its users now than a century ago, when it was a tiny fraction of that size.

TRUESWELL'S THEORY

Too many books and too few. Trying to slip through those horns, or failing that to saw them off, I remembered reading, nearly a decade ago, an astonishing statistical theory of library use published by an industrial engineer named R. W. Trueswell.[5] Among other unsettling heresies, Trueswell blandly predicted that one could remove nearly half of an academic library's collections and reduce the holdings of *wanted* books by only a trifling 1 percent. "By God this is impossible!" I said, repeating Thomas Hobbes' famous exclamation upon first reading Euclid's geometry. Reading Euclid made a philosopher out of Hobbes. Reading Trueswell has made an optimist out of me, for his remarkable discoveries light the way to a sovereign remedy both for our space and our performance problems.

Trueswell discovered in his elaborate investigations of library use that the best criterion for predicting future demand on any book is its last recorded circulation date—not the number of times it was borrowed, nor language of text, nor date of publication, nor subject matter, but simply, and elegantly, the last date it was used. The criterion itself has found little favor among librarians since Trueswell announced it ten years ago. And no wonder. For one's immediate impression is that it has no more relevance to future demand than does the color of the binding. And Trueswell, being an engineer, has never exerted himself to explicate a statistical phenomenon that I suppose is self-evident to engineers but inscrutable to librarians.

A practical illustration may help. Assume a library has a thousand books returning from loan each day. Looking at the date-due slips daily in those books, you discover that all but ten have circulated at least once in the last seven years, in addition to the current loan. You continue your survey for several weeks, getting essentially the same results, and so conclude that 1 percent, or ten out of a thousand, of your current and predictably all future loans will consist of books that had not previously circulated once in the last seven years. Thus, you may also predict that if you remove from your collections all books whose last circulation date is seven years ago or longer, you would lower the holdings rate of wanted books in your library by exactly 1 percent.

The criterion takes on immense practical value when you discover what percentage of books in your collection exhibit a last-circulation-date of seven-plus years. Trueswell's investigations in several libraries indicate you will find perhaps 30 percent of your collection falling into that category.[6] And if that is so, then removing that part of your collection will lower your holdings rate by an imperceptible 1 percent.

Trueswell chose an unfortunate time to publish his theories, for the *Zeitgeist* of the 1960s favored only those who could find ways to make libraries bigger. Everything in academia was expanding in those days—not least the appetite for vainglory—and Trueswell excited no more interest than a mountain climber who scales a sand dune. And then as now, for a librarian to propose to any faculty a strategy for reducing holdings rates by even 1 percent would be a sure invitation to professional ruin. So Trueswell was heeded only by the theorists, who had nothing at stake except a reputation for mathematical competence, and that was never in jeopardy. The logic of Trueswell's formulations is absolute, unassailable.

Along with his discovery that vast numbers of academic library books get little or no use, Trueswell corroborated an inversely related phenomenon that others had observed, though it too has elicited scant practical response, namely, the fact that a small portion of any library collection is in such heavy demand that these books are often unavailable when wanted. So often that the average rate of unavailability for all wanted books owned by an academic library appears to be in the range of 50 percent.

Think about that one for a moment, for it is the practical clue to our escape from the Tower of Babel, whose foundation stones Dr. Trueswell has been pulling out from under us. *Fifty percent of the cataloged books your patrons want are not available when they want them.* Placed against that giant scale of failure, the 1 percent drop in availability that would result from removing 30 percent of your collection looks absurdly inconsequential. And indeed it is, except where money and building space are concerned.

For the avoidance of that 1 percent drop is costing you many times what it would cost by other means to bring the availability rate of books you own from a dismal 50 percent to a gratifying 90 percent.

Avoiding that 1 percent drop, or trying to gain 1 percent in a mature library's holdings rate, necessitates the endless and unproductive addition of new floors to the Tower of Babel. For it is with groups of readers as with individuals: they can only read so many books in a lifetime, and to provide more than that number in the library merely increases the weight of ballast.

The law of diminishing returns applies with astonishing force to the growth of library collections. Doubling the number of titles in a library of any size will add not 100 percent to its usefulness, but something more on the order of, say, 1 or 2 percent. On the other hand, keeping its size constant while periodically revising its stock in response to actual reader demand can have the effect of doubling its utility.

To help you grasp the plausibility of these impossible-sounding generalizations, consider a simple illustration. First, some definitions of a few essential and unfamiliar terms. *Holdings Rate*: By this I mean the percent of all books your patrons want to read that are held by your library. *Availability Rate*: This is the percent of wanted books held by the library that are available on your shelves when your patrons want them. *Performance Rate*: This is the product of Holdings Rate times Availability Rate, and it measures the percentage of all books your patrons may want that are on the shelves when they want them.

Now for the illustration. Assume a university library with the following characteristics:

Collection size	1,000,000 vols.
Shelfload factor	100 percent
Current additions	50,000 vols./yr.
Enrollment	20,000 students
Holdings Rate	90 percent
Availability Rate	50 percent
Performance Rate	45 percent

The Performance Rate, which is what your patrons really care about, is poor, but probably typical. You decide to improve it by miraculously creating the total Library of Babel, right down to the commentary on the commentary on the Gnostic Gospel of Basilides. Everything is there, and your Holdings Rate climbs to 100 percent. The first impression is one of extravagant joy. But your Performance Rate moves only from 45 to 50 percent because you did nothing to improve the Availability Rate. The relatively few high-demand books are still off the shelf more than half the time your patrons want them, so they perceive things now to be even worse than before, because they must walk ten times as far to suffer about the same number of disappointments. The uncommon hope was followed, naturally enough, by deep depression.

Now let's go the other way 'round to improve the Performance Rate by lowering the Holdings Rate and raising the Availability Rate.

Since our library is already 100 percent loaded, with no money in sight for a new building, we start by removing 300,000 volumes from the collection, using the Trueswell criterion of last circulation date to ensure removal of only the low-demand books. The Holdings Rate drops just 1 percent, from 90 to 89, and nobody can tell the difference—yet. Then we identify among the remaining volumes those that need multiple copies to lift the Availability Rate from 50 to 90 percent. Computer simulation indicates we need 100,000 multiples to do this, and we buy them, and there is plenty of space to shelve them now, after removing the 300,000 little-used books. Collection size has shrunk to 800,000 volumes, and the Performance Rate leaps from 45 to 81 percent.

THE PHOENIX LIBRARY

The Tower of Babel has fallen to the ground, but few mourn its loss because the new library that replaces it, which I shall call the Phoenix, satisfies *real*, measurable patron demand at nearly twice the level of its predecessor. And at a small fraction of its cost.

The keepers of the Tower of Babel may forever lament its passing because their ambition to storm heaven and make a name for themselves has been crushed in the rubble. By the waters of Babylon they will hang up their harps and weep. But their patrons never had any wish to storm heaven. All they wanted was certain books—not an indiscriminate overwhelming heap of books. Just the books they wanted to read, and in the new Phoenix they are twice as successful in finding them.

This new Phoenix is both self-regenerating and self-limiting. Its content is ever changing, but never growing. As new books, and multiples of books are added to the collections, older books (and multiples) are continually removed from the library by the ongoing application of the Trueswell criterion, keeping outflow in precise equilibrium with intake. When Holdings and Availability Rates are kept constant, collection size becomes a function of enrollment and breadth of curriculum. Assuming they will fluctuate only within narrow limits, you have achieved a no-growth library, and may keep it so indefinitely, while delivering twice the service you provided in the old Library of Babel.

What I am proposing may sound disagreeably mechanistic, high-handed, and insensitive to the rich variety of human interests a library is created to serve. But upon close reflection I think you will see it is just the opposite. For what in fact will happen is this: the patrons of the library will determine for themselves what its content shall be by the indelible record of the use they make of it, stamped on the date-due slip of every book in the collection. The application of the Trueswell criterion for withdrawal is merely a convenient device for removing books they indicate no interest in, to make way for the others that they will use, and in sufficient copies that one will nearly always be available when it is wanted.

This approach differs radically from the traditional practice of letting librarians and faculty decide exclusively, on the basis of shockingly inadequate information, what books shall be available to library patrons. The cost of that practice is moving rapidly beyond society's willingness to underwrite it. And even while they did support it, the results were nothing to boast about, with patrons leaving the library emptyhanded half the time. When patrons are allowed to decide for themselves what books a library shall hold, they will be much better served than they are now, and at much lower cost.

What is to be done with the 300,000 books we removed from the Tower of Babel and with the 50,000 we will remove each year hereafter from the new Phoenix?

STORAGE CENTERS

If I say "Put them in storage," someone will remind me that several years ago Ralph Ellsworth explored that matter in his *The Economics of Book Storage* and found storage to be an uneconomic solution. For the cost of identifying storage candidates, and changing their catalog records, he reckons to be at least a dollar per book,[7] and that exceeds any savings to be realized from housing them in cheaper off-campus real estate.

But Ellsworth omits two considerations that dramatically alter this economic picture. One is cooperative storage, and the other is computerized catalogs and circulation systems.

With a system of national storage centers, the quantity of books actually stored could be reduced by at least 90 percent through outright discard of multiples that would flow in from many libraries. Academic libraries in the United States currently add about 20 million volumes per year, while the *NUC* records some 400,000 new titles annually. The ratio of copies to titles may thus be roughly estimated at about 50 to 1, and it is a fair guess at this point that a similar ratio would obtain among books going to storage.

For the advanced scholar who maintains that his research depends vitally upon access to the sort of book that gets consulted only once in a hundred years, these storage centers should be a precious blessing. For that is the kind of book they will specialize in, and he will find them all under one roof, whereas now he must travel throughout the nation to see even a fraction of what those extraordinary libraries will hold.

The great promise of library automation has yet to be fulfilled. To date, the computer has turned out to be merely a new way of doing old things in libraries: generating copy for card catalogs, compiling serials lists, maintaining acquisitions records, controlling circulation. And the economic payoff has been disappointing, or worse.

UNCATALOGING—UNBUILDING

But when the computer is put to the task of large-scale *un*cataloging, and systematic collection *un*building, things we never did before, then it will truly be a new thing under the sun, and the economic payoff enormous.

We have already taken a long step in that direction, with computerized circulation systems and the fabulous OCLC experiment in computer-based cooperative cataloging. The next step will be to let the computer systematically process circulation data and identify titles either to be removed to storage or duplicated to satisfy current demand. Then, when the card catalog is fully displaced by the computer, as it is bound to be in a few years, the computer can uncatalog a book for what it now costs to circulate one, and complete the collection development cycle for a fraction of Ellsworth's estimated cost.

People ask me how we can accurately predict the future demand on a new book before we buy it, to avoid the expense of adding to the Phoenix Library a book that will not be used. My answer to that is simple: I don't know. For it is with books as with men: in their infancy it is hard to guess what their worth will be at maturity. Sizable errors of judgment seem inevitable at the outset, and where library acquisitions are concerned, it bothers me very little.

Over a period of decades, the majority of our acquisitions turn out to be "errors" anyhow, since the level of reader interest in them eventually approaches zero, whatever it may have been at the outset. The cost of buying some books that will never be read is negligible in relation to the cost of housing all the books that have ceased to be read. When the latter problem is dealt with, I favor making large errors in selecting new books, to lessen the probability of making a worse mistake: failing to acquire promptly a high percentage of the new books your patrons want to read.

There is nothing about the concept of the Phoenix Library that compels a reduction in present intake rates of new books. Indeed, the intake rate may rise sharply, if the need exists, without any effect at all on the size of the Phoenix collection. For when intake rates rise, so will outflow rates, and the system remains in equilibrium. Conversely, if it turns out that the intake rate is greater than the demand situation warrants—and I believe this is certainly the case in all academic libraries where serials are concerned—then the intake rate should be reduced, as a matter of common sense, and still the collection size remains constant, for there will be a corresponding drop in the outflow rate.

As to the Library of Babel, there is much about its concept that will soon require a sharp reduction in current intake rates. It has been well said that anything growing at exponential rates aspires to take over the whole planet. Academic libraries have been doing just that in the twentieth century, and if we do not apply the brakes ourselves, somebody else will do it for us. The brakes in fact are already being lightly pressed by others, as witness the progressive disappearance of capital funds for creating new building space. The next logical step in that process will be a sharp curtailment of acquisitions funds, but not because of any absolute scarcity of money for that purpose. Considering its relatively trifling size in relation to total unviersity budgets, money for acquisitions will not disappear through any difficulty in raising it. It will vanish because nobody will care to provide money to purchase books we cannot shelve.

It looks like a Hobson's choice to me: either we abandon Babel for the Phoenix Library, or we forsake the acquisition of new books.

Having declared there are only two choices open to us, I immediately hear a voice asking, "But what about microfilm? If we cannot enlarge our buildings, then let us drastically reduce the unit size of their contents." But that is no choice at all, for experience has already discredited it. The highest growth rates in the history of libraries occurred simultaneously with the ascendancy and flourishing of microtechnology, a paradoxical result that a moment's reflection will lay bare. For we typically acquire materials in microformat only when, for whatever reason, we cannot or will not acquire them on paper. So microcollections usually turn out to be things we would not have acquired at all, had they not been available in microformat; and in that sense what microtechnology has actually accomplished is a micro-increase in our total space problem.

Underlying most decisions to purchase microcollections is, I believe, an instinctive realization that such things will, with few exceptions, get little or no use once they are acquired. We all know that in those rare instances where a significant demand arises for repeated use of any item we own on microfilm, demand invariably arises to convert the microfilm to paper copy, because of its superior legibility, and then we are right back where we started. Would it not make more sense to forego the purchase of the majority of our microfilm collections, and obtain such items from a lending center only when a specific demand for them arises, either in micro or paper format, depending on the nature of the demand?

Doing that returns us directly to the Phoenix Library concept, with low-demand items housed in a national cooperative, where they will be promptly available to anyone on request, preferably in hard copy. Like technology in general, microtechnology has allowed us to do things that are both grandiose and useless, when closer thought would enable us to accomplish more useful ends through more modest means. Technology is not in itself bad, but any misuse of it ceratinly is; and while microtechnology provides some substantial benefits to libraries—as in, for example, the preservation and storage of newspapers—the widespread misuse of it has helped no one.

Of "The Library of Babel," Borges says that "other men, inversely, thought that the primary task was to eliminate useless works. . . . Their name is execrated, but those who mourn the 'treasures' destroyed by this frenzy, overlook two notorious facts. One: the Library is so enormous that any reduction undertaken by humans is infinitesimal. Two: each book is unique, irreplaceable but (inasmuch as the Library is total) there are always several hundreds of thousands of imperfect facsimiles—of works which differ only by one letter or one comma."

REBUILDING BABEL

Where will you find those books? Where else but in the national storage system I have proposed as a device to relieve us of the duty to create the Library of Babel on every campus in the nation.

So the joke, you see, is on me. In prophesying the destruction of the Tower of Babel, I have only succeeded in urging its recreation and its indefinite survival. But there will be just one of them, not the 2,000 we have labored to create in the twentieth century. And when that one threatens to grow intolerably large, we can properly reduce its least used portions to microfilm, and thus approach equilibrium in its size too.

"Where there is no vision," the Proverb says, "the people perish." A clear look downward at what is going on today around the foundations of our lofty Tower may help us see, in time to avoid them, the hazards and the folly of building too high. The narrator of the Book of Genesis says a confusion of tongues seized the men who built that first Tower of Babel on a plain in Shinar. Does anyone imagine a brighter destiny for the builders of our times, who sought to make a name for themselves by making 2,000 replicas of that original mistake?

"We all make mistakes," Will Cuppy observed. "But intelligence enables us to do it on purpose." Maybe intelligence will also enable us to stop on purpose, before others compel us to call a halt, in ways that will damage our mission as librarians. José Ortega y Gasset, who has been called the greatest philosopher of the twentieth century, wants us to become Policemen of the Book, an organization of censors, to guard against the simultaneous existence of both too many books and too few. I maintain there is a better way than that. The road to it was paved years ago by the unnoticed but momentous discoveries of an industrial engineer named Richard Trueswell, who cares enough about libraries to find ways to make them work better in the service of real human needs—work better, and at less cost too, than they have worked in the recent past.

Sweet are the uses of adversity. When "lean-looked prophets whisper fearful change," that is the time to turn bleak adversity into bright opportunity. If philosophers insist we become policemen, then engineers can show us how to become better librarians.

NOTES

1. Jerrold Orne, "The Renaissance of Academic Library Building, 1967-71," *Library Journal,* (December 1, 1971): 3947. The quoted passage refers to the five-year period 1967-1971.

2. See Appendix (by Claudia Schorrig) for analytical details. Certain turns of phrase have also been adapted here from Schorrig's paper.

3. José Ortega y Gasset, "The Mission of the Librarian," tr. James Lewis and Ray Carpenter, *Antioch Review,* (Summer 1961): 133-154. Reprinted as a separate article in 1961 by G. K. Hall.

4. Jorge Luis Borges, "The Library of Babel," in his *Ficciones,* ed. Anthony Kerrigan (Grove Press, c1962), pp. 79-88.

5. Trueswell has published a number of papers over the last ten years elaborating his statistical theory of optimal collection size. The principal study is R. W. Trueswell, *Analysis of Library User Circulation Requirements, Final Report,* January 1968. N.S.F. Grant GNO 435.

6. In at least one library, Trueswell found that only 40 percent of the collection accounted for 99 percent of the recorded use, but he believes that to be at the far end of the range for all libraries. To be on the extremely conservative side, I have based illustrations in this paper on the assumption that 70 percent of a collection will account for 99 percent of recorded use, an assumption that should meet or exceed any actual library's use pattern.

7. Ralph E. Ellsworth, *The Economics of Book Storage in College and University Libraries* (Metuchen, N.J.: ARL and Scarecrow Press, 1969), p. 81.

ANALYSIS OF AGGREGATE BUILDING AND COLLECTION GROWTH DATA, 1967-1974 BY CLAUDIA SCHORRIG

SHELVING CAPACITY ADDED, 1967-1974

Data here are taken from Jerrold Orne's series of American academic library building reports, which appear in each December 1 issue of *Library Journal,* and cover·(with the exception of the five-year cumulation noted below) building completions of the calendar year in which the report appears. Orne excludes two-year college libraries from his report, but includes Canadian senior institutions.

According to Orne (*LJ,* December 1, 1971, p. 3947), the total shelving capacity added in the five-year period 1967-1971 was 127,377,821 volumes. This figure also includes Canadian libraries, whose added capacity must thus be subtracted to obtain a figure for U.S. academic libraries. Adding Orne's individual listings for Canadian libraries on p. 3967 of the *LJ* issue, I get a rounded total of 8,929,000 volumes added shelf capacity. Subtracting this sum from Orne's grand total, and rounding the result, gives us 118,499,000 volumes new capacity in American academic libraries (excluding two-year institutions) for the period 1967-1971. I obtained data for subsequent years simply by adding all the listings in Orne's reports and in all categories except Canadian libraries. I count a renovation project as new capacity, except where Orne has made a specific distinction between new and renovated capacity in connection with a renovation project. Any error of interpretation here would have the effect of making new building capacity appear somewhat larger than it actually was.

From her "Sizing Up the Space Problem in Academic Libraries," in *Farewell to Alexandria: Solutions to Space, Growth, and Performance Problems of Libraries,* ed. Daniel Gore (Westport, Conn.: Greenwood Press, 1976), pp. 14-17.

Completion Date of Building	Capacity Added (volumes)	Number of Buildings
1967-1971	118,449,000	445
1972	15,770,000	36
1973	8,979,000	29
Built but not reported prior to 1973	1,396,000	6
1974	15,805,000	52
Built but not reported prior to 1974	1,704,000	4
Totals:	162,103,000	572

VOLUMES ADDED TO COLLECTIONS, 1967-1974

Data for this section come from *The Bowker Annual of Library & Book Trade Information,* 19th edition, 1974, p. 258. There is a difficulty here, because these summary data for college and university libraries include data for two-year colleges, lumping all into one category. But Orne's building data exclude two-year colleges, so to make the data comparable one must either discover building data for two-year colleges (which I believe is not obtainable for the period in question) or find some means to segregate collection data of two-year colleges from the total. There is little in the literature to help here. But Theodore Samore, a recognized authority on academic library statistics, calculates that for the period in question the acquisitions of two-year college libraries represent 10 percent of the reported total. (Personal communication from Mr. Samore to Daniel Gore.)

To arrive at a net growth figure for any given period, one must also take into account the number of volumes withdrawn. A complete sample of the "Volumes Withdrawn" columns on four pages, taken at random from the Fall 1969 *Library Statistics of Colleges and Universities: Data for Individual Institutions,* shows that volumes withdrawn came to 7.0 percent of those added. Data reported in the *Bowker Annual* ("Volumes at end of year" and "Volumes added during year") also provide a basis for calculating withdrawal rates, but gross anomalies in those correlations make that approach useless. So in the calculations below I have used the 7 percent withdrawal rate figure developed from individual library reports. Aggregate data from the seventy-eight ARL university libraries over a nine-year period yield approximately the same withdrawal rate. Data are taken from *Academic Library Statistics, 1963/64 to 1971/72* (ERIC ED 082 791; Washington, ARL, 1972) and are as follows:

Year	Vols. Added (Gross)	Vols. Added (Net)
1971-1972	7,847,305	7,169,308
1970-1971	7,989,803	7,484,446
1969-1970	7,969,505	7,474,590
1968-1969	7,691,036	7,238,611
1967-1968	7,141,718	6,727,224
1966-1967	6,451,956	6,043,102
1965-1966	5,117,388	4,772,504
1964-1965	4,861,678	4,480,864
1963-1964	4,284,850	3,613,049
	59,355,239	55,003,698

The difference between gross and net indicates a withdrawal of 4,351,541 volumes over the nine-year period, or 7.3 percent of the total added.

For volumes added during 1974, I have used the estimated figure of 24 million, since the Bowker data only go through 1973. That estimate is 1 million less than the figure reported for 1973.

Calculations

Volumes added, 1967-1973 (from Bowker Annual)	174,000,000
Volumes added, 1974 (estimate)	24,000,000
TOTAL:	198,000,000
Less 10 percent (estimated intake of two-year colleges)	19,800,000
Volumes added, 1967-1974, to four-year colleges and universities	178,200,000
Volumes withdrawn, 1967-1974, from four-year colleges and universities (based on 7 percent of intake)	12,400,000
NET ADDITION TO COLLECTIONS	165,800,000vols.
NET ADDITION TO BUILDING CAPACITY	162,103,000vols.
Space Deficit Created During Boom Years:	3,697,000vols.

Things Your Boss Never Told You About Library Management

Several years ago I read a news item about a subway token agent who was retiring after twenty years' service. The token agent, as you probably know, is the man who sits in the little barred cage underground on the platform near the turnstiles and sells you tokens. Besides making change correctly, he is also supposed to be able to give you route information, though ordinarily he will only wave you towards the wall chart, as he's too busy making change, or it's too noisy to be heard.

Now this particular agent had done nothing else in his twenty-year career. He began as a change maker and he ended a change maker. The reporter asked if opportunities had ever come his way to do anything else.

"Yes, I was once offered a promotion as station agent in this same station—but I turned it down."

The reporter asked what was different about the station agent's post and was told that, besides selling tokens, he was responsible for keeping the platform clean. And that was more responsibility than the token agent would feel comfortable with. Why?

"Well, you see, we have this porter named Louie. He sweeps the platform, and he always does a good job. But I says to myself, some day Louie might not sweep up too good, and then if it was me that was the station agent, then I'd have to say, 'Louie, looka here. You ain't swept up behind this post too good,' and Louie might get mad. So I decided I'm better off just doing my hitch as a token agent."

The anxieties of a managerial assignment were too strong for that token agent's imagination to bear. He preferred steady boredom unrelieved by sporadic anguish. The story gives some color to Erich Fromm's speculation, in *The Anatomy of Human Destructiveness,* that humans, like other animals in hierarchical societies, achieve positions of leadership not so much through any great individual ambition, but simply because nobody else would have the job.

Reprinted from *Library Journal* (April 1, 1977), pp. 765-770. Copyright © 1977 by Daniel Gore.

I think Fromm is right, and certainly it is a saving feature of library management that ordinarily no one else on the staff really wants the director's job. The director will usually have enough worries without suffering the inconvenient presence of a subordinate who not only believes it must be a nice thing to have the director's job—but is foolish enough actually to *seek* it.

MANAGERIAL ANXIETY

The anxieties of management are insufficiently appreciated by those in subordinate positions. Until, like the token agent, they are offered some managerial responsibilities and the imagination is suddenly awakened to the realization that something may go wrong. What then? Well, Harry Truman's folksy advice, as you surely remember, was "If you can't stand the heat, stay out of the kitchen." Fromm thinks most people can't—or prefer not to—and that is why most working people can spend their lives more or less comfortably in subordinate posts. The heat is less, and they know it, and they prefer it that way.

But staff members are always, to some degree, great or small, fearful of the boss. On any urgent occasion, or even perverse whim, he can suddenly place uncomfortable burdens on them and demand that they be carried too far or too fast. There are numberless things he may do to increase their miseries—or diminish them—and in any organization he can injure their career hopes, if not deprive them of work altogether. Fear of the boss is an existential fact. Some bosses prefer to maximize it, others prefer to do the opposite, and still others just ignore the matter, with unpredictable results.

No matter what the boss is like, or what he says or does, there is always some measure of fear or uneasiness among the staff—and it needs no prophet come from heaven to tell you that. You knew it the day you started work.

What is not so well known, maybe because managers as a type have no great impulse to confess publicly what may be viewed as weakness, is the fact that the boss usually suffers a good deal more anxiety than the staff. If they are mildly anxious—a condition he can normally prevent if he has any sense at all—then the boss will be in a panic. If *they* are in a panic, he should be in an airplane, leaving town to look for another job.

I think bosses are generally more aware of the anxieties of their staff than the other way around. Not that bosses are better people, but that the structure of the organization leads to that result. When the boss is in trouble—the normal condition—the staff can at least laugh about it. They can always get another boss if things don't work out. But when the staff are in trouble, that means great trouble for the boss, who won't be laughing. If he is smart enough to understand where his own interests lie, he will do his utmost to minimize *their* troubles.

In an Op-Ed article in the *Times* (December 11, 1975), Erich Fromm drew a useful distinction between "paranoid" and "normal" personalities. The paranoid, he says, is wholly concerned with possibilities, while the normal concern is with probabilities. Rationality does not figure in the distinction. The bacteriaphobe who places a handkerchief over the doorknob before turning it is perfectly rational in his claim that there *may* be noxious bacteria on it and that skin contact with them *may* bring a dangerous or deadly disease. The possibility exists, and you will waste your breath trying to talk the paranoid out of it by appealing to the science of bacteriology. It confirms what he is telling you: the possibility exists. Q.E.D., and hence the handkerchief. The paranoid is entirely rational with respect to possibility. And that is his problem.

The "normal" person, in Fromm's distinction, limits his concern to probabilities. While he knows there is a possibility that touching a bare doorknob may open for him a doorway to eternity, he also knows that the probability is infinitesimal, and unthinkingly he open doors with his handkerchief in his pocket.

I have asked myself the interesting question: "What institution is most like a library, in terms of the temperament and outlook of its managers?" My answer: the Pentagon. Let me explain.

Fromm observes that the thinking of the Pentagon, of the Joint Chiefs of Staff, is entirely paranoid where the question of "national security" is concerned. Anything is *possible*—even Soviet conquest through superior techniques of parapsychology; therefore, *everything* should be done. In their paranoid outlook, the Joint Chiefs can make a very strong case for putting the entire GNP at their disposal. Only the normality of the citizenry prevents that from happening. Our concern is with probabilities, and we think the probability of parapsychological conquest is very low. But Pentagon managers, chronically anxious about the endless possibilities of an attack, never let up in their demands for more money, more personnel, more equipment, more everything.

Academic library managers commonly develop a similar anxious concern about possibilities. In a bibliographical universe that presently contains some 50 million titles and adds several hundred thousand new ones each year, what security can one feel even with a collection the size of Harvard's, which now lacks 40 million books and falls farther behind every year? The possibilities of being asked for something you don't own are vast, and if possibilities are what concern you, then the only way to hold your anxieties at a bearable level is to keep hammering away at the administration for more money, more personnel, more computers, more books, more everything. The faculty will at least know you were trying, although they are never satisfied with the results. The administration will come to loathe you for your persistent demands upon the treasury; and between their loathing and the faculty's habitual dissatisfactions, you find yourself being pulverized between the upper and the nether grindstone. In university libraries the process takes about five years to complete; a little more in smaller academic libraries. The director can extricate himself only by taking off for another assignment, and that is what embattled directors invariably do—often, I have noticed, to teach administration in library school.

(They make me think of those Egyptian wise men who, according to Will Cuppy, "invented mosquito netting, astrology, and a calendar that wouldn't work, so that New Year's Day finally fell on the Fourth of July. They believed that the sun went sailing around Egypt all day on a boat and that a pig ate the moon every two weeks. Naturally, such people would wish to record their ideas, so that others could make the same mistakes." And so they invented hieroglyphic writing.)

The director can save himself by vanishing at the critical moment, but the staff cannot. And they, too, must suffer a good bit from the anxieties that pervade an institution when it becomes intensely focused on possibilities. The managerial staff especially will be afflicted by the director's mounting anguish, as will the entire public services staff, whom he will constantly pressure to carry out the impossible task of being prepared to respond instantaneously to all possible service demands. So the director, the other managers, and the public service people will be chronically scared stiff, while everybody else—mainly the catalogers and clerks in the back rooms—will be bored stiff. It is an explosive mixture, and I have seen enough of its grim consequences in academic libraries to wonder what might be done to make working life more agreeable both for those who are scared and those who are bored.

RELIEF MEASURES

In speculating on measures for relief, I make no pretense of speaking scientifically, of developing universal laws of library management. Neither will I try to impress you with learned allusions to scientific treatises on management theory, for I have read just enough of such things to understand that by careful selection one can find authoritative statements to substantiate any view he cares to advance. Until we have a total, unassailable theory of human personality, I do not see how we can have a totally satisfactory theory of management, universally applicable as, say, we understand the law of gravity to be. Meanwhile, I content myself with such instruction and general vision as we find in documents like the Sermon on the Mount or the Tao te Ching. What I mean to do here is merely reflect upon what I have seen hither and yon over my seventeen years in librarianship, and what I believe has worked for me in trying to help my staff find satisfaction rather than frustration in their library work. I can do that and will try to do nothing more.

The main problem with libraries is the director. If he cannot take some heat without passing the warmth on to everybody else, then he should never go into the kitchen at all, for nothing gets cooked without some fire. His problem is to control the fire so he doesn't get himself or anyone else burned up. Library directors who concern themselves with possibilities quickly grow paranoid, making a nuisance of themselves with their superiors and a pestilence to everyone else. The bibliographical world offers far too many possibilities for them to cope with. Dealing with probabilities offers a way out of that predicament.

What in fact makes the practice of librarianship possible is the narrow range of interest that any library clientele will have in the totality of published writings. Put another way, the distribution of interest from one book to another is exceedingly uneven. That is a very lucky thing for us. If the case were otherwise, librarianship would be an impossible calling. Consider this simple logical proposition: If any group of readers held the same degree of interest in each of the 50 million books printed since Gutenberg's time, then even a library of a million books would be largely useless to them. Ninety-eight percent of their searches would end in failure, and no institution can survive that level of frustration.

That we survive at all points to a radically different reality, which happily becomes clearer to everyone as the statistical evidence keeps coming in to show that among any group of readers the majority of interests can be satisfied by relatively small book collections, on the order of a hundred thousand titles or less. Increases in size beyond that level bring ever-diminishing margins of utility, and once a director clearly grasps that immutable phenomenon, he can begin to think calmly about probabilities rather than possibilities, and do something that actually works to respond to those probabilities.

One of those probabilities is that a relatively small proportion of books in any collection will be in such high demand that multiple copies *must* be provided if readers, and the staff who receive their complaints, are to be spared endless disappointments and frustrations. Testing that probability at Macalester, we found that by spending about 3 percent of our annual operating budget on multiple copies, we had cut the frustration rate by a third in just one year. Of course, that was a welcome result for our patrons. But imagine what a blessing it was for the whole public services staff, who heard far fewer complaints that year, and who, when they did hear complaints, could offer the patron more than a shrug by way of explaining what causes the problem, and what we are doing to overcome it.

Library directors, like people, do not enjoy anxiety either, and I was much relieved myself to discover that something useful could be done to cut disappointment rates without having to pester the administration for ever larger book budgets. Had we gone the usual route of trying to meet possibilities head-on, we would have insisted upon vastly enlarged collections and a new building to hold them, and would have wound up with the same level of patron and staff frustration, but greatly intensified dissatisfaction among the administration that provided so much money to buy no practical benefit.

I have known directors who, bent upon impressing the administration with their capacity to increase productivity, simply turned the heat on the staff by measures too ordinary to merit review. The underlying motive may be simply desperation or the malice of vanity. Either way the technique works in the short run. It is no great thing making a sweatshop out of a library or any other institution. Keeping it that way indefinitely turns out to be impossible. Through some miscalculation the director pushes the staff to the panic level, and the revolt is on. "There is nothing more terrible than a revolt of sheep," Balzac said. Some library shepherds come to the realization of that vital truth only as they climb aboard the next plane for anywhere.

SWEATSHOPS AND SUCCESS

I abhor the sweatshop technique. I despise being sweated myself and am willing to believe everybody else does too. I do not know what time any of my staff are supposed to start or quit work, and all I know about the length of their lunch period is that I tell them that their own needs, not college policy, should settle the matter, since the taking of food is a sacrament and ought to be sheltered from the idiot rules of bureaucratic procedure. The one thing I'm reasonably sure of is that nobody spends *more* time on the job than the college's rules require. When the staff have to work longer or faster than what is customary, it is a sure sign the director doesn't know what he's doing. Even if I don't know, I try hard not to let it show.

If one desires to increase productivity—and I believe that is ordinarily an excellent goal since it is the best way to go about getting the typically dismal salaries of library staff improved—there are better ways to do it than sweating the staff. You can help them find simpler ways to do what must be done, and together you can probably find—if you only look—some burdensome tasks that don't need to be done at all. The *possible* tasks of a library staff are infinite. I know of one that had the Sisyphean assignment of compiling indexes for reference books that lacked them. The number of *necessary* tasks is always less than is commonly supposed. But it is no rare thing to find library staffs so burdened by superfluous tasks that they can never keep up with the necessary ones. Anxieties flourish, and real productivity declines.

By improving techniques and dropping unnecessary tasks, we were able to double staff productivity at Macalester, and we could prove to the administration, as well as ourselves, that we had done it. Nobody sweated in the process but me, and that is what I am paid to do, since as a director I am incapable of doing any work.

While I have absolutely no interest in the number of hours my staff work—
so long as it stays within college minimums—I maintain an abiding interest
in what they accomplish in the course of each week's work, and so do they.
That way all of us know routinely that everything is going well, and everyone feels relaxed and comfortable about the work of the library. On those
rare occasions when accomplishment appears to sag, a casual conversation
suffices to clear up the mystery: a number was wrongly recorded, student
staff vanished early on spring break, etc. There are no crises of performance.
I have always found that staff enjoy reporting on their accomplishments,
provided you have done your duty and created for them a situation in which
good work *can* be done. Not asking for staff reports implies their work isn't
worth hearing about, and once you convey that impression, that is the kind
of work you are likely to get.

Annual reports of institutions tend to be pale, lifeless things, generally
unreadable and unread. They don't have to be that way, of course, unless
the people who write them are also pale and lifeless. I look upon the annual
report of a library as a unique and indispensable occasion to create, and
re-create, the complex reality of the library for the several constituencies it
serves: students, faculty, and administration, and of course the library
staff themselves. A library is bound to be perceived by its patrons as the
elephant in the old Hindu fable was perceived by the blind men: as anything
and everything but what in reality it is. A library is too vast and various in its
parts to be correctly perceived by almost anyone but the library director,
who *must* see clearly what it is and what each part is properly supposed to
do—lest he wind up trying to lead the elephant by its tail. Anybody who
can write a dull report of the year's work of a library either doesn't know
what is going on or doesn't care.

A lively, accurate, and comprehensive account of a library's accomplishments is the best way to secure for an entire staff the esteem and rewards
their work merits. "Production" is a dirty word in academic circles, maybe
because of a widespread uneasiness that if someone should be mean enough
actually to measure it, a scandal would result. But I find that even academic
people are capable of understanding that a library produces something, and
they are favorably impressed when you will take the trouble to show them
what it has produced, and at what cost.

Traditionally, we have placed great emphasis upon reporting on what
goes *into* a library: dollars, books, staff positions, and new building space—
as if that demonstrated anything but our capacity to spend other people's
money for them. Much less is said about what comes out, in terms of services
provided, materials lent, operating efficiencies, holdings and availability
rates, and net performance rates in producing those materials that are
actually wanted by the people who use the library. When close attention is

paid to that end of the process, productivity rises, institutional effectiveness increases, and library staff are better paid for doing better work.

Macalester contributes annually to a compilation of library statistics for thirty-nine distinguished colleges—institutions like Amherst, Haverford, and Wellesley. There are twenty-one separate categories for reporting all the things that go into those libraries. There is not a single category for reporting *anything* that comes out. The same extraordinary deficiency can be observed in national compilations of academic library statistics. And, of course, in such reports as we occasionally get from the Pentagon. In our great anxiety about the possibilities for failure, we neglect to say anything at all about our successes.

Have you ever asked yourself what nonlibrarians must think of an institution that launches a barrage of statistics, but has absolutely nothing to report about the work it has done? If nowhere else, that negative impression can be remedied on your own campus by writing and distributing a lively, intelligible report each year of what the library staff have actually contributed to the enterprise of teaching and learning. Faithful reporting not only creates the reality of a library, it induces everyone spontaneously to perfect that reality. Once that process is set in motion, it largely runs of its own accord, for it takes the friction out of the system. Nobody has to be told or goaded to do what is necessary, when the situation has been rendered fully intelligible. Your staff as a whole are at least as smart as you are, and you can count on their doing well what must be done, if you will just allow them to see where and how it fits into the whole reality of the library.

Academic library staff are particularly vulnerable to abuse from the faculty, a few of whom, you can always be sure, are incapable of distinguishing between what is possible and what is not, and ill-mannered enough to take out their frustration on your staff when informed that it is not possible to fulfill their perverse wish. That kind of abuse can reach serious proportions if the director is not willing to state generally what is possible and what is not, and let it be known on campus that the library is not designed to respond to all *possible* requests, and will make no apologies for maintaining a deliberate, rational, and economically necessary margin of failure. Some badgering will nonetheless take place, and the director will just have to put a stop to it, giving full support to his staff no matter what the facts of the situation may be. Faculty who are not satisfied with staff performance can always take the problem up with the director, but should never be allowed to harass the staff, much as some of them would love to do that. A director who will not spare his staff that kind of heat by taking it on himself should seek a cooler line of work.

In that wonderful collection of essays entitled *Small Is Beautiful: Economics As If People Mattered,* E. F. Schumacher chooses a fine phrase,

"The Principle of Subsidiary Function," to indicate the abiding requirement that the manager stay out of his subordinates' hair. He borrows the phrase from—of all things for an economist to be reading—the Encyclical "Quadragesimo Anno" and quotes the argument in its favor as follows: "It is an injustice and at the same time a grave evil and disturbance of right order to assign to a greater and higher association what lesser and subordinate organizations can do." For our present concern, that means that a director should ordinarily be doing none of those things the operating departments are capable of doing, and that he should intervene in their work only in exceptional instances. By definition that means rarely. It is not necessarily a bad sign if staff grow a little edgy when the director walks into their department. If things are being managed as the Pope and Schumacher and I think they should be, then the director's presence in an operating department *ought* to signal that something at least a little unusual is going on, and that fact in itself is sufficient to put everyone momentarily on the alert. If staff are totally relaxed when you enter their turf, it may mean that you have subverted their morale by frequent usurpations of their function, and instead of momentary tension, you have aroused steady contempt.

I do not mean to imply that every library management problem admits of a happy solution, although I believe that most do. In fifteen years of managerial assignments, I have actually fired three people, and I imagine I will always remember their names and the exact circumstances that led to the firing, so painful is that duty when it must be done. Still I believe it was as much a favor to them as to the library, for some folks cannot stand to do the work that must be done, but lack the gumption to give it up for something more congenial.

Even among your very best performers you must expect some occasional failings. When they occur, I follow the uncivilized example of the Mbutu tribe, that charming group of Central Congo pygmies Colin Turnbull has written about in *Wayward Servants* and elsewhere. Instead of seeking to blame an individual even when he is clearly at fault, the Mbutu make elaborate and sometimes comical efforts to deflect the blame on some impersonal or utterly ridiculous cause. They are wise enough to know that placing blame only worsens the original problem. Deflecting or diffusing the blame allows everyone to quickly forget the offense and resume harmonious relations. When mishaps occur in the library, my main concern is to see what I can learn from them. More often than not, they come about because I did not properly anticipate a novel predicament requiring more understanding of a policy or practice than I had conveyed to the person caught in the predicament.

Administration, it is said, consists of a series of minor crises punctuated here and there by major crises. I've always thought that saying was even more foolish than it was funny. Certainly there is no necessity for crisis atmospheres to prevail in organizations as small as academic libraries. Even the largest have staffs numbering no more than several hundred people, and at that size crisis ought not be the dominant atmosphere, for people are certainly capable of understanding and carrying out the mission of such a small organization in a calm and purposeful way.

Twenty-five years ago, as a boot ensign directing Coast Guard search and rescue missions in the Gulf of Mexico, I held, with some other young men, much broader command responsibilities than you find in libraries, and the only crises were those we were trying to help other folks survive. We knew what we had to do, and we did it, unruffled by the probability that there would occasionally be failures, even fatalities. But I have seen catalogers work themselves up into worse frenzies over the inconsequential choice of a corporate name entry than we suffered even when, as once happened by some mischance, we sent a helicopter full of congressmen out to watch a buoy tender work all day, when we were supposed to have had them rendezvous with a cutter at the scene of an airliner crash. The night I phoned the district commander to report that gaffe, all he said was "Thank you, and just keep your damned mouth shut and the congressmen will never know." And that was that. Had the skipper been a cataloger, I might have been keel-hauled.

The tensions in the workrooms of libraries may arise from the repetitive nature of most of the work and the fact that most of the workers are usually alienated from the results of their labor. In large libraries you are likely to see many such people, bored stiff and irritable, relieving their frustration through daily bickering and backbiting. Their work suffers too. I believe that wherever the introduction of OCLC has effected real reductions in cataloging costs, it is merely from the refreshing force of novelty, acting through the sudden presence of a television screen in the workroom to rupture a mass boredom of maybe a half-century's duration. When the novelty wears off and the grip of boredom tightens up again, production costs will climb right back where they used to be. Early warning signs are already appearing in the news we read about libraries developing blacklists of other OCLC members that are contributing inferior catalog copy to the data base.

What can be done to cure the boredom and alienation of the people in library workrooms? In academic libraries, which exist mainly for the sake of students, a guaranteed permanent cure for those ills is available to anyone willing to try it. All that is needed is to involve students as fully as may be in the work of the library. Since they are after all what the work is all about, their heavy participation in the library's work is bound to prevent regular staff from feeling alienated from the results of their work: for the results are right there in the middle of it. Teaching young people to work in fruitful cooperation with others is certainly no less vital than teaching them chemistry or French. Learning to work that way is for college students the indispensable rite of passage between adolescence and adult responsibilities, and the library is better able to administer that rite than any other unit on campus.

Student staff hours typically run 10 to 20 percent of the total worked in an academic library. At Macalester they are 50 percent because I believe wholeheartedly that library work is a superb educational experience for young people.

I've also discovered that maintaining a high percentage of student workers is a sovereign cure for the characteristic boredom of regular staff. At Macalester, each staff member has five or ten students to train and supervise each term, so a considerable part of everyone's time is devoted to instruction, which can never be boring, even if you are only teaching someone to sort and file catalog cards. Sorting and filing are indeed boring activities themselves, but students aren't doing it on a career basis, nor even for many hours a week. Some of them welcome those interludes of repetitive work, as a relief from the mental strain of studying.

In the course of a year, some 10 percent of all students at Macalester will work for the library. And at any one time probably one-fourth of the students on campus will be present or past library workers. With that kind of participation in our work, students cannot and do not regard the library as an indifferent, uncaring, bureaucratic preserve. The library is not just made for them. It is made by them too, and everyone prospers under that arrangement.

When staff are neither bored by their work, nor alienated from it, nor made anxious by it, productivity is bound to soar. And when that happens, a library director has the best possible case for making compensation rise too.

"A feast is made for laughter, and wine maketh merry," said Ecclesiastes, preacher in Jerusalem. "But money answereth all things."

The best hope I can see to remedy the sad salary situation of library staff is to find agreeable ways to bring about quantum leaps in real productivity, and then prove to your administration that you have done it. The happiest time of year for me is when seasonal negotiations get underway with the college administration for staff salary improvements. That is an excellent time to celebrate the work my staff has done for the college. And when a celebration is going on, you can cheerfully abandon caution and the restraints of modesty, let your hair down, and do with all your might the thing that must be done to brighten everyone's prospects for a better year ahead.

Going Out of Bibliographical Control: A Theory of Library Organization Based on Human Principles

Many years ago I worked in the serials cataloging department of what in those days was regarded as a very large research library—about 2 million volumes. My boss was an intelligent, worried-looking fellow whom I shall call Bill. His talk was always full of the ear-catching phrase "bibliographical control," and his arms were often loaded with cataloging "snags"—items that had thwarted the attempts of us junior catalogers to get them cataloged according to Bill's (and the Library of Congress's) exacting standards for serial monographs.

When I started work there, the department had about 5,000 of these snags on wall shelves awaiting cataloging, and nobody but Bill would touch them. Others had already tried to catalog them and failed. Bill had two desks about 10 feet apart. Old-timers told me that some years back the first one got covered by as many snags as Bill could stack on top of it. Then he brought in a second desk, and when it too vanished beneath a ragged mound of monographs in series, Bill began to work directly from a book truck. He organized his work in such a way that the desks were used only as intermediate storage facilities. You could not easily get up to the desks anyhow, as each was fully ringed by a palisade of snags that had gradually drifted down from the top of the desk pile and then begun to grow upward in a pile from the floor, like a cylindrical wedge.

So Bill worked from a book truck—actually several of them, organized on the same principle as the desks, and including your book truck too, if you didn't retrieve it soon after Bill quietly wheeled it off to make more work space for his growing collection of snags. Bill started the morning's

Hitherto unpublished, this essay is a slightly revised version of a speaking text I have used at a variety of library gatherings around the country.

work by removing an armload of snags from a book truck, and then he set out on an itinerary of library departments that might furnish the necessary clues for getting these publications unsnagged. Reference, Acquisitions, Descriptive Cataloging, Bibliographical Search, the Public Serials Catalog— these were the usual stops, and at each of them, in the course of some absorbing conversation that eventually got around to Bill's favorite theme of bibliographical control, Bill would make a small, inadvertent deposit of snags on the nearest table or desk and then be off to the next stop. In this way, the whole armload of snags would be disposed of by lunch, and Bill would equip himself afterwards with a fresh armload for afternoon distribution. Snags thus deposited would occasionally be returned to our department by a well-meaning colleague, and we would add them to the top of a desk pile, to repeat their slide to the floor, from which Bill then transferred them to a book truck, when an aisle became blocked by the widening circle of floor-level snags.

The saving feature of Bill's system of bibliographical control was that none of the snags had to be cataloged. That would have required desk space, and Bill had none. Instead, the snags just got perpetually shifted from place to place, and since they were much harder to read than to catalog, the system worked no hardship even on the most advanced researchers using the library. They were too busy writing just such things themselves to waste their time trying to read somebody else's impenetrable monograph.

Bill often carried with him, in a ring notebook, the manuscript of a treatise he was developing on bibliographical control. He loved to read from it to anyone who would listen. Newcomers like myself were favorably impressed by the urgency of his concern and stunned by the complexity of his undertaking. But our awe diminished when we came to see the practical outcome of Bill's theories of bibliographical control.

He once attempted to maintain separate bibliographical control for a journal and its covers. Our library was desperately short of shelf space, and Bill correctly deduced that less of it would be required if journal issues were bound with their covers removed. So Bill instructed the bindery preparations clerk to remove the covers. Then some fastidious soul confided to him that the covers of scholarly journals sometimes carried vital information not repeated in the journal itself. How would scholars get at it if Bill removed the covers?

Nothing to it. Bill decided we would keep the covers in our workroom. Then when a scholar needed one, he had only to ask us for it. Bill would later figure out a system of bibliographical control for the covers; meanwhile, they would be stripped and stored neatly in a pile by the bindery clerk's desk. In those days, we were receiving perhaps 2,000 journal issues a week. The bindery clerk, a woman who had served in the Marine Corps, had anxious fantasies of being encircled by, and then buried under, the journal

covers, and she told Bill so. "It'll work out all right," Bill said. The strip-
ping began, and those covers sprang upwards from the floor like some
tropical vine. In the third week, the clerk's desk vanished, and the clerk
announced that she too would soon vanish—one way or the other—if Bill
didn't change his mind about saving those covers. Seeing that they weren't
coming under bibliographical control nearly so fast as he had hoped, Bill
decided we would just have to discard them. To deposit those covers on the
daily rounds, along with the monographic serials, was too much even for Bill.

So the covers went: a melancholy end to an ambitious experiment in
bibliographical control. No one has dared to repeat it, though nowadays we
have computers to help out—as Bill did not—and the space problem is more
desperate than ever. Had Bill's queer genius carried him just a centimeter
farther in that quixotic enterprise, he might have rescued us all from one of
our more pressing predicaments. He might have decided to bind the covers
and discard the innards of, say, all but 5 percent of those journals, and
nothing of value would have been lost, while an enormous amount of shelf
space would be saved.

Maybe he was reserving his genius for the last of his bibliographical
innovations I shall tell you about. It is a thing that to this day—nearly two
decades after the event—still teases me out of thought with its metaphysical
profundity. It is rather like a Zen *Koan.* One day we catalogers realized that
all new volumes on the "To Be Cataloged Shelf" had begun to contain not
only the usual printed routing slip, but also a perfectly blank pink slip of the
same dimensions. At first we just ignored it. But finally someone's curiosity
got the best of him, and he asked Bill, "What does that pink slip mean that
you're putting in all the new books?"

"Oh," said Bill, "That means the book is here." After that we decided
to leave Bill alone. If the pink slip is in the book and the book is here—well,
I ask you, what is wrong with saying that the pink slip means the book is
here? Incessant thinking about bibliographical control had transported
Bill to a sphere beyond our reach as well as our grasp, and none of us cared
to ask what it would mean if a book showed up with *no* pink slip in it. After
all, we were catalogers, not philosophers. And any time we wanted to re-
assure ourselves of the essential craziness of the bibliographical world, we
had only to peek beyond the title page of whatever it was we happened to be
cataloging. We didn't need to bother Bill with crazy questions.

All of that stuff that Bill used to shuffle from place to place is probably
under firm bibliographical control by now. But it is hard to imagine who
has benefited from that monumental effort, since no one ever bothered us
to produce for him any of those 5,000 snags that for years had been waiting
on our workroom shelves to be cataloged. Like Gogol's wily comic hero
Chichikov, we were merely trying to support ourselves through the acquisition and formal registration of a growing flock of dead souls.

The concern with bibliographical control is, of course, ancient. I need mention only the clay tablet catalogs of the Sumerian royal libraries, as well as the lost "Pinakes" of Callimachus, thought to be a catalog of the enormous Alexandrian Library. The necessity for formal, rational control naturally arises whenever a collection grows to inconvenient size, simply because the human mind cannot recall either the identity or the whereabouts of any one of a large number of objects. Systems of control have been based on a narrow range of principles. Books may be arranged on shelves by subject, size, author, date of accession, date of publication, or some combination of these. Catalog records for them may be arranged alphabetically by author, title, subject, or class number, and subarranged in various ways. Whatever the principle of organization may be, it will be seen to refer directly to some bibliographical feature of the book itself. Its relation to human principles may begin and end with the fact that the system was originally devised to remedy the inability of humans to remember large numbers of things.

After that, the system usually develops on strictly bibliographical principles, with some secondary concern for linguistic principles, as in the formation of subject catalogs. The system chosen is intended to be effective no matter how large the library may grow. Scale is irrelevant.

On that basis, one might also surmise that through prolonged overfeeding a single-celled amoeba could be made to grow into a satisfactory whale, with no elaboration of structure along the way. The amoeba, of course, knows better than to let such an absurd thing happen. So does a whale, and everything else in nature. Libraries do not, and we have seen thousands of them grow from amoeba to whale size without any change in structure. Collections and catalogs grow steadily larger with no internal changes in their organization. The bibliographical principle governs all, while the human principle that necessitates bibliographical control is largely forgotten.

Robert Ornstein, in his widely used and refreshingly lucid text *The Psychology of Consciousness* (Viking, 1972) speaks of the vital functioning of the brain (and other parts of the sensory system) as a reducing valve, designed "to reduce the amount of 'useless and irrelevant' information reaching us and to serve as a selection system." Thus, the human eye is by design capable of sensing only a tiny fraction of the entire electromagnetic spectrum. What it sees is necessary for biological survival. What it does not see— cosmic rays, X-rays, radio waves, etc.—is (or was) irrelevant to survival and would only bedevil us with fruitless, ceaseless distractions if it could be seen. And the brain by design forgets nearly everything that it appears perfectly capable of storing, given the enormous number of its neuronal connections. The need to forget must far outweigh the need to remember. Ornstein quotes C. B. Broad (a physiologist) to this effect:

The function of the brain and nervous system is to protect us from being overwhelmed and confused by a great mass of largely useless and irrelevant knowledge, by shutting out most of what we should otherwise perceive and remember at a given moment, leaving only that very small and special selection that is likely to be practically useful.

How then does this protective, reductive function of the brain bear on the problems of library organization?

We are hearing regularly now from the people in the largest libraries that their card catalogs have grown too large for convenient use. Similar concerns are less often stated about overlarge collections, but there are great problems in using them too. The solutions that are being proposed contemplate no essential change in the structure of the catalog or the organization of the collections. Rather, the existing bibliographical system will be automated and, if possible, vastly enlarged by bringing the catalog records of many libraries into a single computerized catalog. It seems to me that this way of proceeding is bound to worsen the problem it sets out to solve, for it ignores the underlying human principle that creates the problem in the first place: namely, the disposition of the human mind to "protect us from being overwhelmed and confused by a mass of largely useless and irrelevant knowledge." Ever-growing catalogs (and collections) fly squarely in the face of that human principle. The principles now heeded are mainly bibliographic and electronic, and these are insufficient for serving human needs.

A simple cure to overgrown card catalogs is to elaborate their structure by splitting them into three files (author, title, subject), thus reducing the length of each file by about two-thirds. It is easily proved that this very inexpensive structural upgrading greatly simplifies both catalog use and catalog production. Yet, large libraries are evincing more interest in automating their catalogs, at enormous effort and expense, than they have ever shown in the tried and tested alternative of elevating catalog structure from the amoeba level to that of a three-cell organism. The Library of Congress's card catalog—the world's largest—is an amoeba grown to whale size.

Reducing file length by splitting the catalog into three alphabets responds directly to the mind's need for protection against "being overwhelmed and confused by a mass of largely useless and irrelevant knowledge." If one is searching for a title entry, it helps greatly not to have that search overwhelmed and confused by the irrelevant presence of author and subject entries in the file. And so for the other two possible objects of a search: authors or subjects. But I believe the greatest benefits to be gained through the restoration of human principles to library organization will come through the structuring of book collections in such a way that most users can bypass the catalog altogether in most of their searches.

Several years before I learned from Ornstein that the brain functions as a reducing valve, I blundered my way into a principle of collection organization that answers precisely the brain's need to be sheltered from the "mass of largely useless and irrelevant knowledge." I say blundered because the special collection I am speaking of was formed without any such object in view. It was formed rather to reduce cataloging costs and to make new books more quickly available to readers. Both objects were accomplished through the creation of the FASTCAT collection. Cataloging staff has been reduced from eight positions to two, and all new books are on the shelves ready for loan within forty-eight hours of their arrival in the library. Total unit cataloging and processing costs appear to be even less than the cost of procuring a set of catalog cards from OCLC, while the time required to make new books available to readers is much less with FASTCAT than with OCLC.

Even more interesting than these economies of time and money is the FASTCAT collection itself. The idea for it was, of course, stolen from my friend Marvin Scilken, who stole it from his friend Harry Dewey, who stole it from God. Scilken turned Dewey's idea into the Frontlog Collection of the Orange, New Jersey, Public Library, by moving the cataloging backlog out front where patrons as well as catalogers could get at it. FASTCAT started with the same idea but took some unexpected turns, both as to size and structure.

Our original approach was to give each new book a temporary FASTCAT call number which would simply be the six-digit order number customarily assigned when a book was ordered. Since the order numbers followed a straight serial sequence, books shelved by those numbers in the FASTCAT collection were arranged chronologically by their order dates. Subject relationships were entirely random and chaotic. Thus, *Love Story, The Selling of the President,* and *The Peter Principle* would be shelved side by side if they were ordered in that sequence. I had some curiosity to find out just how large a chaos of new books our clientele would tolerate before someone protested. People at Macalester have a great love of reading and a great love of protesting, so I expected to be hearing from them soon. A year passed, and this randomly arranged collection grew to about 5,000 volumes. But nobody objected. Yet, the collection was being heavily used, at a rate double that of the general collections despite its chaotic arrangement and despite the lack of catalog access either by authors or subjects. A copy of the order slip was filed as a temporary entry in the title section of the card catalog, and that is all the catalog access there would be so long as a book remained in the FASTCAT collection. Something was happening that appeared to run exactly counter to the orthodox teachings of librarianship: a collection in total subject disarray, and with grossly deficient catalog access, was getting substantially heavier use per volume in it than the general collections, which were shelved in rational subject order and fully cataloged.

When I described the FASTCAT technique in the September 1, 1972, *LJ,* several thoughtful people wrote to assure me that it would add greatly to our cataloging costs and that the absence of full catalog access to FASTCATs would prove an intolerable handicap for our patrons. What these anxious souls did not know was that in the first year of its life the FASTCAT collection did not even have any subject structure, for by the time I wrote the essay for LJ we had built structure into the collection, and I described only that second stage in the evolution of the FASTCAT.

Patron protest had nothing to do with the decision to create a subject structure for FASTCAT, for there never were any protests. But there were expressions from the faculty of great satisfaction with the ready access FASTCAT gave them to new books. When the original collection reached a size of 5,000 volumes, I began to find it disagreeably cumbersome to pursue in it my own interests in new books, so I decided to elaborate its structure. We created general subject groupings by constructing order numbers beginning with some twenty-five different alphabetical prefixes, corresponding to LC notation. Thus, the order number (as well as the FASTCAT call number) for a math text begins QA, followed by a straight serial sequence within that category, while the number for a psychology text begins BF, and so on. The number of volumes in any category will clearly be only a small fraction of the original unstructured collection of 5,000 volumes. I had surmised that developing the structure of the collection would bring immediate increases in its use, but that did not happen. Two years later, a student suggested we leave dustwrappers on FASTCATs, and we did just that—also remembering that it is a time-tested axiom among booksellers that what sells a book is its wrapper, not its content. In the year that practice began, the use rate of the collection jumped by a staggering 50 percent, and it continues to rise. Presently, the use rate of FASTCATs is five times that of the general collection; among the faculty, it is thirteen times that of the general collections. Although FASTCATs now represent just 2 percent of the total bookstock, they account for 10 percent of all general loans.

Following the advice of Sextus Empiricus, the codifier of Greek skepticism, I shall suspend judgement on just what caused the great jump in FASTCAT use rates in the fourth year of the collection's existence. Maybe it stemmed mainly from a growing awareness among our clientele of what and where the collection was—and the special satisfactions to be had in using it. I do not know.

What most intrigues me about this unusual collection is that in the first year of its life it yielded a use rate double that of the general collections, although it violated practically all of the canons of bibliographical organization and control.

From that experience with FASTCAT, and a later experience with an uncataloged collection of more than 1,000 new phonograph records (which exhibited use rates ten times that of the fully cataloged regular collection), I have become a true believer in the following principles of library organization:

People have a much greater average interest in new books than in old ones.

A collection of 5,000 books in a state of near-zero bibliographical control is not so large that the brain feels "overwhelmed and confused by a mass of largely useless and irrelevant knowledge," provided that the brain knows that a relatively high proportion of the books in that collection will be more than ordinarily useful and appealing.

A special collection of books formed on human principles is more useful to readers than one formed on bibliographical principles.

People hate catalogs and love to bypass them as much as possible.

The FASTCAT collection has yet another quite special feature. It is a no-growth collection, and it is up to whoever forms it to decide what size it should be. My intuitive choice is that it should represent between one and two years' intake of new books. Once the criterion is met, older books are permanently cataloged as the newest ones are added, thus keeping collection size in equilibrium. Less than a year's intake would, I believe, insufficiently satisfy the strong human curiosity about new books. But I should note that most of the sixty libraries I know of that use FASTCAT take the position that its ideal size is zero. That is to say they regard it wholly as a cataloging stratagem—and if LC copy were available for each new book as it arrived, they would send nothing to the FASTCAT shelves. That approach ignores human concerns and makes bibliographical principles paramount.

In large libraries, more than two years' intake on the FASTCAT shelves might prompt the mind to begin acting as a reducing valve. I am not at all sure what the upper limit may be. I do know we had not reached it with 5,000 volumes in random shelf order. With twenty to forty general subject groupings, an upper practical limit could turn out to be 100,000 volumes or more. It would be well to test that figure empirically, but I am not situated to do so. For a large library with a strong sense of administrative self-confidence—almost a contradiction in terms—such an experiment could yield enormously valuable findings, favorable or otherwise.

I am inclined to think that the average age of FASTCAT books may be a more potent limiting factor than the mind's incapacity to tolerate large numbers.

Keeping more than two years' intake in the FASTCAT collection might adversely affect one's perception of it as a *new*-book collection. A ten-year intake, for example, obviously would. An upper age limit definitely exists, but I have not tested to find out what it is, as our space situation at Macalester pretty well imposes on us a limit of two years' intake.

FASTCAT manifests a principle of library organization based on the universally observed interest that people have in books because they are new. If that interest did not commonly exist among readers, the FASTCAT collection would not receive such extraordinarily heavy use. Indeed, it would not exist without that strong interest, for it would not be needed: not even for the purpose of expeditious processing, for there would be no demand for that either. FASTCAT responds to the perennial human thirst for novelty and to the mind's desire not to be overwhelmed by large masses of irrelevant objects.

Another class of book that lies at the other end of the time spectrum, and generates equal or greater human interest, is the book that has withstood the test of time: in George Orwell's opinion, the only reliable test for isolating that handful of books, among the tens of millions that have been written, that may be confidently called classics. Several years ago, I was stirred to thought about those books by the unpleasant realization that the worth of libraries, like the worth of banks, is usually measured by the size of their holdings.

Books become abstracted into mere numbers because of their great quantity, and librarians are tempted to regard them all as exactly equal in value, like dollar bills. Does your library own a million books? Excellent! Then it is ten times a better library than the one down the road with only 100,000. Spend $20 million to add another million books to it, and it will be twice as good a library as it used to be—and twenty times better than the one down the road. In reality it may be worse, but appearances are in the saddle and hold the reins.

Competition among libraries inevitably drifts into a rivalry of mere size. Quantity signifies quality, *more* is synonymous with *better,* and *most* is *best*— as if the Astrodome were a better building than the Parthenon.

Librarians see the folly of quantitative values as clearly as other persons. We make no claim that a thousand murder mysteries are better than one *Hamlet,* ten volumes of Eddie Guest more precious than one "Ode on a Grecian Urn." But the values of sheer quantity become inescapable for us—and those who judge our efforts—in a world that has already produced 50 million books and adds 500,000 new ones to the heap each year. A librarian who aspires to build a small library excites no more applause than a mountain climber who scales a foothill. The conditions of his calling compel him to think big.

For the welfare of his patrons, it would be well if, in the midst of superfluity, he could also think small. Especially so if his patrons are students making their first tentative explorations in the forest of books. A moderate-sized library of several hundred thousand books, even if perfectly cataloged and staffed by amiable experts to guide the perplexed, is still a bewildering maze for the beginner. Where do you start in a library that already holds more books than you can read in a thousand years, and each year adds more than a lifetime's new reading?

Well, a student starts where his professors tell him to start, and that's that. The library is only an adjunct to the classroom. It is the kitchen, and the faculty furnish the recipes for the intellectual cookery that goes on in it.

The picture is plausible, orderly, reassuring—and wrong. One careful investigation of the actual reading habits of students disclosed the startling fact that nearly half the books they borrow from a library may have nothing to do with the courses they are taking. (Irene A. Braden, *The Undergraduate Library* [Chicago: American Library Association, 1970], p. 56.) For them the library is no kitchen, but the site of the self-made, uncoerced curriculum, where each decides for himself how he will stretch his mind, what intellectual itch he will scratch next, what beckoning curiosity he will heed today, and what tomorrow, and tomorrow, and tomorrow (and in no petty pace). The library is the place for the unfettered intellectual growth of the young. It is a region for spontaneous exploration and discovery—and a lot of it is going on, as we know from the observed reading habits of undergraduates and from our recollection of what our own intellectual excitements were like in our youth.

But in a library of hundreds of thousands of books, the discovery of "the best that has been thought and said in the world" can be a disheartening task. It is like trying to find two grains of wheat hid in two bushels of chaff. The card catalog gives no help in distinguishing wheat from chaff, being merely a record of what is there, and not an indicator of its value. Nor is there help from the subject classification of books, which simply arranges them on the shelves by type without disclosing anything of their relative merit. A student or, for that matter, most users of a public library gazing at a collection of 5,000 novels will be hard put to discover that precious few of the calibre of *Tom Jones* or *The Brothers Karamazov*. If one is not a literature specialist he may never discover them, although he is seeking just such books and they lie right before his eyes. If he is not a biologist, he will miss Fabré's classic work on insects, just as the biologist is likely to miss Plato's *Republic,* or the philosopher Plutarch's *Lives.*

Do people really want to be plainly told what the great books are, and then go on to read them? The financial success of such enormous publishing ventures as the "Great Books of the Western World" proclaims emphatically that they do. People will spend large sums of money to possess such sets, even though the editorial work may be unsatisfactory, the typography inferior, and the bindings unlovely. People want to be *shown* the great authors. Librarians, prompted by worthy motives of neutrality, instead show them everything. In public libraries, I have often noticed special collections of detective stories, murder mysteries, science fiction, and romantic novels, but never a comprehensive collection of great authors. The giants fade from view amid a swarm of pygmies.

Academic librarians also lose sight of the giants. Pressed as we are to keep up with the tens of thousands of new books coming out each year, it is no scandal if we do not realize that there is not one good reading edition of Keats in the library, not enough copies of *War and Peace* to satisfy the demand, and no copy at all of the Upanishads. Glaring omissions are usually discovered, if at all, when a reader notices them and raises a question. Continuing qualitative review of a collection of hundreds of thousands of books becomes a practical impossibility.

If the great books of the world were drawn together in one special collection, then readers could discover them effortlessly, and librarians could maintain a continuous survey of those books to make sure that each one was available in sufficient copies and in textually and typographically superior editions. How large might such a collection be? Genius is rare. Of the millions upon millions of books that have been published, the number of those that have withstood the test of time—the only certain measure of greatness—approximates 2,000. Add to those the 500 or so tentative candidates from the last century—works so recent that one cannot conclusively say they have failed the test of time—and you have a collection that fills only one side of a standard 24-foot stack unit. The estimate of 2,500 books, if in error, errs on the side of liberality. Robert Hutchins' "Great Books" series, for example, represents the work of less than a hundred authors, while the "Harvard Classics" compresses all into fifty volumes.

Critics have developed numerous aesthetic criteria by which they claim to distinguish classic works from all others; as one example, take Matthew Arnold's "touchstone" test of "high seriousness." Their criteria, however, have often been used to seal with immortality books that scarcely lasted the lifetime of the critic. The test of time works infallibly. It is Mind-at-Large working as a grand reducing valve "to protect us from being overwhelmed and confused by a great mass of largely useless and irrelevant knowledge."

With 2,500 books chosen systematically from the standard bibliographical guides, one can be sure of including all authors of world stature. With so small a collection, one can also take the considerable pains necessary to see that every author is represented in the best editions—editorially and aesthetically—that are available. Assume an average requirement of two copies of each work—since the loan demand in such a collection will be predictably greater than the norm—and a collection of about 5,000 books is called for, representing fully "the best that has been thought and said in the world."

Would such a collection be actively used? That much can be guaranteed. For librarians, like grocers, know that the prominent display of any attractive portion of their stock increases the demand for it. Place such a collection of books in a heavy traffic area and a use rate several times greater than the usual may ensue. People who would otherwise never read a word of Homer, Sophocles, Horace, or Tolstoy would almost certainly do so under these circumstances. Under any other circumstances, short of majoring in literature, they are almost certain not to do so, except on the lucky counsel of a well-read friend. My strategy is consciously subversive. It intends the injection of quality into the educational enterprise.

The documented fact of heavy, independent, voluntary student use of libraries implies that students, and perhaps others, will eagerly acquire a liberal education on their own initiative, if given a convenient starting place. That is what libraries never give them. Instead of offering them somewhere to start, we offer everywhere, which is the same as nowhere in a collection of hundreds of thousands of books.

We are presently developing a Greats collection at Macalester College. When it reaches its full size of about 5,000 volumes, it will then constitute perhaps 2 percent of the total book collections. I am prepared to forecast that it will eventually account for 10 percent of all general loans. That, of course, is partly an expression of personal faith in the classics, but only partly. Keep in mind that the underlying reason that we call those books classics is that they have passed the test of time. Human interest in them has proved to be enduringly greater than in the ordinary mass of books. The inference is irresistible that in a library, too, people will show far greater interest in them—especially if they are made easy to find.

Note that the Greats collection, like FASTCAT, will also be essentially a no-growth collection. If my estimate of 2,500 titles produced over roughly the last 2,500 years is anywhere near accurate, then the growth rate of a Greats collection should work out to an average of about one title per year. The size of the collection will not change perceptibly, even over the course of a century.

Also like FASTCAT, the Greats collection will be small enough that readers will not ordinarily be expected to consult the catalog to gain access to the books in it. As a gesture to tradition, however, we will indeed provide full catalog entries for those books since, unlike FASTCATs, they will remain permanently in a special collection.

Now we have two collections totaling about 10,000 volumes and representing about 4 percent of our total bookstock. Taken together, they should account for 20 percent of all general book loans, but patrons will make little use of the card catalog or any other bibliographical record to discover them. For the organization of the collections takes into account the human principles of the enduring thirst for novelty, the abiding interest in the relatively few authors who (like Shakespeare) are "for all time," and the mind's tendency to function as a reducing valve and thus blot out large masses of "useless and irrelevant knowledge." The organization of the library begins to mimic the structure of the mind itself.

What of that great mass of books that lies between either end of the time spectrum, between the Greats and the FASTCAT? At Macalester we have more than 200,000 of them already, and more are on the way. University libraries and the great public libraries, of course, have millions of such books. Most are rarely or never used. Yet, thousands of them, neither great nor very new, are nonetheless used often enough that it should be an enormous help if the reducing valve principle were also applied to isolate them from the vast numbers of rarely or never-used books. Can it be done? Statistical studies of collection use patterns by the industrial engineer Richard Trueswell clearly show that it can be done. I will not review his findings in detail here because that has been done elsewhere. Rather, I will speak of one particular application of his theory to the problem before us.

Trueswell has discovered that in any mature library collection—that is, a collection that holds around 85 percent of the titles a local patron is likely to ask for—30 to 50 percent of the collection is so little used that it actually fills only 1 to 5 percent of the total demand. If that portion of the collection should be sequestered from the relatively active collections, readers would scarcely notice either its separate status in some remote area of the library building or even its total removal—so little does it contribute to satisfying the aggregate needs of the whole group of library patrons. In its present unsegregated condition, what that little-used portion of the collection does contribute is a "great mass of largely useless and irrelevant knowledge," which overwhelms and confuses the minds of most readers. They are looking for something else. A reducing valve is needed, and I will indicate in very general terms how it may be applied, once again using the Macalester Library as an example. Other libraries can determine for themselves how far, or how much farther, the example may apply to their own differing circumstances. I should note that I am describing a contemplated organization of collections at Macalester, some parts of which presently exist, while others are in development.

As noted above, at Macalester, the general book collection totals about 200,000 volumes. Based on the Trueswell theory, we may reasonably hypothesize that 40 percent of those 200,000 books (80,000 volumes comprising the Phoenix collection) will account for, say, 75 percent of total book loans. FASTCATs and Greats will each account for another 10 percent. Taken together, these three collections—FASTCAT, Greats, and Phoenix—account for 95 percent of all loans. The Phoenix collection is made up of middle-demand materials that we can conveniently identify through the straightforward statistical application of Dr. Trueswell's last-circulation-date criterion. I call this collection the Phoenix because it is continually in a process of regeneration. As FASTCATs that have reached the shelf-age criterion of about 1.5 years are withdrawn from FASTCAT for regular cataloging, they are then added to the Phoenix collection. At the same time, a like number of volumes will have met the Trueswell criterion for withdrawal from the Phoenix, and they will then be added to that large collection comprising 120,000 little-used volumes, which for convenience I will call the Lazarus collection—made up of books that are functionally dead but subject to infrequent, intermittent, and astonishing episodes of revivification.

The Phoenix collection of 80,000 volumes is constantly being regenerated. but although its constituency is always changing in response to changing reader interests, its size remains fixed at 80,000. It is a no-growth collection. So are FASTCAT and the Greats. While the total size of these three collections hovers indefinitely at about 90,000 volumes, their content is always such as to account for about 95 percent of all book loans. The only factor likely to have any significant effect on that total size is enrollment. Modifications of curriculum will have only a negligible effect on size, but they will strongly affect collection makeup. Only increases or decreases in the number of users will theoretically affect total size.

A certain percentage of total loans will, or should, be made up of inter-library loans, since no library is or ever will be able to satisfy from its own collections all the demand that it *must* satisfy. At Macalester, some 3 or 4 percent of all loans are supplied through interlibrary loans, and that per-centage is probably optimal. To go higher appears uneconomic; to go lower might generate intolerable frustrations among our readers.

Let us now summarize the contribution of each supply source to the total number of loans actually made. FASTCAT, 10 percent; Greats, 10 percent; Phoenix, 75 percent; and interloan, 3 percent—or a total of 98 percent of all loans *that are made.* The other 2 percent comes from the Lazarus collection. Before describing that moribund collection more fully, I want to return briefly to the Phoenix collection.

At a fixed size of 80,000 volumes arranged on the shelves in subject order, the Phoenix collection is small enough that most patrons will be able to make good use of it without a confusing or overwhelming encounter with our catalog—which will nonetheless contain entries for books in this col-lection for those occasions when a patron finds he *must* use it. Not only is the Phoenix collection conveniently small, but it also contains sufficient copies of all relatively high-demand titles to assure that one is nearly always available when wanted. It is a superb browsing collection, for it ordinarily contains most of those books one would hope to discover through the browsing approach, and very little to distract and overwhelm the reader with "largely useless and irrelevant knowledge." Compare for a moment its browsability with that of the collection we traditionally provide, where the books one would hope to discover through browsing are very often gone from the shelves and in some other reader's hands, while most of the books that *are* on the shelves constitute that overwhelming and confusing "mass of largely irrelevant and useless knowledge" from which the mind instinctively recoils. Michael Buckland has aptly termed this perverse browsing phenomenon "collection bias," for the conventional collection is biased *against* the browser by virtue of mainly containing books one would prefer not to discover, while routinely lacking a very high proportion of those books one would hope to stumble upon through browsing. The Phoenix collection, like FASTCAT and the Greats, is ideally suited to the browsing approach. Indeed, their superior browsability is a cardinal reason for the existence of all three collections.

The Lazarus collection differs from these three in that it has no browsing appeal at all. It consists wholly of books that humankind have generally agreed to forget. Not only that, it is the only one of the collections that continues to grow. Having segregated it from the other three, we can now begin to form some clear impression of the economic consequences of our disposition to maintain this collection's growth indefinitely.

As mentioned earlier, our hypothetical Lazarus collection contains 120,000 volumes. About 15,000 of these volumes are presently in a separate storage collection, and 115,000 are still part of the general collection in the main library, where they ought not to be. As a first step in segregating them, we propose to convert two of our five general stack floors to compact shelving and to put Lazarus there in its entirety. When Lazarus begins to outgrow these accommodations, we expect by then to be able to remove the overflow directly to some local or regional cooperative storage facility. Such an arrangement should remove any remaining political resistance from the faculty to the idea of a no-growth library. Such resistance as exists today is minimal and is fast withering in the face of economic reality.

At today's real estate and maintenance costs, it costs the college $24,000 per year merely to provide shelf space for Lazarus. Its 2 percent share of all general book loans made will remain constant no matter how large the collection may grow. Even if the Lazarus collection were allowed to reach a size of 5 million volumes, it would still yield only 2 percent of total loans.

We currently make about 50,000 general book loans per year. Two percent, or 1,000, will come from the Lazarus collection. The mere real estate cost of providing each such loan is now $24. If the collection is allowed to grow at conventional rates, by 1992 the real estate cost of lending one book from the Lazarus collection will be $48. By comparison, the real estate cost of lending a volume of Homer or Shakespeare from the Greats collection will eventually work out to about fifteen cents. That cost will be the same fifteen years from now, too, for the Greats collection does not grow.

The people who pay for library services will some day catch on to the interesting fact that while it costs fifteen cents per loan to house Homer, it costs $24 per loan to house a 1955 *Introduction to Principles of Office Management*. Before they think to ask me why I am spending 150 times more of their money on Lazarus than on Homer, I hope to have sent Lazarus back where he belongs. If I cannot find a way to do that, I may have to give up Homer altogether, so great is the expense of maintaining Lazarus's growth.

Librarians are wonderfully sentimental about Lazarus; they become pugnacious at the mere suggestion that he be returned to the sepulchre. It is not hard to get an argument to the effect that, while this ever-growing collection of moribund books satisfies only 2 percent of reader demand—and will never satisfy more than that despite its continuing growth—still that 2 percent, the argument goes, somehow represents the saving and indispensable remnant. But your sentimental opponent will never illustrate for you just how. Homer is not there, nor Sophocles, Vergil, Dante, Chaucer, or Shakespeare—and certainly not the Bible—nor any work published in say the last seven or eight years. What *is* in that Lazarus collection is a growing mass of material that, soon or late, failed the test of time and became "alms for oblivion, a great-sized monster of ingratitude."

If Lazarus must be preserved, then better it be done systematically and properly in a handful of libraries here and there, than uneconomically and improperly in every library in the country. I say improperly because it is common knowledge that most books published in the first half of this century are rapidly disintegrating, since the very people who rhapsodize about their intrinsic worth will spend nothing on their material preservation. This contradictory behavior merits fuller examination than I can give it here. Let it suffice here, however, to ask why the spokesmen of our profession so warmly resist the idea of economically segregating, centralizing, and thus preserving the scattered, heavily duplicated mass of unused books they are allowing to disintegrate in their own libraries? And why do they beckon us down a path that leads to the certain destruction of all those books whose preservation, they tell us, is indispensable to the advancement of learning? Would it not make more sense to preserve just one or two copies of that 1955 *Introduction to Principles of Office Management* than to allow hundreds of copies to continue disintegrating in hundreds of libraries, in the name of "collection completeness"? Even those elite few who devote their lives to the study of historical minutiae are badly served by the self-defeating resolve to preserve everything everywhere. Meanwhile, the rest of us, having no interest in such things, are losing our way in a growing pile of sawdust.

In his luminous study entitled *The Myth of the Eternal Return,* Mircea Eliade tells us that the majority of mankind has been ahistorical throughout the thousands of centuries of human life. To the present day, most of us still live by the myth of the eternal return. We are sustained by the idea of renewal and regeneration, and we prefer to forget altogether what Eliade calls the cumulating "terrors of history." The growing mass of historical detritus that constitutes our Lazarus collections everywhere serves only the interest of that extremely small elite who are captivated by "the terrors of history." What the majority of readers want—and are finding it increasingly difficult to discover in our libraries, hidden in the sprawling heap of "largely useless and irrelevant knowledge"—are those books that speak to us of regeneration, of new beginnings, and of human and divine deeds that are exemplary and archetypal, free of the bewildering and endless particularity that makes up "the terrors of history." Where will one find these exemplary, archetypal, and regenerative books? Where else but in our Greats, FASTCAT, and Phoenix collections, which shut out "most of what we should otherwise perceive and remember at a given moment, leaving only that very small and special selection that is likely to be practically useful."

When libraries are organized on human principles, the great mass of readers will have slight need of the elaborate, increasingly computerized instruments of bibliographical control. The organization of the library will be in harmony with the organization of the mind itself.

Computers forget nothing and they value nothing. In libraries, they should be mainly useful to that small elite whose minds are simlarly disposed. With computers they can call up the spirit of Lazarus from the vasty deep—and he will come!

But the millions of people who seek refreshment and renewal, comfort, wisdom, and joy in books need something better than Lazarus and the computer: they need a library organized to lead them directly to the books that serve those universal and enduring human needs. We surely have the material resources to make such a library for them. The cost is nothing in relation to what we are spending to house a rapidly growing horde of dead souls. If bibliographical principles serve mainly to keep control in the house of the dead, while human principles of library organization serve the needs of the living, it should not be difficult to choose where the bulk of our dwindling resources should hereafter be employed.

The Mischief in Measurement: A Caveat on the Hazards of Using Faulty Instruments to Measure Library Performance

"But let them measure us by what they will,
We'll measure them a measure and be gone."
—SHAKESPEARE, *ROMEO AND JULIET*

The first rule in using any measuring instrument is to be wary of its accuracy. A pilot relying upon a faulty altimeter is in greater peril than a pilot flying by the seat of his pants, for the latter's head is always wary of what his seat is telling him. Where much is at stake, redundancy in measuring instruments is indispensable, for conflicting results will alert you to the fact that at least one instrument is wrong, and possibly all of them. That is why airliner navigation systems commonly exhibit multiple redundancy, to reduce the probability of generating a sudden loud noise at flight's end.

The second rule of measurement is that the more complex the phenomenon being measured, the more difficult it will be to obtain precise, accurate, and reliable measurements. That is why the instruments of medical diagnosis are so intricate, elaborate, and full of redundancy. The probability of error increases with the increasing complexity of the thing being measured.

Librarians do not need to be convinced of the complexity of libraries, nor of the great difficulties inherent in attempts to measure their performance. Daily experience confirms those facts to us and makes us properly skeptical of all techniques of measurement—to the extreme degree that, until recent years, we have largely forsaken any efforts to measure library performance, except for gross measurements of volumes circulated, volumes acquired, dollars spent, and the like.

While a seriously faulty measuring device for libraries is worse than none at all, an approximately accurate one, capable of calibration and cross-

Published here for the first time.

checking against other evidence, would clearly be much better than none at all. Lately we have witnessed a variety of efforts to measure library performance, none of them perfect, but all of them valuable in that even the worst of them has awakened us to the possibility that useful measures of library performance can be obtained and presumably improved upon through the stringent test of experience. Richard Trueswell,[1] Michael Buckland,[2] Philip Morse,[3] Ben-Ami Lipetz,[4] and Ernest R. De Prospo[5] are names that immediately come to mind in respect to serious efforts to obtain usable measures of library performance. I have made some modest efforts in this field myself[6-8] and will report briefly here on subsequent efforts at performance measurements, drawing attention both to their benefits and especially to their shortcomings.

While libraries rightly concern themselves with a variety of services, I think it fair to say that their cardinal mission is to provide recorded materials (books, journals, phonorecords, etc.) to library users, and that among this variety of materials the provision of books is in most libraries the paramount concern. The efforts at measurement I report upon here are exclusively concerned with the provision of books to readers. At Macalester Library I have attempted to measure the following phenomena, which I briefly define to avoid confusion in nomenclature:

Holdings Rate: The percentage of all books your patrons want to read that are held by your library.

Availability Rate: The percentage of wanted books held by the library that are available on your shelves when your patrons want them.

Performance Rate: The product of Holdings Rate times Availability Rate, or the percentage of all books (both those you own and those you don't) immediately accessible to patrons when they want them.

The results of my first effort to measure Availability Rate are presented in "Let Them Eat Cake While Reading Catalog Cards" (p. 42), but the technique of measurement was not described.

For a period of three weeks in 1974 (March-April, when demand peaks), we placed stacks of "Reader Satisfaction Survey" slips at all catalog consulting tables, asking readers to complete and return them. A copy of the slip, which is self-explanatory, is reproduced on p. 98. Over the three-week period we obtained reports on about one thousand searches for books we owned, of which only 58 percent were successful. The measuring technique is simple and virtually cost-free; it is also a good deal less than perfect. The following shortcomings are immediately apparent:

• Apparently only one-third of actual catalog-based book searches made during the survey period were reported on by patrons. There is no certainty that the one-third who did report represent a random sample. Self-selection of respon-

WEYERHAEUSER LIBRARY
READER SATISFACTION SURVEY

We are trying to find out how often books the library owns are not available when you want them, so we can do something to improve the situation if it turns out that we need to.

To help us find out what the situation is, please write down the call numbers you found in the catalog for books that you need either to examine or to borrow. Then take this list to the shelves and indicate by each call number whether you actually found the book.

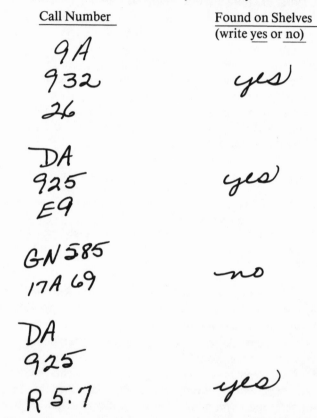

Call Number	Found on Shelves (write yes or no)
9A 932 26	yes
DA 925 E9	yes
GN 585 17A 69	no
DA 925 R 5.7	yes

Please leave this sheet at the Circulation Desk, whether you found a book to borrow or not. Thank you for the help. We'll report the results in the Mac Weekly shortly after the survey is completed.

Date_____

dents obviously occurred, some (or much) of it by persons who had frequently been frustrated by the nonavailability of owned and wanted books.
- The survey gives no clue as to how much of the failure to find books on the shelves is assignable to patron error.

Both of these shortcomings would tend to indicate a lower Availability Rate than the true potential maximum. The extent of error is not measurable. Nonetheless the survey findings did confirm what we already believed to be the case from the frequent and sometimes bitter complaints, registered at the Circulation Desk by frustrated patrons.

From these two pieces of evidence, we concluded that systematic duplication of high-demand titles was urgently needed to lower the frustration rate, and such a program was accordingly inaugurated (p. 49).

One year after the first availability survey was conducted, we made a second survey in April 1975 in all respects identical to the first. By that time we had added about one thousand high-demand multiple copies to the collections. We had also reduced the general loan period from about five weeks to about three. The second survey indicated that over a twelve-month period the Availability Rate had risen from 58 to 70 percent—a very satisfying result, even though the second survey suffered the same shortcomings as the first and furthermore could not be used to *prove* a causal connection between the remedial actions we had taken and the subsequent improvement in Availability Rates. We infer that such a connection did exist, but we cannot prove it.

Patron complaints about unavailable books dropped sharply over the same period, confirming the second survey's indication that Availability Rates had improved substantially.

The program of systematic duplication was continued, and in April 1976 we conducted a third availability survey, identical to the first two. This survey yielded only about one-tenth of the returns received from each of the first two and showed an Availability Rate of about 75 percent. Although satisfying in itself, we regard that result as totally unreliable because of the very small response. The meagerness of response is however significant, for it implies a sharp reduction in general patron concern about the availability problem. That supposition is also confirmed by the fact that complaints of nonavailability made to circulation attendants had virtually ceased.

The availability surveys obviously told us nothing about the library's Holdings Rate: the percentage of wanted books the library actually owned. One way to precisely determine the Holdings Rate is to follow the elaborate methodology employed by Beni-Ami Lipetz in his conclusive study of catalog use at the Yale Library. The difficulty with that method is that it costs a great deal of money to carry out properly, and the money was not available to us.

Still it seemed vital to get some approximate reading of our Holdings Rate in order to arrive at some judgment about the adequacy of our holdings to our patrons' needs. We seldom heard complaints on that score but desired some better confirmation, if it could be inexpensively obtained, that our holdings were indeed satisfactory. Several years' speculation on the matter led me to the conclusion that there was probably no method for measuring Holdings Rates that was both cheap and scientifically valid. I therefore decided to seek a cheap instrument of measurement, something akin to a thermometer, which in the event of a fever will signify that something definitely is wrong, although it will not tell you what, or in the absence of fever allows at least a reasonable supposition, if other symptoms are absent, that all is well.

The thermometer-like device I finally hit upon is a student-kept diary, recording the results of all book searches in the Macalester Library over an entire academic semester. A sample page of the diary, and of instructions for keeping it, are reproduced on the following two pages.

To insure faithful student work on the diary, some quid pro quo seemed necessary, and we offered a payment of ten dollars to each student who completed the work. On that basis we were not prepared to involve all 1,600 students in the project, nor even a statistically valid random sample, given our then uncertainty about the magnitude of the problem or even its existence.

The group actually invited to participate were all those members of the junior class who were eligible for membership in Phi Beta Kappa—presumably active users of the library. Of the forty-six students thus eligible, twenty-five agreed to participate, and nineteen actually completed their diaries at a cost of $190 to the library. The project ran from February to May 1977.

The only data I have tabulated thus far are those related to Holdings Rates, Availability Rates, and interlibrary loans. The methodology employed has no scientific validity whatever. One might, for example, expect to derive from it an artificially high Availability Rate, on the assumption that these bright juniors are more likely than the average student to seek relatively low-demand, abstruse materials for research papers, etc. One might also expect the indicated Holdings Rate to be lower than it is for duller students and much higher than it would be for faculty engaged in rarefied research, and so on. We were only using a simple thermometer, which might at least be counted upon to tell us whether a fever was, or was not, present.

The results were about what I anticipated as regards Holdings Rate, and a good bit higher as regards Availability Rate. Of a total of 422 books sought by these students, we owned 378, yielding a Holdings Rate of 90 percent, which coincidentally matches the Holdings Rate determined by Ben-Ami

Lipetz for the whole population of users of the enormous Yale Library. That strong showing also suggests why we so rarely hear complaints that the library does not *own* the books our students want to read.

Of the 378 books we owned, 331 of them were on the shelf when wanted, yielding an Availability Rate of 88 percent. As noted, this figure is probably higher than one would obtain from a truly random sample, but it nonetheless adds some confirmation to what we had previously learned from the three availability surveys already described: Availability Rates show strong improvement since the time when the duplication program was inaugurated and the general loan period shortened. A further explanation for the con-

Diary #_____

Diary of Library Book Searches

It has but one purpose: to help library staff measure and improve their success in providing for you the books you want when you want them. When the project is over we'll give you a written summary of the group's results.

Reading, like thinking, is a personal matter, so your name shouldn't appear on the diary. The master cross-list of names and diary numbers will be seen only by me, and I will consult it only if a question of interpretation arises and I need help from an individual diarist.

So you'll be sure to have your diary with you whenever you use the library, please place it (in numerical order) in the Diary Box at the Circulation Desk when you leave the library—and of course pick it up there too when you come back.

If you run into problems or have any questions about the project, just drop in to see me at your convenience. Thanks very much for your participation.

Daniel Gore
Library Director
Macalester College
14 February 1977

Notes on Diary Entries

Column headings:
- Received interloan
- Requested interloan
- On shelf
- Call #
- In catalog
- Course related
- Brief title & Pub. Date if known

Record only *book* searches made at the *Mac* Library.

A brief title will ordinarily suffice. Occasionally an author's name will be needed, as with "The Plays" of Shakespeare, where the name makes the title specific.

Course related: Are you seeking the book for a course you are presently taking? Answer yes or no.

In catalog: Write A, T, or S if you locate an entry in the *Author, Title,* or *Subject* catalog. Write "no" if you find no entry in a catalog search. Write B if you locate a book through shelf-browsing rather than a catalog search.

Call #: leave blank if you find no catalog entry or book. For a Reserve book, write "Res." after call #.

On shelf & interloan squares: Write yes or no or leave blank, as appropriate.

Use footnotes to explain special situations: e.g. a book turns out to be in the Olin branch, and you decide against making the trip to fetch it.

Fill in here the date you began the diary: _____

and the date you concluded it: _____

On the concluding date (or soon afterwards), deliver your diary to Mrs. Dorothy Barnes, Library Secretary, and she will present to you the honorarium of ten dollars for your contribution to our joint effort to measure and improve library performance.

If you find diary keeping a nuisance and want to give it up, be quick to say so! No harm is done by simply dropping out. But haphazard participation will blur the group results.

tinuing improvement in the Availability Rate is that in February 1977 we installed electronic exit controls. That was done because data collected over the previous year showed that 15 percent of our general loans were not charged out—and were presumably kept out much longer than the three-week general loan period. Preventing the occurrence of so many long-term loans would predictably bring strong improvements in the Availability Rate.

The net Performance Rate is expressed as the percentage of books obtained against the totality of books wanted (331/422), or the product of Holdings Rate times Availability Rate (90 percent × 88 percent). Either way you figure it, the same result is obtained: a Performance Rate of 79 percent. That is to say, these students actually found about four out of five of the books they went after—a result that leads me to the conclusion that no fever exists and that the library apparently is in healthy condition.

The Macalester Library presently owns about 200,000 book titles. That works out to about four-tenths of 1 percent of all titles thought to have been published since Gutenberg. If our acquisitions program throughout the years had been conducted on a strictly random basis, one might then expect our actual Holdings Rate would also have worked out to a figure of four-tenths of 1 percent. The reason it comes out instead (provisionally) to 90 percent is of course that the collection was developed not randomly but on the basis of the perceived needs of our own clientele.

In the same diary project, the data show that of the ninety-one books that were not available (for whatever reason) when wanted by the students, twenty-three (or 25 percent) were requested on interloan. Expressed as a percentage of the books they actually borrowed, the figure is 7 percent. For the total population of users, that figure runs around 4 percent—a result that suggests that bright students are much more likely than others to take the trouble to pursue unowned or unavailable books through interloan.

These students also turned out to be far more unlucky than our general user population in receiving delivery of requested interloan books. Of the twenty-three books they requested, only thirteen were delivered, for a decidedly poor showing of 55 percent. On an annual volume of about 1,800 books requested on interloan by all Macalester patrons, our success rate runs an average of around 80 percent. The data obtained from the diary project furnish no clue as to the cause of these nineteen juniors' extraordinary bad luck with interloan service. The very small number of requests involved might well be expected to yield statistical discrepancies—a deficiency that might also be imagined to a lesser degree with the indicated Holdings and Availability Rates, except that the latter two are approximately corroborated by independent evidence, while the diaries' interloan results are definitely undermined by our wholesale data on total interloan activity.

The methods I have described here for measuring Holdings, Availability, and Performance Rates fall a good deal short of yielding absolutely reliable results for the reasons I have stated and no doubt for other good reasons that people more statistically adept than myself will readily perceive. Although these methods plainly lack scientific validity, they nonetheless proved to have considerable managerial usefulness: They enabled us to confirm approximately a rather serious deficiency in Availability Rates and to correct the problem at relatively low cost (about $24,000 over a four-year period, or about 2 percent of our total library budget over the same period). They also confirmed that no serious problem exists with our Holdings Rate, despite the fact that over the last seven years our volume of annual additions to the collections has dropped by about 50 percent.

In the absence of these admittedly crude performance measures, we might well have leapt to the conclusion that what caused great problems for our patrons was a deficiency in the Holdings Rate rather than the Availability Rate. Had we in fact reached such a mistaken conclusion, we would have argued for maintaining the acquisitions volume at the high level of seven years back. And had we carried the argument successfully with the administration, we would have spent about $500,000 more on adding even more new titles instead of the $24,000 actually spent on duplicates. And the patrons' problem would still not have been resolved, for the problem was with the Availability rather than the Holdings rate.

And still I wish we could hit upon better methods for measuring Availability and Holdings Rates: methods that would give more reliable results, but at the same low cost of the methods we have been using. I will return to this point later.

Other methods have indeed been proposed, and I turn now to those lately developed by Ernest De Prospo et al. and published in *Performance Measures for Public Libraries*. I examine these methods in detail because they promise to be widely used among public and perhaps other types of libraries, and because the methods specifically proposed for measuring Holdings and Availability Rates manifest gross defects, which, if not clearly recognized by library managers employing these methods, are likely to lead to courses of action exactly the opposite of those warranted by a library's actual situation.

As a by-product of the original De Prospo work, Ellen Altman et al. have recently published *A Data Gathering and Instructional Manual for Performace Measures in Public Libraries*.[9] Workshops in the practical use of these measures will be conducted around the country to promote their utilization.

A further strong impetus to the widespread use of the De Prospo methodology is its recent incorporation in condensed form in a chapter in *Measuring the Effectiveness of Basic Municipal Services*,[10] which is the bible for city managers interested in gauging the performance of various municipal institutions—public libraries of course among them. To state my concern once more, I believe that city managers who regard the De Prospo methods as canonical—as they are likely to do—may impose courses of action on public libraries that will lead to their becoming less effective institutions than they are at present.

Of the variety of measurements proposed by the De Prospo group, I will confine myself to those designed for ascertaining a library's Holdings, Availability, and Performance rates, because they are the only ones that fall within my area of experience and the only ones I feel qualified to discuss with any confidence.

To determine Holdings Rate, the De Prospo group advocate drawing a random sample of 500 book titles from the five most recent years of the *American Book Publishing Record* and checking those titles against one's own catalog to determine the percentage held. (De Prospo et al., p. 35) Thus, if one discovers 200 of the 500 *BPR* sample titles in the local catalog, the Holdings Rate is alleged to be 40 percent.

To determine Availability Rate, the De Prospo group takes the titles actually held among the 500 title *BPR* sample and makes a shelf check to determine what percentage of actual holdings are then available on the shelves.

In a *Library Quarterly* review of De Prospo's *Performance Measures for Public Libraries,* Michael Bommer briefly, but convincingly, analyzes gross defects inherent in De Prospo's methods for measuring Holdings and Availability rates.

Another indicator purports to measure "the chances that a user has in obtaining recently published books" (p. 34). This indicator is derived by determining the proportion of books a library has available from a list of 500 randomly selected titles drawn from *American Book Publishing Record (ABPR)* for the years 1966-70. Obviously, in general, libraries with the greater expenditures for books will have a greater proportion of these sample titles available. In addition, this measure in no way reflects the quality of a library's collection. A library that randomly selects books from *ABPR* will receive a rating comparable to that of a library of similar size that may make great efforts to select books that are of most interest to its users. This same criticism applies to the measure of the probability of availability of periodical articles (p. 35). The tendency toward bias inherent in these measures is probably best illustrated by the measure of satisfaction reported by patrons of these libraries. In general, users of smaller libraries, where a smaller proportion of books and periodicals were available, reported a higher satisfaction rate than users of larger public libraries (72 percent versus 66 percent).

Similarly, a title-availability measure purporting to measure the probability that a user will successfully find a book owned by the library (but actually measuring the probability that any book is available) contains an inherent bias. It is generally known that the majority of demands are for a small proportion of a library's collection. Thus, the probability that an actual demand will be satisfied (considering that a greater proporiton of these high-demand books will be out on loan) will be much less than the probability that any book selected at random will be available.[11]

Bommer's terse critique merits fuller exploration. Using a *BPR* sample (or a sample from any other extensive bibliography, such as *Books for College Libraries, NUC,* or the *Standard Catalog for Public Libraries*) clearly tells you nothing whatever about an actual patron's probability of finding the book he wants in your catalog, unless the range of total patron interest extends evenly throughout the entire contents of *BPR* or any other listing used as a criterion. The probability of that being the case is approximately zero, except perhaps among the patrons in a city as large as New York or Los Angeles.

Using the *BPR* sample only tells you, by an indirect and cumbersome route, about how many dollars you are spending each year on the purchase of current American imprints. Looking at your current budget allocation will tell you the same thing more easily and more precisely.

Consider now the case of the public library in Lake Wobegon, Minnesota, "the little town that time forgot." The reading interests of its citizens are almost wholly confined to hunting, fishing, baseball, auto repairing, country music, the making of powdermilk biscuits, and, curiously enough, to the work of a *New Yorker* staff writer, Mr. Garrison Keillor. Measuring that library's catalog against the *BPR* random sample would probably yield a Holdings Rate of less than 1 percent. Yet Raoul (driver for the Warm Car Service), the redoubtable Jack himself (owner of Jack's Auto Repair), and most other citizens of Lake Wobegon all attest that the library owns virtually everything they wish to see. Even Barbara Anne Bunson, now an undergraduate at the University of Minnesota, states the little library of Lake Wobegon always had the books she wanted when she was growing up there—although of course now that she is a university student, she does have to depend on the University Library for advanced sociology texts and the like that her professors require her to read.

The true Holdings Rate of the Lake Wobegon Library, as confirmed by its patrons, is around 95 percent, rather than the scandalously low 1 percent rate indicated by the *BPR* sample. For Lake Wobegon to achieve a 95 percent showing from the *BPR* sample, the town would have to buy some 25,000 new American imprints each year at a cost of about $375,000 per year, a sum that exceeds the entire municipal budget for the last ten years. Even if Lake Wobegon contrived to do such a foolish thing, the *real* Holdings Rate of its library—as measured against its own patrons' reading interests—would not rise more than a percent or two, and the town would be in hock from now to kingdom come.

For most towns and cities in the United States, the *BPR* method will clearly yield a wild and erroneously low Holdings Rate. For all twenty libraries (ranging from "small" to "large") measured in De Prospo's pilot survey, the indicated Holdings Rate ranged from a low of eight-tenths of 1 percent (possibly Lake Wobegon) to a high of 58 percent. Indeed, one of the large libraries surveyed showed a Holdings Rate of only 13.6 percent. (De Prospo et al., p. 47) Is anyone prepared to believe that the true Holdings Rates (as measured against actual patron demand) are thus shockingly low in all sizes of American public libraries? If city managers are foolish enough to believe that and to act upon their belief, then they will order extravagant increases in the library's acquisition of new titles and accomplish little or nothing by way of increasing actual patron satisfaction.

It would be well for the De Prospo group to validate their *BPR* measure by taking real Holdings Rate measures against actual patron demand (much as Lipetz did at Yale) and comparing their results. To date no such cross-validation has been attempted (personal communication from Dr. Ellen Altman) nor is any contemplated. Having nothing to guide me but my knowledge of the great competence generally found among book selectors in public libraries, I am willing to predict that if the true Holding Rates were measured, they would fall generally in the 75 to 90 percent range in most American public libraries.

As noted (implicitly) by Bommer in his review article, the De Prospo method of measuring Availability Rates will very likely yield artificially high results. That is because of the classic inventory phenomenon, where one commonly finds that only 20 percent of the items in a given inventory will receive 80 percent of total demand, while the other 80 percent of inventory items satisfies only 20 percent of the demand. Thus 80 percent of the *BPR* sample is likely to be in very low demand, and the majority of those books will be on the shelves when wanted. Of the remaining 20 percent of high-demand titles, half or more of them are likely to be off the shelves. But the overall Availability Rate, so heavily biased by the 80 percent portion of low-demand titles, will probably work out to around 60 percent, even if no systematic duplication program exists.

Availability Rates in the De Prospo pilot study of twenty libraries ranged from a low of 56 percent to a high of 81 percent. These figures are almost certain to be artificially high. The true range of Availability Rates, if measured against actual patron demands, would probably be significantly lower, say from a low of 45 percent to a high of 70 percent.

To recapitulate: In practically all public libraries, the De Prospo method of measurement will yield artificially low Holdings Rates and artificially high Availability Rates. The net effect of multiplying these two rates to obtain the net Performance Rate is impossible to predict accurately, since the two errors in opposite directions will in some degree cancel each other out. But in most instances it might be expected to yield an artificially low Performance Rate (which is the equivalent of De Prospo's "Probability of Availability").

The median range of Performance Rates in the large, medium, and small libraries included in De Prospo's pilot survey worked out to an astonishingly low figure of 27 percent for large libraries and eight-tenths of 1 percent for small libraries. (De Prospo et al., p. 47) Does anyone believe that the American public would tolerate such gross inefficiency in the performance of their public libraries?

Let us assume now that a public library manager does indeed have great confidence in the results obtained by applying the De Prospo measurements to his own library. He discovers a Performance Rate of only 21 percent, resulting from the product of a measured Holdings Rate of 30 percent and a measured Availability Rate of 69 percent. Looking at these data he naturally concludes that the best remedy for his intolerably low Performance Rate is to bring the Holdings Rate up by vast infusions of new titles. But the real source of difficulty is more likely to be the Availability Rate, which looks so comparatively satisfactory that he decides to do little or nothing to improve it. Actually, the derived Availability Rate is artificially high, while the derived Holdings Rate is artificially quite low.

So instead of laying out a modest amount of funds on duplicate copies necessary to improve an Availability Rate that in reality may be only 50 percent, he spends a huge amount of money to improve a Holdings Rate that may in reality already be at a very satisfactory level of 90 percent. The misleading properties inherent in the De Prospo measurement methodology cause him to spend a great deal of money to accomplish minuscule improvements in the true Performance Rate, when by spending a little money instead on high-demand duplicates, he would have achieved very substantial increases.

The De Prospo measuring instruments may be likened to a thermometer with its fluid bulb placed at the wrong end.

It is my conviction that the only trustworthy measures of Holdings and Availability Rates are those that are applied directly to the actual users of any given library, whether it be public, academic, or special. I have described a particular type of such measures that were applied in the Macalester College Library and indicated their shortcomings and my moderate dissatisfaction with them. My dissatisfaction is such that I am not willing to advocate their use in any other library, although I am quite satisfied with the useful results they produced for us.

I believe that better methods than those I employed can be designed by better minds: methods that will yield more reliable results and at a cost that can readily be borne by any library. If such improved methods can indeed be devised, they would yield inestimable benefits to all kinds of libraries.

So interested am I in promoting the creation of such methods and so convinced that young, creative minds are more likely to hit upon them than are older and wearier heads, I am publicly offering a prize of $1,000 to the one library-school student who develops, in my judgment, the best new methods for inexpensively measuring Holdings and Availability Rates in both public and academic libraries.

The deadline for submitting methods to me is September 1, 1978. If in my judgment none of the submissions substantially improves on existing methods, no prize will be awarded. It is my optimistic forecast at this writing that a winning method will be created, because the need for it is so urgent, and there are so many fine young minds capable of rising to the challenge if properly stimulated.

NOTES

1. Richard W. Trueswell, "Growing Libraries: Who Needs Them? A Statistical Basis for the No-Growth Collection," in *Farewell to Alexandria*, ed. Daniel Gore (Westport, Conn.: Greenwood Press, 1976), pp. 72-104. Trueswell's various investigations of library performance measurements began about two decades ago. The paper cited here is a compendium of his mature views on the subject.

2. Michael Buckland, *Book Availability and the Library User* (Elmsford, N.Y.: Pergamon, 1975).

3. Philip M. Morse, *Library Effectiveness* (Cambridge, Mass.: M.I.T. Press, 1968).

4. Ben-Ami Lipetz, "Catalog Use in a Large Research Library," in *Operations Research: Implications for Libraries*, ed. Don R. Swanson and Abraham Bookstein ("University of Chicago Studies in Library Science"; Chicago: University of Chicago Press, 1972), pp. 129-39.

5. Ernest R. De Prospo et al., *Performance Measures for Public Libraries*. PLA/ ALA, 1973.

6. Daniel Gore, "Zero Growth for the College Library," *College Management* (Aug./Sept. 1974), pp. 12-14.

7. _____, "Let Them Eat Cake While Reading Catalog Cards: An Essay on the Availability Problem," *Library Journal* (January 15, 1975), pp. 93-98.

8. _____, "The View from the Tower of Babel," *Library Journal* (September 15, 1975), pp. 1599-1605).

9. Ellen Altman et al., *A Data Gathering and Instructional Manual for Performance Measures in Public Libraries* (Chicago: Celadon Press, 1976).

10. Urban Institute and The International City Management Association. *Measuring the Effectiveness of Basic Municipal Services: Initial Report* (Washington, D.C., 1974). The relevant chapter is "Library Services," pp. 33-37.

11. Michael R. W. Bommer, Review article in *Library Quarterly* (July 1974), pp. 273-75.

MACALESTER COLLEGE

Annual Report

of

THE LIBRARY

1970/71

St. Paul, Minn.

December 7, 1971

Dr. Kenneth Goodrich
Vice-President for Academic Affairs and Provost
Macalester College
St. Paul, Minnesota 55101

Dear Ken:

    I am pleased to submit herewith the Annual Report of the Library
for fiscal 1970/71. The year was eventful and productive, and the
changes carried out are so numerous that I have taken some pains to
chronicle them in fuller detail than may be customary.

    Let me take this opportunity to express my deep appreciation for
the good support the Library received from the College Administration
and the Educational Resources Advisory Committee during a year of continuous experiment and reorganization.

                                        Cordially,

                                        Daniel Gore
                                        Director

DG:db

I.   INTRODUCTION

That was the Year of the Phoenix in the Library. And the fuel that fired the hatching of the Phoenix turned out to be not money but hard creative work by a talented staff.

The reclassification project, virtually halted in 1969/70 for want of special funding, was reactivated in 1970/71 without special funding, and 26,000 volumes were reclassed during the year. The card catalog, containing 750,000 cards in one alphabet, was split into three (Author, Title, Subject), making it easier to use, and reducing the typing load for all future cataloging by 75 percent.

A computer-based acquisitions program was developed to bring new books to the Library shortly after publication, and the Acquisitions Department devised a rapid-processing system so patrons may borrow new books the day after the Library receives them, instead of waiting the customary three or four months.

Loans to patrons increased from 85,000 in 1969/70 to 102,000 in 1970/71; exit checks were introduced to improve collection security; and a new fine policy was established to encourage timely return of all loans and thus assure better access to high-demand items.

Shelf space was created in Weyerhaeuser to accommodate some 30,000 additional volumes, and the practice of transferring books to a storage collection was abandoned. Reserve collection procedures and layout were overhauled to reduce delays in putting materials on reserve, to provide easier access to materials, and to cut staffing requirements nearly in half.

The card catalog was moved from the Main Reading Room to the Reference Room, where expert help is conveniently available to patrons. A display-type index was created for the Reference Collection so students can rapidly determine the shelf-location of most reference works, and the physical arrangement of the reference collection was altered to place call-numbers in straight-forward, rather than broken, sequence. Interlibrary loan service, a vital element in any academic program, was expanded ten-fold, delivering 3,399 books and journal articles to Macalester students and faculty, in comparison to the several hundred delivered in 1969/70.

While all of these things were taking place, total permanent staff complement diminished by about twenty-five percent. Some details of how this was done are given in the following chronicle of the Year of the Phoenix.

II. STAFF

A. Reference Department

Both reference assistants had resigned by the end of December, leaving the department without a regular operating staff. Minimal service was provided by staff members filling in from other departments, and in February, 1971, Mr. David Ondercin was appointed to the post of Bibliographical Intern, to provide bibliographical, reference, and inter-loan service to Macalester patrons. Authorization to appoint a second intern was not obtained, so Mrs. Joyce Gobb, Acquisitions Librarian, contributed substantial time to help reference services keep pace with growing demands.

B. Acquisitions Department

There were no changes in personnel, but Mrs. Jean Francis, who formerly gave full time to the gifts and exchange program, devoted half-
time throughout the year to provide courier service for interloans
from the University of Minnesota. Mrs. Cobb, head of acquisitions,
devoted much of her time (as noted) to reference services.

C. Cataloging Department

One clerk-typist resigned and was not replaced. Mr. Un Chol Shin,
Cataloger (half-time), was transferred to Circulation (half-time). A
microfiche cataloging system, leased in the previous year for $5,000
per annum, in exchange for one cancelled staff position in the department, was discarded in 1970/71.

D. Circulation Department

Two circulation assistants resigned and were not replaced. The shelving supervisor resigned and was not replaced. Mrs. Rosemary Salscheider,
who began the year as full-time Curriculum Lab Supervisor, was assigned
part-time to both Circulation and Curriculum Lab. Mr. Shin, as noted,
was transferred from Cataloging (half-time) to Circulation (half-time).

E. Reserves & Periodicals Department

Mr. Robert Cramer was appointed to supervise this department, with
Mrs. Bernice Oliver and Mrs. Peggy Rude as part-time assistants. In

the course of the year, as operations in this area improved, Mrs. Rude, who had also been working part-time in the Olin Science Library, was assigned to work full-time in Olin; her position in Reserves was filled for several months by Mrs. Corinne Kellar, who is regularly assigned to cataloging, and at the end of that period the post could be, and was, permanently vacated.

During the first half of the year, Mr. Cramer gave a good deal of his time to the Circulation and Reference Departments, as well as his own.

F.   Summary of Staff Reductions

Staff Roster

Fall 1970

Daniel Gore
Jean Archibald
Wendy Adamson
Dorothy Barnes
Louis Buggs
Joyce Cobb
Robert Cramer
Regina Crouse
Jean Francis
Will Harri (1/2 time)
Mary Hampl
Corinne Kellar
Maryann Kerr
Louise Kiscaden
Rosemarie Leonard
George Meyn
Lois Nelson
Ruth Newcomb
Bernice Oliver (1/2 time)
Ann Pressman
Peggy Rude
Rosemary Salscheider
Un Chol Shin (1/2 time)
Elli Sorensen (1/2 time)
Marymina Stenger
MICROFICHE CATALOGING DEVICE
(in exchange for one staff position)

24 FTE

Fall 1971

Daniel Gore
Jean Archibald
Dorothy Barnes
Joyce Cobb
Robert Cramer
Regina Crouse
Jean Francis (1/2 time)
Robert Haberkorn (1/2 time)
Mary Hampl
Corinne Kellar
Rosemarie Leonard
Lois Nelson
Ruth Newcomb
Bernice Oliver (1/2 time)
David Ondercin
Peggy Rude
Rosemary Salscheider
Un Chol Shin (1/2 time)
Elli Sorensen (1/2 time)
Marymina Stenger

17 1/2 FTE

G. Student Staff

Total hours of student labor (all categories) in 1970/71 came to 29,387,
as compared with 24,927 hours in 1969/70. Nearly 8,000 hours of the
1970/71 total were spent in staffing two exit-check stations in
Weyerhaeuser Library, for the first time in its history. Student staff
represent nearly 50 percent (in FTE) of the Library's work force. While
in some libraries student labor is regarded as an incidental feature
of the whole operation, students clearly occupy a central role in the
operation of their library at Macalester, and their contributions are
highly regarded by the Library's permanent staff. Although a good deal
of staff time is devoted to training and supervising students, everyone
feels the time is well spent in terms of educational benefit to the
students, of whom some 100-150 work in the Library each year. The student
staff as a whole are diligent, responsible, strongly motivated workers,
and the Library reaps large benefits from their varied services.

H. Staff Organization

When the year began, there existed no formal means of communication
among the staff, and there was some confusion about areas of responsibility and authority, since the previous director had involved himself
personally and directly at all levels of the operation. To remedy the
problems arising from this situation, and to encourage staff initiative
and participation in the decision-making process, lines of responsibility and authority were clearly drawn for each of the Library's
several operating units; persons held accountable for the performance
of each department were delegated broad authority in the management
of that department, and weekly reports of department activity were

submitted to the library director by the department heads.

Mrs. Jean Archibald, in her capacity as Associate Director, was given general supervisory and coordinating authority for all departments.

An Executive Council, made up of library staff carrying major responsibilities for the operation, was appointed to assist the director in making decisions, to keep him informed on personnel and operational matters, and to ensure smooth and regular two-way communication between staff and administration, and open communications among the staff. The Council met weekly throughout the year, participated actively in developing the many decisions that had to be taken in a year of total re-organization, and in communicating those decisions, and the reasoning behind them, to the staff and the Library's patrons. The Council's work was a crucial element in the successful reorganization of the Library.

Although a similar body was not created within the student staff, the need for one has become apparent and will be attended to in fiscal 1971/72.

In addition to weekly Council meetings, and irregularly scheduled meetings held by Council members with department staffs, monthly meetings with the whole staff were held to ensure that everyone fully understood the changes that were taking place, and had an opportunity to express views, reactions, and recommendations on all matters of policy and procedure. With the pace of change now much reduced, it appears that quarterly, rather than monthly staff meetings will be scheduled for 1971/72.

Steps taken thus far to improve communications and define areas

of accountability and authority have resulted in more harmonious staff
relations, improved performance, and very good staff morale.

Mrs. Dorothy Barnes, Library Secretary, plays an indispensable
role in maintaining good day-to-day communications among the staff.
Knowledgeable in all areas of library activity, she pinch-hits in any
department when emergency help is needed, alerts the director to
anticipated problem spots, and generally assists in keeping the entire
organization running smoothly and on schedule. Without her varied
skills and detailed knowledge of the organization, the task of reorganization would have been infinitely more difficult to carry out.

I. General Appraisal of the Staff

This Library is far more fortunate than most in its staff. Industrious,
innovative, adaptable and fully dedicated to their mission, as a group
they accomplished last year nearly twice what one might expect from
the usual library staff. They adjusted readily to the numerous and
often sweeping changes that were made in every aspect of the Library's
operation; they participated actively and imaginatively in the endless
decisions that had to be taken in the course of extending and improving library services; and they finished the year's work in a state of
high morale. It is no exaggeration to say that the College now has,
on the whole, a library staff as talented and loyal as could be wished
for.

I conclude this section with a special word of praise for Mrs.
Jean Archibald, who carried most of the burden of seeing to it that
all decisions respecting the whole range of library policy and procedure
were properly carried out. This is an enormously difficult task in a

complex organization undergoing rapid change in all its branches. It

requires expert judgment in matters of timing and coordination; a

high order of diplomacy; eternal vigilance in matters of detail; end-

less patience and unflagging diligence. I wish to record here a very

special debt of gratitude for Mrs. Archibald's distinguished contri-

butions to the Library, and to the College.

III. THE 1970/71 BUDGET

Operations were complicated throughout the year by instabilities in

the total budget. The original budget request of $349,000, submitted

in March of 1970, was not finally acted upon until December of 1971,

three months after the fiscal year began. At that time it was reduced

to $312,500, causing some difficulties in devising and supporting a

suitable acquisitions program. Then in April, 1971, the budget was

further reduced to $282,500 ($15,000 cut in the salary budget, $15,000

cut in the acquisitions budget), and expenditures for retrospective

buying (except from History Chair funds) were terminated, with the hope

that the current-imprints profile program could be continued through

the fiscal year (as it in fact was).

A summary of expenditures for 1970/71 is here presented:

Title		Expenditures
1. Salaries & Wages		$149,638
2. Acquisitions & Binding		101,158
Books	$ 78,862	
Periodicals	20,647	
Binding	1,649	
3. Operations		34,151
Student payroll	18,706[1]	
(Regular session)		
Supplies	6,072	
Telephone	263	
Printing	1,265	
Travel	733	
Equipment purchase	5,427	
Equipment repair	609	
Photocopying	1,086	
Grand Total		284,947
Lost Book Credits		1,982
Net:		282,965

Three major items of equipment were purchased:

An IBM Selectric typewriter for book-labeling; a Minolta

Enlarger photocopier for the Cataloging Department

($1,895.00); and a Minolta reducer-photocopier for the

Periodicals Room ($1,295.00), which previously had no

photocopy equipment.

IV. Departmental Activities

A. Acquisitions Department

Following lengthy deliberations with the faculty and discussions with the

Richard Abel Co. (a book jobber), the department implemented in

---

[1] Actual expenditures were $23,897. Credits of $5,191 from overdue fees
yield a net of $18,706.

January, 1971, a profile program for acquiring new imprints as they are published. In broad outline, the program works like this: the College draws up a very detailed set of categorical specifications (a "profile") of its new book requirements. The profile is keyed into the jobber's computer. The jobber systematically reviews the output of some 5,000 publishers the world over, and every book of potential interest to an academic library is profiled and also keyed into its computer. (Some 40 to 50,000 new books are thus profiled each year by the jobber). When a book's profile matches the College's profile, the computer generates a set of detailed announcement slips that are then forwarded to the Library for later distribution to the faculty. The faculty return the slips to the Library indicating a buy or don't buy decision, and the Library proceeds accordingly.

Statistical results of this program, January - August, 1971, are as follows:

	Number	Dollars	Average
Notice slips from Abel	8,115	$74,028	$9.15
"Buy" slips from faculty	3,221	26,818	8.35
"Don't Buy" slips from faculty	2,153	22,453	10.50
Total slips from faculty	5,374	49,271	
Acceptance rate	60 percent	54 percent	
Rejection rate	40 percent	46 percent	

For evaluative purposes, faculty were invited to compile their own desiderata lists of current imprints to check against Abel offerings. We have received one such list to date, covering about 30 titles, all of which were either in the Library or on order when the list was submitted.

Faculty response to the program has generally been favorable. Several professors who opposed it at the outset now strongly endorse it. And several regard it as neither better nor worse than a conventional acquisitions program.

In conjunction with the profile program, one of whose principal virtues is early receipt of new books, the Acquisitions Department developed a "Fastcat" processing system for getting new books on the shelves the day after they reach the Library. Instead of holding new books in the workroom awaiting the availability of Library of Congress catalog copy (which often arrives months after the book) the Acquisitions Department assigns a simplified LC number to each book, tags it for the FASTCAT shelves where it is available for loan, and allows it to remain in the FASTCAT collection until LC copy is published. Since the Catalog Department keeps a new book off the shelves only a day or two when LC copy is at hand, new books are never tied up more than three days in the total acquisitions/cataloging process. The combined effect of the profile plan and the FASTCAT method is to get new books into borrowers' hands about one year sooner than is possible with conventional procedures. *

Acquisitions expenditures were fully distributed by subject this year, with ten percent of total purchases assigned to the "Library and Miscellaneous" category. Since in previous years less than thirty percent of purchases were distributed by subject, no comparisons can be made between this year's distributions and any other.

Expenditures were as follows:

_____

* A comparison of our total acquisitions, May - Aug., with those of another Twin City college library, similar in size and character, shows that 80 percent of our receipts in that period were 1971 imprints, while the other library's showing was 6 percent.

Departmental Book and Periodical Expenditures 1970/71

| Division | Expenditure by Division | | |
	Books	Periodicals	Total
1. Social Sciences			
Geography	$ 1,436.32	$ 412.27	$ 1,848.59
Political Science & Simulation	5,627.17	1,310.75	6,937.92
Psychology	1,965.25	1,637.22	3,602.47
Sociology & Anthropology	3,880.15	740.61	4,620.76
Totals	12,908.89	4,100.85	17,009.74
2. Business and Economics	2,687.56	869.70	3,557.26
3. Education	3,291.84	683.79	3,975.63
4. Fine Arts			
Art	2,583.94	220.00	2,803.94
Journalism	390.78	40.00	430.78
Music	1,722.18	117.95	1,840.13
Speech	863.00	184.15	1,047.15
Totals	5,559.90	562.10	6,122.00
5. Humanities			
Classics	1,261.97	159.25	1,421.22
English	7,770.76	548.82	8,319.58
Foreign Languages			
French	1,733.19	195.07	1,928.26
German	2,778.26	472.01	3,250.27
Russian	808.03	164.02	972.05
Spanish	1,004.06	167.45	1,171.51
History	16,863.78	737.15	17,600.93
Language (General)		290.00	290.00
Philosophy	3,073.24	243.59	3,316.83
Religion	1,294.53	406.78	1,701.31
Totals	36,587.82	3,384.14	39,971.96
6. Physical Education	848.64	171.50	1,020.14
7. Science and Mathematics			
General		174.00	174.00
Biology	4,024.35	1,878.88	5,903.23
Chemistry	2,141.97	2,975.50	5,117.47
Geology	1,165.18	937.80	2,102.98
Math	914.00	1,189.00	2,103.00
Physics	1,449.25	1,757.40	3,206.65
Totals	9,694.75	8,912.58	18,607.33
8. Library & Miscellaneous	7,282.80	1,962.19	9,244.99
Grand Totals	$ 78,862.20	20,646.85	99,509.05

As the profile plan started late in the fiscal year, and accounted for less than 1/3 of total book purchases, its effect on subject distributions is not reflected in the above analysis.

Expenditures from endowed funds (included in the total distributions given above) were as follows:

Wallace History Chair $15,002

Classics	$ 340	
English	1,282	
French	956	
German	1,007	
History Dept.	1,347	
Wallace History Chair	8,194	
Philosophy	1,050	
Russian	566	
Spanish	260	

Anonymous	807
Richardson Memorial	1,030
Class of 1902	75
Class of 1965	137
Davenport	15
Doubleday	1,505
Gillette	106
Gunderson	39
Harper	700
MacRae	836
Morrow	486
Thompson	979
Wood	476

Total book expenditures from endowments: $22,193

Budget control in the Acquisition Department has been vastly improved under Mrs. Cobb's supervision. She has made order out of chaos, keeping total expenditures within limits set by the College, and recording them in such a manner that everyone can see just how book funds were spent.

Other operational improvements in the department enable it to function smoothly with approximately one less FTE staff than it had the previous year (a reduction of about 25 percent). Adopting the profile plan accounts for a good deal of the gain in efficiency. Should it be abandoned, one additional FTE staff member would be required to take up the added load of conventional order work.

Gifts and Grants

A gift of $1,000.00 from the Macalester Alumni Association covered the purchase of in-house binding equipment, the use of which will reduce total binding costs about $6,000.00 per year.

A grant of $5,000.00 was received from the Kellogg Foundation, to be used over a three-year period for the purchase of materials in the field of environmental studies.

Gifts of 3,626 books, journal issues, etc. were made to the Library by 335 donors. Of these items, 2,497 were added to the permanent collections. Estimated total value is $7,500.00. All gifts are promptly acknowledged in writing by the Library Director.

An outstanding collection of scholarly and literary works (411 volumes in all) was presented to the Library in the summer of 1970 by Mrs. David W. Aberle. Containing such valuable and hard-to-come-by books as Falconer Madan's Books in Manuscript, Joseph Conrad's Marcel Proust, Robert Graves' The Feather Bed, and George Meredith's Works (16 vols.), this collection constitutes a notable addition to the Library's resources.

Over the last several years Mr. Charles W. Ferguson, of Mount Kisco, N. Y., has made cash gifts to the Library of $5,545.00. These funds have been designated as seed money for "The Word Library," a special collection of materials illustrating the history of meanings and the transmission of the word in written, printed, and spoken texts. Mr. Ferguson has also given generously of his time and ideas in helping the Library formulate long-range plans for developing this collection.

B. Cataloging Department

This department, which cataloged and reclassed 13,000 volumes in 1969/70, cataloged and reclassed 37,000 volumes in 1970/71 - nearly tripling production while the staff was reduced about 25 percent. How that was done takes some telling.

The first step was to divide the card catalog into three parts (Author, Subject, Title), a task that required the labors of all available staff during August, 1970. When it was done, some 3/4 million cards had been sorted and re-filed by type of entry. Then 50,000 raised guide cards were typed for the subject catalog - one guide for each subject heading, so any new catalog card for an existing subject can be filed without typing a heading on it. Thus when new cards are made for a reclassed book, no typing is required on the subject cards.

Since title entries in the divided catalog are filed in a separate alphabet, new cards are simply filed in title order without typing a raised entry at the top. Thus when new cards are made for a new or reclassed book, no typing is required on the title card.

Using the divided catalog, typing workload per book is so sharply reduced that total production is sharply increased.

While the department made numerous other innovations during the year, the most consequential one (after the divided catalog) was the purchase of a Minolta enlarger-photocopier. This device permits direct retrieval of full-size LC catalog copy from the condensed entries in the printed LC Book Catalogs. The unit cost is less than 1/10 that of any of the several other existing methods of retrieving copy. Without the Minolta, total production would have fallen perhaps 20 percent below actual results.

The catalog staff convinced the Xerox Company that a Xerox machine could be modified to make high quality catalog cards cheaply. At times the lobby of the Library looked like a Xerox convention hall, with servicemen, technical experts, and district representatives swarming around the machine and more than once announcing to the staff that the machine was not designed to do what was wanted. In the end, the machine did exactly what was wanted. And in the course of the year some 150,000 catalog cards were produced, at a total cost of about $1,500.00 - at least $6,000.00 less than a commercial processor would charge, and with the risks of mailing loss, processing confusion, etc., totally eliminated.

Finally, the adoption of the FASTCAT method of processing new books spared the Catalog Department the frustrations and wasted time of making repeated searches for LC cataloging copy that isn't yet produced. New books remain on the FASTCAT shelves for at least 6 months before the Catalog Department makes a first search for LC copy, and by that time it is usually available and repeat searches are unnecessary. The result is a substantial reduction in unit-times for cataloging new books.

Summary statistics for the cataloging operation are the following:

	1969/70	1970/71
Volumes reclassed	1,908	25,923
Volumes cataloged	10,909	11,094
Volumes withdrawn	3,331	3,524 *
(Includes lost and stolen)		
Net additions	7,578	7,570
Size of the collections	189,988	197,558

Besides carrying on the usual duties of the department, the cataloging staff was frequently called on to staff other positions (reserves, circulation, reference) when resignations and illness left them vacant. Under Mrs. Stenger's supervision, the staff adapted readily, and enthusiastically, to the procedural changes that were constantly being made in the operation. It is probable that these changes would have had little beneficial effect without a top calibre staff to implement them. The complexity of the operation, and the pace of change were such that an untalented, or unwilling, staff would have made chaos out of the intended improvement.

C. Circulation Department

Total loans in Weyerhaeuser came to 99,072, as compared to 81,751 in 1969/70 - a gain of 21 percent, achieved while staff complement was declining by 25 percent. Some of the increase may be attributed to speedier acquisition and cataloging of new books, and reclassification of a large block of the collection from Dewey to LC, all of which theoretically enhance use of the collections. Other contributory

---

*For the most part this count represents volumes discovered missing in the course of reclassificatipn, which might have vanished from the Library at any time in its history.

factors are these: (1) Physical re-arrangement of collections to
get them in nearly straight class sequence (A-Z) from top to bottom
stack levels; (2) Installation of exit checks to discourage theft;
and (3) Adoption of a fine policy to encourage timely return, and
thus permit more frequent use, of books in heavy demand.

The most notable gains in circulation occurred in the Reserve
Collection, to be discussed in a later section.

The method of recording loan transactions was revised in the
Fall of 1970 to protect the privacy of our readers. Under the old
method, the record of who had borrowed the book was placed in the
book pocket when it was returned, making it a fairly simple matter
for investigatory agencies to construct a history of a person's reading interests. (Several instances of such activity were reported in
the press during the summer of 1970.) Under the revised method, the
loan record is destroyed when the book is returned. A side benefit
is a significant reduction in labor required to process new and reclassed books: there is no charge card to be typed, and no book
pocket to be glued in.

Finding a place to shelve books was a constant problem for the
department throughout the year, although it is now much alleviated.
Last Fall the shelf-load factor was nearly 90 percent, with scarcely
2,000 ft. of vacant shelving in the stacks. By July, 1971, the load
factor was brought down to 60 percent, by adding some 2,000 ft. of shelving in stack areas where carrels had been placed (the carrels were removed to reading rooms), and by discarding or transferring to storage
nearly 5,000 shelf feet of duplicate journals, and journal backruns
more than three years old. The shelving situation in Weyerhaeuser
as of July, 1971, was this: 21,270 feet of stack shelving, carrying

13,000 feet of books, for a load factor of 61 percent. While the shelving situation remains critical, we have gained some temporary relief, and the practice of transferring monographs to storage has ceased (journal backruns go there instead).

The new overdue fine policy, developed with the close cooperation of the student members of ERAC, was introduced in November, 1970, with the immediate effect of cutting overdues about 70 percent. While the policy met with some anticipated resistance, it was generally so well received, and so effective, that it remained in force, unmodified, for the rest of the fiscal year.

The loan desk staff, under Mrs. Leonard's supervision, merit high praise for making the transition so smooth when it could have been so rough.

These are the summary circulation statistics for Weyerhaeuser and Olin Libraries:

| | Weyerhaeuser | | Olin | |
	Students	Faculty	Students	Faculty
Books (General)	49,565	4,919	1,429	247
FASTCATS	1,039	350	5	10
Paperbacks	488	284		
Government Documents	228	49		
Curriculum Lab	1,863	171		
Juvenile	3,856	744		
Pamphlets	299	77		
Phono records	1,871	211		
Art rentals	81	56		
Periodicals	12,095	(student & faculty)	101	24
Storage	664	" "		
Reserve	20,162		1,005	
Totals	92,211	6,861	2,540	281

Combined: 99,072   2,821

Both Libraries: 101,893

The Curriculum Laboratory, administratively a unit of the Circulation Department, recorded declining activity for the last three years as follows:

	Loans	Dropped
1967/68	4,627	
1968/69	3,841	986
1969/70	2,659	1,182
1970/71	2,034	625

Because of declining demand in this area, and declining staff complement in others where demand was growing, staffing of the Lab was maintained on a part-time basis throughout the year, to release some staff time urgently needed elsewhere. It is perhaps noteworthy that the smallest drop in circulation recorded over the last three years occurred in the year when supervisory staffing was reduced from full to part-time.

Mrs. Salscheider, appointed supervisor of the Curriculum Lab in 1970/71, has worked very effectively in weeding the collection of outdated materials, assisting students using the collection, and mounting sizeable exhibits of curriculum materials. Three such exhibits, consisting in all of more than 2,500 books, were on display at various times in Weyerhaeuser, and attracted wide attention among educators in the Twin Cities.

Other exhibits and displays created by Circulation Department staff exceeded one hundred in number, covering such matters as recent staff and faculty publications, new books on current issues, new library services and policies, and campus cultural life.

Despite substantial reductions in staff, the Library maintained
its usual 103 hour per week schedule throughout the regular sessions.

D. Periodicals & Reserves

At the end of fiscal 1969/70 the periodical subscription list numbered
1,616 titles - substantially more than are commonly found in libraries
the size of Macalester's. Faced with the potential dilemma of having
to forego some necessary book purchases to maintain such a list in a
tight-money year, the faculty recommended dropping 395 journals that
had little or no value to the College. At the same time 30 new ones
were added, leaving a net list of 1,251 periodical titles renewed at
the beginning of 1970/71.

To further reduce needless expenditures on the periodical collection, the Library bought its own binding machine (with money given
by the Alumni Association) in the summer of 1971, with the expecta-
tion of reducing annual binding costs about $6,000.00. Off-shelf
time of periodicals being bound will be reduced (once the catch-up
period is over) from the usual 6 weeks to 1 week at the most, and
internal record keeping will be greatly simplified.

Physical arrangement and control of the periodical collection
were much improved during the year, although the storage collection
of periodicals is still in poor order, in consequence of some emergency
shifting that had to be done last spring when stacks were removed to
prevent further cracking of the floor in the Main Reading Room.

The reserve operation (administratively joined to the periodical
operation simply because they occupy the same room) showed an enormous

increase in activity - from 8,363 loans in 1969/70 to 20,162 in 1970/71.
The reasons for this are not entirely clear, but improved record keeping and other procedural reforms may be partly responsible. In any
event, following total reorganization of reserves in the Fall semester,
staffing requirements dropped off so much that Mrs. Peggy Rude, who
had worked part-time in both reserves and the Olin Science Library,
could be transferred full time to Olin. The reserve operation is now
run almost entirely by student staff.

Both the periodical and reserve operation are running so smoothly
that full-time professional supervision is no longer required.

E. Reference Department

The reference collection was completely rearranged to put all books
in one straightforward call-number sequence, rather than many broken
ones. The card catalog was moved into the Reference Room from a spot
nearly one hundred feet away, so patrons needing expert help in using
this complex device would have it close at hand. The staff prepared
a large display index to the reference collection and mounted it in
a prominent spot in the Reference Room. Persons unfamiliar with the
content of the collection find it an extremely handy guide.

The pamphlet file was weeded of obsolete material, and reduced
in size by 50 percent. Materials acquired by and formerly housed in
the Simulation Center were transferred to the Reference Room, where
they are kept in locked cases.

The staff compiled two specialized bibliographies, one on
Vietnam for general distribution, another as a research guide for

students in the social sciences.

Several instructional tours of the Library were given, and library staff taught an interim course in bibliography.

By far the most momentous development in the Reference Department was the large-scale expansion of interlibrary loan services. Amounting to no more than two or three hundred deliveries per year in times past, interloan activity suddenly leaped to 5,885 requests in 1970/71. The cause of this amazing leap was the availability of good service. Most items were delivered in one or two days after being requested - in contrast to the usual waiting period of two or three weeks.

The foundation of the program was the courier service to the University of Minnesota Libraries. Each working day the Library sent one of its own staff to the University Libraries to borrow books and photocopy journal articles on behalf of Macalester students and faculty. There was no charge for the service or for photocopies (up to $2.00 per item). The courier service yielded the following results:

	Requested	Delivered	Not owned by Univ.	Not * Available
Books	2,124	1,144 (54 percent)	435 (20 percent)	549 (26 percent)
Articles	2,074	1,571 (76 percent)	274 (13 percent)	240 (11 percent)
Combined	4,198	2,715 (65 percent)	709 (16 percent)	789 (19 percent)

* Owned but in circulation, at bindery, etc.

Total photocopy cost of the 1,571 articles was $924.00, or an average
of $.59 per article. Some idea of the size of the bargain may be form-
ed by calculating what it would cost Macalester to buy, house, and service a 15,000 title journal collection like the one our courier had
access to: very conservatively, the cost would be not less than
$300,000.00 per year.

In addition to the courier service, the Library obtained interloans from CLIC and numerous other libraries; total results are the
following:

	Requested	Delivered	Success rate
Courier	4,198	2,715	65 percent
CLIC	1,445	513	35 percent
Western Michigan University	60	50	83 percent
All others	182	121	67 percent
	5,885	3,399	58 percent

Besides handling nearly 6,000 requests from Macalester patrons, the
reference staff also processed 868 interloan requests from other libraries,
of which 438, or 51 percent, could be delivered.

Libraries contemplating an interloan program of this scope would
normally plan 4 or 5 staff positions to handle interloans exclusively.
Macalester had no one to assign full time to the program, and so assigned
one person half-time from Acquisitions (Mrs. Jean Francis, our courier)
and one person half-time from Reference (Mr. David Ondercin, Bibliographical Intern). Their accomplishments in this joint undertaking go far
beyond what anyone could reasonably hope for; such an avalanche of interloan requests might fairly be expected to overwhelm a staff several
times the size of ours.

The success of the interloan program has far-reaching implications for the basic principles of collection development at Macalester. Heretofore the principle appears to have been, "Buy everything you are asked to, as long as the money holds out." That the money will never hold out long on that basis is self-evident in the fact that the universe of books comprises some 50,000,000 titles, with half a million new ones added each year, while some 100,000 journal titles are also being currently published.

With ready interloan access to a major research library, collection development may now proceed (experimentally, at least) on the principle that the Library should acquire all needed publications not conveniently available on interloan - which means all relevant current imprints, all standard works of scholarship and literature, and all high-use books and periodicals, whether current or retrospective. Within the limits of that principle, it appears that a book/periodical budget in the range of $115,000 will suffice. On the "Buy everything" principle, the riches of Croesus would not suffice.

The post of Bibliographical Intern was created in the Reference Department as an alternative to hiring (what our budget restricts us to) inexperienced library school graduates, who usually have had little or no teaching or research experience - both of which are indispensable in providing high quality reference service. Candidates for the internship are required to have teaching and research experience, but not library-school training, since on-the-job training quickly makes up for that deficiency. Only distinguished graduate students nearing completion of a doctorate are considered for the post.

The post was created on the assumption that it would yield substantial benefits both to the Library and the intern, and the assumption has been fully borne out by the performance of the first incumbent, whose accomplishments surpass those of the two reference assistants whom he replaced.

Authorization was sought to appoint two interns to fill the two positions vacated by the two reference assistants, but owing to financial difficulties it was not obtained. So the new intern found himself in a far more demanding situation than either of the two reference assistants, having double the load to carry, and no specific training or experience as a reference librarian. As expected, his solid background in teaching and scholarship, together with a few weeks' intensive training on the job from Mrs. Archibald, equipped him to carry a double load with excellent results. The validity of the internship concept was well supported in this stressful situation.

F. Olin Science Library

During the Spring semester Mrs. Rude, who formerly divided her time between Olin and Reserves, was assigned full time to Olin. In her absence the Olin Library is staffed by students.

Total circulation was 2,827, a slight drop from the 3,034 loans recorded in 1969/70.

Shelf space for the Olin periodical collection is about to run out (shelf load factor is 84 percent), and transfer of parts of this collection to a storage area in Olin has begun. The general shelving situation in Olin is fast becoming critical. Total shelf capacity (including periodical stacks) is 939 lineal feet; the collection presently contains 753 lineal feet of books and periodicals. Assuming a growth rate of about 100 ft. per year (600 - 700 vols.), Olin shelves will be packed tight within the next two years. The broad policy questions posed by this fast-approaching problem should be taken up at an early date by the Educational Resources Advisory Committee.

As is the case in virtually all branch libraries on American campuses, unit operating costs are higher than those for the main library. While Olin accounted for about 3 percent of total recorded loans, it absorbed 6 percent of the total library budget (including costs for staff, books, periodicals, and processing).

V. THE COLLECTIONS

The Library, with more than 197,000 volumes, is recognized as one of the best in the Twin Cities. While collection building is carried on primarily for the benefit of Macalester students, faculty, and staff, the Library is frequently used by students and faculty of other colleges, as well as residents of the Twin Cities. Graduate students from the University of Minnesota, in education and other fields, often obtain books here when they cannot find them elsewhere in the Twin Cities.

An up-to-date and extensive reference collection of 5,000 volumes, unusually large and comprehensive for a small college library, provides an excellent foundation for research activities at Macalester.

To assist the Education Department in preparing for a 1972 NCATE review, the Library made a special analysis of its materials in the

field of professional teacher education. The following statistics
were compiled:

Holdings

Monographs	6,000 volumes
Children's literature	5,000 volumes
Curriculum materials	6,000 volumes (plus 48 file drawers of pamphlet materials)
Bound periodicals	2,300 volumes
Total:	19,300 volumes

Using a random-sampling procedure, the Library found that it
holds 50 percent of the 60,000 titles listed in Books for College
Libraries, and 61.5 percent of the titles listed under "Education" in
the same source.

119 current periodical subscriptions in the field of education
are in the Library, as well as 66 titles that have ceased publication.
The Library holds 61.5 percent of "Education" periodicals listed in
Magazines for Libraries.

These data indicate strong basic collections, amplified by extensive research materials.

During the past nine years, the Library's holdings in the humanities
have been greatly enriched through the James Wallace History Chair funds,
administered by Professor Boyd Shafer. One area developed extensively
by Dr. Shafer is the French Revolution. Macalester history students
have at hand an unusually comprehensive collection of books dealing
with all aspects of French history and culture. Numerous other areas
in the humanities have been improved by careful analysis of the collections and selective purchasing.

During 1970/71, Library staff evaluated music holdings at the request of the Music Department. The National Association of Schools of Music <u>Basic Music Library</u> was checked to indicate all items held by the Library. All important missing items were ordered to bring resources up to satisfactory standards. $850 was spent on this project.

Library expenditures over the three previous years in the field of music were found to be $2,717.49. Figures from the survey of the Library's music collection are:

> 2,800 volumes in the main music collection
>
> 482 titles in the Arthur Billings Hunt American Hymnology Collection
>
> 982 phonograph records
>
> 27 reels of microfilm (Mozart's and Beethoven's works)

It was recently announced that the Music Department has been accredited as an Associate member of the NASM. Dr. Hammer, Chairman of the Music Department, states that the Library's support was one of the vital factors in the Music Department's achieving accreditation.

Macalester College has been noted for its strong emphasis on political science, and this is well reflected in the collections. The book collection is very comprehensive and is supported by a selective government document collection of more than 3,000 items. The Library keeps in touch with Minnesota's senators and representatives in Congress and is on their mailing lists to receive many committee reports and

hearings. Other government publications are regularly ordered by the
Reference Department.

Microfilm collections are receiving notably heavier use after being moved to a more prominent location, where help is available in using them. Microfilm of the New York Times is heavily used. The Library
has microfilm runs from 1946 to date, and hopes eventually to have the
complete backrun (1851 through 1945) to meet constant reference demands.
Over 500 reels of census reports issued by the U. S. Bureau of the
Census are in the microfilm holdings, covering the period 1820-1870
for many midwest states, and are of great value to history and geography students and faculty. A significant title added to the microfilm
collection during the past year is the "Times" (London) for the years
1900-1920. As possible, acquisition of additional years' runs will
be made to serve more fully the needs of history students.

Years before there was a high demand for materials on minority
groups, the Library was systematically acquiring books concerning the
Negro in Africa and America, the American Indian, Chicanos, and other
minorities. These collections now number more than 2,100 volumes, and
include such outstanding sets as The American Negro Series, published
by Arno Press and the N. Y. Times (44 vols.), The North American Indian,
by Edward S. Curtis (20 vols.), and the Slave Trade series of the
British Parliamentary Papers (97 vols.)

VI. PHYSICAL PLANT

The Weyerhaeuser building leaks in various places despite numerous repair jobs; the stack walls are cracking in several places; and the main
floor of the south wing developed such dangerous cracks in one area
that stacks were removed from it last March on the recommendation of

a structural engineer. Cause of the cracking was not established; however, it appears that floor loading was well under design capacity,
and is not to blame. (The stacks in the area of worst cracking weighed
3500 lbs., and carried 16,500 lbs. of books, in an area of 500 sq. ft.
The load thus came to about 40 lbs. per sq. ft., while the design
capacity is 80 lbs. per sq. ft.) The area vacated by the stacks is
now used for seating, which keeps the load well within the 60 lb./sq. ft.
limit recommended by the structural engineer.

In the summer of 1971, two window fans were installed in the
Main Reading Room, bringing temperatures down from intolerable to
reasonably comfortable levels. In previous summers it was virtually
impossible to use this area after 11:00 a.m. because of the fierce
heat, but the room was well used this summer after the fans were installed.

The Circulation Desk was relocated in the main lobby to improve
exit control and general traffic flow.

Maintenance and custodial services have been above average despite
the difficulties posed by an aging structure. Mr. Heuer's maintenance
and custodial staff are reliable, diligent, and courteous, and it is
a great satisfaction to know that when help is needed, it will arrive
in good time.

VII.   STAFF ACTIVITIES

All staff are encouraged to attend Minnesota Library Association
meetings, and nearly everyone does so.

Mrs. Jean Archibald served as Program Chairman of the Academic
Division of the MLA during 1970/71, and was elected Chairman of the

Division for 1971/72, and board member of MLA.

The Macalester Library was host for the Spring meeting of the Academic Division, and many of the staff assisted in the hospitality arrangements. Mr. Gore and Mr. Hernandez presented a slide show on the reclassification project at Macalester.

Mr. Gore and Mrs. Archibald offered an interim term course in bibliography.

Publications, Speeches, etc.

Cobb, Joyce, Vietnam Bibliography.

Francis, Jean. "Free to be an Individual" Enquiry, March-May, 1971, pp. 18-20.

Gore, Daniel. "How the Vikings Forced King Alfred to Invent the Reserve Book Collection," paper presented at a Workshop on Reserves, University of Minnesota, August 24, 1970. To be published in American Libraries.

"The Minolta and the Fastcat," speech presented to the Technical Services Section, Minnesota Library Association, Rochester, Minn., Oct. 16, 1970.

"Library Censorship and the AAUP," speech presented to the general membership of the New York Library Association, New York City, November 11, 1970; and to the Library Staff Forum, University of Minnesota, December 16, 1970.

"Against the Dogmatists: A Sceptical View of Libraries," American Libraries, Bulletin of the American Library Association, Vol. 1, No. 10 (November, 1970), 1953-57.

Advances in Understanding Approval and Gathering Plans, edited by Peter Spyers-Duran and Daniel Gore. Kalamazoo: Western Michigan University, 1970. 220 pp.

"Understanding Approval Plans," in Advances in Understanding Approval and Gathering Plans, pp. 3-17.

"The Minolta and the Fastcat," Bulletin of the Minnesota Library Association, Vol. 20, No. 1 (February, 1971), 2-3, 10.

"Faculty Status for the Librarians at Arbuthnot," American
Libraries, Bulletin of the American Library Association,
Vol. 2, No. 3 (March, 1971) 283-95.

"A Library Lacking 49,800,000 Books?" Macalester College
Bulletin, Vol. 59, No. 2 (Winter 1970-71), 22-23.

"Adopting an Approval Plan for a College Library: The
Macalester College Experience," paper presented at the
Third International Seminar on Approval and Gathering
Plans, West Palm Beach, Fla., February 12, 1971.
To be published by Greenwood Press as part of the seminar
proceedings.

"High-Speed Reclass in Slow Motion; A Media Presentation,"
slide show presented to the Minnesota Library Association
Academic Section, Macalester College, May 8, 1971.

Ondercin, David. The Social Sciences Guide.

VIII. PROBLEMS PRESENT AND DISTANT

A serious immediate problem is the books/periodicals budget. Continuous efforts were made throughout 1970/71 to streamline the operation and thus reduce staff requirements, with the result that the salary/
wage budget for 1971/72 is $29,000.00 less than in 1970/71. However,
the total library budget was cut by $37,000.00, so instead of being
able to augment the book budget, as hoped, we had to make some modest
cuts. From our experience to date, it appears that our book budget
requirements are the following:

Profile Plan:	$65,000
History Chair:	15,000
Other retrospective & miscellaneous	10,000
Periodicals	25,000
$	115,000

While we may weather 1971/72 with a book budget $13,000 below that level
(by postponing most "other retrospective & miscellaneous" purchases),
either the book budget will have to be increased in 1972/73, or the
profile program abandoned in favor of some formal allocational procedure.

. Library staff salaries appear to have been substandard at Macalester
even during the years of plenty. They are about 25 percent below the
scales for comparable positions at the University of Minnesota, although staff productivity rates at Macalester appear to be somewhat
higher. Maximum efforts should be made to correct library staff salary
deficiencies in 1972/73.

Solutions to some of the major operational problems were found
and implemented in 1970/71, but in some areas - e.g. reclassification -
several more years may pass before work begun is completed. While
some temporary relief has been found from the recurrent shelving crisis,
collection growth over the next three years will bring it on again.
By that time, and ideally long before, the Library should acquire
sufficient compact shelving (about $40,000.00 worth) to expand
Weyerhaeuser capacity 40 to 50,000 volumes, thus adding 3 or 4 years
to the useful life of the building, and permitting comfortable lead
time for planning, funding, and constructing a new library building.
It appears that by 1977 all measures for extending the usefulness of
the Weyerhaeuser building will be exhausted, and a new building must
be ready for occupancy at that time.

IX.   A Concluding Personal Note

Probably no one has been more surprised than myself at the accomplishments of the library staff over the past year. When changes are so
numerous, and the pace so swift, the ensuing confusion and anxiety
normally drag achievements well below theoretically possible levels.
What so surprises me is that the staff accomplished everything that
seemed theoretically possible at the start of 1970/71, and they did
it with fewer people than I had counted on to do the work at the outset. I speak with the authority of wide experience when I say
Macalester has a college library staff second to none in talent,
loyalty, and accomplishments. It is a pleasure to be held accountable
for their performance.

———————————

Individual reports of the Acquisitions, Cataloging, Circulation,
Periodicals and Reserves, and Reference Departments, and of the
Curriculum Lab and Olin Science Library are on file and available
for inspection in the Library Office. These reports give a more detailed account of certain aspects of the Library's operations.

Macalester College

Annual Report
of
The Library
1971/72

St. Paul   Minnesota

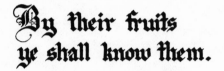

By their fruits
ye shall know them.

Matthew 7:20

MACALESTER COLLEGE

SAINT PAUL, MINNESOTA 55101

February 7, 1973

Dr. Kenneth P. Goodrich
Vice President and Provost
Macalester College
St. Paul, Minnesota 55105

Dear Ken:

I am pleased to submit herewith, for your review, the Annual Report of
the Library for fiscal 1971/72.

Statistical data necessarily make up a large portion of such a report,
since it is in the nature of a library to deal with quantities of considerable
magnitude--things that are largely intelligible only when reduced to numbers.
But behind the bare bones of these dry statistics there lies, of course, an
eloquent testament to the day-in, day-out labors of faithful and talented
people--something that may easily be lost sight of in a maze of data. The
work done, and credit for its results, must in candor be attributed to my
staff, since I have had little or nothing to do myself with the actual work
of the Library. As its Director, I understand my principal duty to be to
give it direction, and keep it pointed the right way; and that is what I have
tried to do. Here then is the report of the year's work of many able and
willing hands, together with my own appraisal of what has been accomplished,
and my judgment of things that yet need attention in the months ahead.

With this report go my appreciation for your good support of Library programs
over the last two years; my best wishes for success in your new assignment
at Syracuse; and my personal regret at the impending departure of so able and
amiable a colleague.

Cordially,

Daniel Gore
Director

DG:db

I.   INTRODUCTION

That was the year the Phoenix took flight. And in the continuing
rough economic weather, the flight stayed smooth and steady and right
on course.

Despite further personnel cuts the reclassification staff processed
26,778 books--a slight increase over the previous year's work.

The computer-based acquisitions program continued to yield good results. Circulation of new books was double that of the previous year,
while the loan rate of other books from the general collection (excluding
periodicals and reserves) dropped about three percent. These results bear
out the hypothesis that new publications will be in strong demand if
made available for circulation shortly after publication date, and they
justify concentration of resources on buying current rather than retrospective imprints.

Rearrangement of traffic patterns in Weyerhaeuser improved building
security and collection control; provided better access to the periodicals
and reserve collections; and permitted a reduction of 3 FTE student positions formerly required to staff an exit-check station, eliminated as a
result of the changed traffic patterns.

The schedule of open hours remained unchanged in spite of continuing
staff reductions.

The Audio-Visual Center, once a separate entity, was merged with the
Library to become one of its several operating departments. The AV Department continued to produce at its previous peak levels even with staff reduced in the course of the year.

A general survey of Library accomplishments and contributions to the
College's educational mission appears in the pages that follow.

II. STAFF

A. Acquisitions Department

Mrs. Joyce Cobb resigned as head of the department in December, 1972, to move with her family to Kentucky. The position was cancelled and the department merged with cataloging in a single unit, the Technical Services Department. Mrs. Marymina Stenger, who had been Head of the Cataloging Department, was promoted to Head of the Technical Services Department.

B. Audio-Visual Department

Mr. Wynn Lee was named Acting Head of the Department in January, 1972, replacing Mr. Ivan Hernandez, who resigned his position as Director of the Audio-Visual Center. For the remainder of fiscal 1971/72 Mr. Lee's position was 2/3 Library, plus a 1/3 time teaching appointment in the French Department.

In June, 1972, Mr. James Derks resigned his post as Electronics Engineer, and was replaced by Mr. Thomas Browne, who devotes 1/2 time to AV and the other half to maintaining Language Laboratory equipment (formerly handled by a full-time engineer not on the Library payroll).

Mrs. Victoria Hakala resigned her half-time position as graphic artist, and was not replaced.

C. Cataloging Department

No personnel changes, except Mrs. Stenger's promotion, as noted above.

D. Circulation Department

Mrs. Rosemarie Leonard, Head of the Department, resigned in May, 1972 and was replaced by Mr. David Ondercin, who vacated his post as Bibliographical Intern.

E. Reference Department

   Mr. Dennis Dickinson was appointed Bibliographical Intern in January, 1972. In May, Mr. Ondercin became Head of Circulation, and the Intern post he vacated was not filled.

F. Reserves & Periodicals Department

   Mr. Robert Cramer, Head of the Department, resigned in May, 1972, and the post was left vacant, to be filled in September by Mrs. Jean Francis. Throughout the year Mrs. Kellar and Mrs. Nelson (both from Technical Services) devoted substantial time to the work of this unit.

G. Olin Science Library

   No personnel changes.

H. Summary of Staff Reductions

                    Library Staff Roster (excluding A/V)

Fall 1970   Fall 1971   Fall 1972

Daniel Gore   Daniel Gore   Daniel Gore
Jean Archibald   Jean Archibald   Jean Archibald
Wendy Adamson   Dorothy Barnes   Dorothy Barnes
Dorothy Barnes   Joyce Cobb   Regina Crouse
Louis Buggs   Robert Cramer   Dennis Dickinson
Joyce Cobb   Regina Crouse   Jean Francis (3/4)
Robert Cramer   Jean Francis (1/2)   Robert Haberkorn (1/2)
Regina Crouse   Robert Haberkorn (1/2)   Mary Hampl
Jean Francis   Mary Hampl   Richard Higginbotham (1/2)
Mary Hampl   Corinne Kellar   Corinne Kellar
Wilbert Harri (1/2)   Rosemarie Leonard   Lois Nelson
Corinne Kellar   Lois Nelson   Ruth Newcomb
Mary Ann Kerr   Ruth Newcomb   Bernice Oliver (1/2)
Louise Kiscaden   Bernice Oliver (1/2)   David Ondercin
Rosemarie Leonard   David Ondercin   Peggy Rude
George Meyn   Peggy Rude   Rosemary Salscheider
Lois Nelson   Rosemary Salscheider   Un Chol Shin (1/2)
Ruth Newcomb   Un Chol Shin (1/2)   Marymina Stenger
Bernice Oliver (1/2)   Elli Sorensen (1/2)   _____
Ann Pressman   Marymina Stenger
Peggy Rude   _____   15 3/4 FTE
Rosemary Salscheider
Un Chol Shin (1/2)   17 1/2 FTE
Elli Sorensen (1/2)
Marymina Stenger
MICROFICHE CATALOGING DEVICE
(in exchange for one staff position)

     24 FTE

                    A/V Staff Roster

                  Fall 1971   Fall 1972

                  Ivan Hernandez   Wynn Lee
                  Jean Jackson   Jean Jackson
                  James Derks   Thomas Browne (1/2)
                  Victoria Hakala (1/2)   _____

                     3 1/2 FTE   2 1/2 FTE

I. Student Staff

Total hours of student labor (all units except A/V) came to 22,622, or
6,765 hours less than in 1970/71. The reduction, roughly equal to 3 FTE
positions, was accomplished largely by changing traffic patterns in the
building so only one exit-check station had to be manned instead of two, as
in the previous year.

Hours of student labor in the A/V Department came to 5,704, or about
50% of FTE positions in that unit.

Students continue to play a significant and valuable role in the
operation of their library. Comparing our hours of student labor with those
of 38 other liberal arts colleges comparable to Macalester in size and
character, we find the per capita figure (total hours worked divided by
total FTE enrollment) to be 62% higher than the average. Since library
work is a vital educational experience for most students who undertake it--
and also enhances the maturing process--that figure speaks very well for
that part of the Library's total contribution to the College's educational
mission.

J. Staff Organization

The organizational methods outlined in the 1970/71 Report (pp. 5-7)
continued to yield good results in 1971/72 and were not modified.

K. General Appraisal of the Staff

This library continues to be far more fortunate than most in its staff.
Everyone works together in unity and harmony, and morale remains high. With
the pace of change greatly reduced after the rigors of reorganization during
1970/71, and work assignments better stabilized than in that year, there is a
good deal less tension among the staff and productivity continues at peak levels

III. THE 1971/72 BUDGET

A. Library (excluding the AV Department)

The budget for 1971/72 was set at $255,000, not including $20,000
for student help, which was part of the 1970/71 budget total of $312,000
(or $292,000 excluding student help). Late in the fiscal year the
Library was asked to spend below the level authorized, and actual expenditures came to $242,807; about $12,000 less than originally budgeted,
and about $49,000 less than originally budgeted for 1970/71. A full
analysis of budget results for 1971/72 is appended. A comparison of major
categories of expenditure is here presented:

Title	1970/71	1971/72
Salaries and Wages	$149,638	$127,826
Acquisitions and Binding	101,158	105,579
Operations (excluding student help)	13,463	9,402
Total:	$264,259	$242,807

It will be noted that while total expenses dropped nearly ten percent, expenditures on acquisitions increased by about four percent. Total dollar
value of acquisitions and binding, including gifts and grant expenditures,
comes to $128,971.

Library Budget 1971/72

Actual Expenditures

Title		Expenditures
1. Salaries & Wages		$ 127,826
2. Acquisitions & Binding		105,579

Books	$81,965	
Periodicals	22,593	
Binding	1,021	

3. Operations (Expenses less income)   9,402

Expenses

Student payroll	n.a.
Supplies	3,383
Telephone	232
Postage	392
Printing	1,133
Travel	-0-
Equipment purchase	2,376
Equipment repair	533
Photocopying	4,072
Membership (CLIC)	1,750
Interlibrary Loans	711
	14,582

Income

Overdue fees	885
Book sales	88
Picture rentals	131
Lost Books	403
Photocopying	3,673
	5,180

Grand total: 242,807

Budgeted total: 255,000

($275,000 less 20,000 transferred to student aid budget)

The principal expenditure for equipment ($1,480) covered 1,500 feet of stack shelving, to replace shelving stripped from storage in the previous year to expand Weyerhaeuser capacity.

B. AV Department

The authorized budget was $37,919, not including student help. Net expenditures came to $24,827, or about $13,000 less than budgeted. The budget analysis is as follows:

Title	Expenditure
Salaries and Wages	$18,969.00
Distribution	7.00
Office Supplies	3,979.00
Other	478.00
Dues and Memberships	83.00
Subscriptions	174.00
Freight	34.00
Telephone	47.00
Audio Visual	2,001.00
Postage	125.00
Printing	580.00
Travel and Mileage	300.00
Meals	93.00
Furniture	-
Equipment	3,339.00
Repair	2,188.00
Total:	$32,397.00
Income Credits:	7,569.00
Net:	$24,827.00

IV. DEPARTMENTAL ACTIVITIES

A. Technical Services

   1. Acquisitions

      The computer-based profile acquisitions program, inaugurated in
January, 1971, continued to function smoothly throughout 1971/72, although certain refinements were made in profile specifications, where
experience indicated they were needed to meet requirements of certain
academic departments.

      General statistical results for the profile program, fiscal 1971/72, are
the following:

	Number	Dollars	Average
Notice slips from Abel	14,834	145,361	$9.80
"Buy" slips from faculty	5,930	53,292	9.00
"Don't Buy" slips from faculty	8,375	77,540	9.25
Total slips from faculty	14,305	130,832	9.15
Acceptance rate	42%	40%	
Rejection rate	58%	60%	

Price figures reflect an average increase per title of about 8% over the
previous fiscal year.

      Most books received on this program continue to reach the Library, and
be made available for loan, on or very close to official publication date.
The most substantial time lag in the acquisitions cycle is the period of
six to eight weeks (average) required for the Faculty to make an order decision on a title and communicate it to the Library.

      Expenditures by departments (all categories of purchase, including
periodicals) were as follows:

Departmental Book and Periodical Expenditures 1971/72

Division	Expenditure by Division Books	Periodicals	Total
1. Social Sciences			
Geography	$1,680.65	$ 442.71	$2,123.36
Political Science	7,003.32	1,055.41	8,058.73
Psychology	3,139.82	1,601.71	4,741.53
Sociology & Anthropology	4,155.49	413.70	4,569.19
Totals	15,979.28	3,513.53	19,492.81
2. Business and Economics	4,169.50	1,118.08	5,287.58
3. Education	2,408.80	360.75	2,769.55
4. Fine Arts			
Art	3,001.58	319.20	3,320.78
Journalism	228.23	40.00	268.23
Music	1,964.97	101.85	2,066.82
Speech	436.69	123.10	559.79
Totals	5,631.47	584.15	6,215.62
5. Humanities			
Classics	994.93	112.75	1,107.68
English	10,994.63	637.51	11,632.14
Foreign Languages			
French	2,003.43	130.15	2,133.58
German	4,374.68	315.12	4,689.80
Russian	530.21	116.20	646.41
Spanish	944.33	110.95	1,055.28
History	13,822.19	459.38	14,281.57
Language (General)		154.40	154.40
Philosophy	2,018.62	340.20	2,358.82
Religion	2,220.92	213.38	2,434.30
Totals	37,903.94	2,590.04	40,493.98
6. Physical Education	205.25	188.50	393.75
7. Science and Mathematics			
General		92.50	92.50
Biology	2,528.91	3,661.41	6,190.32
Chemistry	2,690.90	5,395.82	8,086.72
Geology	1,220.14	723.44	1,943.58
Math	828.32	1,051.92	1,880.24
Physics	943.61	1,440.45	2,384.06
Totals	8,211.88	12,365.54	20,577.42
8. Library and Miscellaneous	7,454.46	1,872.51	9,326.97
Grand Totals	$81,964.58	$22,593.10	$104,577.68

GIFTS AND GRANTS

A federal grant of $50,000 was awarded to CLIC for 1971/72 for the joint purchase of expensive library materials. After study of numerous recommendations, a purchase list was compiled by the CLIC Grant Committee. These materials are located in the various libraries, and Macalester's collections were enriched with the following items:

London Times. 1785-1899, 1914-1929 (microfilm) Index 1922-1967	$10,178.00
Palmer's Index to the London Times. 1785-1905 (microfiche)	250.00
Evergreen Review. v. 1-14 (microfiche)	56.00
Yale Law Journal. v. 1-25 (microfiche)	170.00
Yale Law Journal. v. 45-67. (Bound vols.)	575.00
Negro History Bulletin. v. 1-20 (Bound vols.)	375.00
English Historical Review. v. 1-43 (Bound vols.)	1,359.00
Historian. v. 1-18 (Bound vols.)	215.00
Partisan Review. v. 1-3 (Bound vols.)	90.00
Western Political Quarterly. v. 1-6 (Bound vols.)	240.00
Guide to Nazi Archive microfilm set	4.50
British Journal of Psychology. v. 1-54 (Microfiche)	480.00
Renaissance Quarterly. v. 1-5 (Bound vols.)	34.20
Phylon. v. 1-13. (Bound vols.)	271.70
Journal of International Affairs. v. 1-8	104.00
	$14,402.40 *

Practically all of these titles extend previous holdings in Macalester's collections, so we are able to provide complete runs of these important serials.

*These expenditures are in addition to those reported on the schedule "Departmental Book and Periodical Expenditures, 1971/72," p.

In April 1971, the W. K. Kellogg Foundation awarded a grant of $5,000 to the College to be expended over a three year period on College Resources for Environmental Studies.

During the period from May 1971-April 1972, the following amounts were spent from the CRES grant:

Books, indexes, abstracts	$1,286.59
Periodical Subscriptions	85.49
Government Documents	25.10
	$1,397.18

In addition to the above purchases, a number of films were ordered for previewing in the fall of 1972, after which final decisions would be made on specific purchases. It is expected that these films on environmental topics will be used extensively by many different classes, such as biology, geography and geology.

Other notable acquisitions:

Two major sets were purchased during 1971/72 with funds from the general book budget.

Encyclopaedia Judaica. Jerusalem, 1972. 16 vols. $500.00

Lewis, Arthur O., editor. Utopian Literature. New York, Arno, 1971. 41 vols. $475.00

3,060 gift items were received during 1971/72 with a total estimated value of $8,989.62. Included in the 3,060 gifts were 2,366 books, with periodicals and miscellaneous documents rounding out the figure.

Among the more notable gifts were books donated by Macalester alumnae. Gertrude Louise Luttgen presented juvenile books to enrich the Wood Collection, and Jean P. Smith gave a select group of books relating to Japan.

About 100 new juvenile books were added to the Wood Collection by the Wood School Alumnae Association.

Boyd C. Shafer (former Macalester faculty member) donated over 500 items, mostly in the areas of history and biography, and Dr. John Bates, Macalester trustee, of Minneapolis gave 113 volumes.

2. Cataloging

Statistics for the last three years, including 1971/72, are the following:

	1969/70	1970/71	1971/72
Volumes reclassed	1,908	25,923	26,778
Volumes cataloged	10,909	11,094	8,298
Volumes withdrawn (includes lost & stolen)	3,331	3,524	2,062
Total units processed:	16,148	40,541	37,138

From the August 29, 1972 census we determined that on that date there were still some 32,000 volumes to be reclassed from Dewey to the Library of Congress system. By the end of fiscal 1973/74 the reclass project should be completed. At that time some 84,000 volumes will have been reclassed (roughly $170,000 worth of work) without any special funding.

Cataloging staff has decreased steadily in numbers over the last three years, to a complement that is about half what it was in 1969/70. At the same time, the more than twofold increase in production over that period indicates a gain of more than fourfold in actual rates of productivity.

B. Circulation Department

Total recorded circulation (Weyerhaeuser and Olin) came to 88,509, an apparent drop of about 11% from the 1970/71 total of 101,893. The drop is more apparent than real, and is accounted for by two things: (1) An "Open Reserve" collection was created so readers might use short-term loan items without charging them; and (2) the physical arrangement of the bound periodicals collection was modified so readers might examine them in open stacks rather than charging them out. Recorded loans in these two collections accordingly dropped by 13,871 transactions--a figure slightly larger than the actual apparent drop in collection use from 1970/71.

These are the summary circulation statistics for Weyerhaeuser and Olin Libraries:

| | Weyerhaeuser | | Olin | |
	Students	Faculty	Students	Faculty
Books (general)	51,982	3,129	1,082	195
Curriculum Lab	1,608	71		
College Cat. and Pam.	266	13		
Paperbacks	243	123		
Cassettes	263			
Government Documents	298	7		
FASTCAT	2,271	703	52	36
Juvenile	3,482	435		
Phono Records	1,811	151		
Art Rentals	89	22		
Periodicals	4,144 (students & faculty)		117	3
Storage	557 (students & faculty)			
Reserve	14,242 (students & faculty)		1,114	
Totals:	81,256	4,654	2,365	234
Combined:	85,910		2,599	
Both Libraries:	88,509			

Circulation of FASTCAT books increased from 1,404 in 1970/71, to 3,062 in 1971/72--partially the result of changing from random to general subject shelf order in this collection at the beginning of 1971/72. Subject grouping facilitates browsing in this collection and thereby increases demand levels.

Because of extremely high shelfload factors, and the rapid pace of the reclass project, it became necessary to shift the entire book collection in Weyerhaeuser (about 160,000 volumes) in the Summer of 1972. This is an

undertaking of great magnitude--comparable to moving the whole library--
but no special budget provisions were made for it. The shift was carried
out over a four-week period by regular staff, with some good assistance
from the Neighborhood Youth Corps. The collections are now evenly distributed over the available shelving, and have been thoroughly shelf-read
to ensure that books are in their correct call-number sequence. Also, for
the first time in at least a decade, the major call number sequences are
in nearly straightforward order, rather than the random sequences formerly
observed.

While the circulation control system functions reasonably well, the
manually maintained files require an inordinate amount of painstaking labor,
and the charging system is cumbersome and time-consuming for the patron.
In fiscal 1972/73 the system will be replaced by a microfilm control unit
that will drastically reduce labor requirements and speed up the charging
process for the patrons.

The department conducted a census count of all collections during the
summer of 1972 twice, since the first count (made by Youth Corps volun-
teers) yielded substantially more volumes than the inventory records showed.
A second, carefully audited count was then made by regular library staff,
and that count yielded more volumes yet than the first one did. At that
point we stopped counting. Summary results of the second census count
(August 29, 1972) are the following:

Census Summary

	Weyerhaeuser	Olin	Storage
Books	180,536	5,559	12,610
Bound Periodicals and Abstracts	5,625	3,394	16,262
Newspaper and Periodical Indexes	337		
Microfilm reels	2,524		
Microfiche	1,489		
Records and Tapes	2,537		
	193,048	8,953	28,872

Grand Total: 230,873

(A detailed analysis of holdings in major subject areas is available for inspection in the Library Office.)

The census total, exceeding by 23,891 volumes the count shown on inventory records, should put to rest any fear that Macalester has, or has had, a serious library theft problem. The problem that was perceived to exist two years ago can fairly be attributed to inordinately long loan terms (full semester) and the lack of any effective policy governing overdues.

Overdue statistics for the year are these:

	Notices	covering	Books
First	2,992		5,817
Second	1,645		3,078
Third	688		1,339
Fourth	119		220

The fourth notice covers all books that have not been returned following the three previous notices, and is in fact an invoice charging the patron replacement and processing costs for the missing items. The above figures indicate that while about 10% of all 4-week loans fall overdue (5,817) only 1/2% are still unreturned after the third notice is sent, and these items must be paid for by the borrowers who keep them.

The Curriculum Laboratory

Circulation activity in this collection continued to decline in 1971/72, as it has done in each of the three preceding years:

Year	Loans	Dropped
1967/68	4,627	
1968/69	3,841	986
1969/70	2,659	1,182
1970/71	2,034	625
1971/72	1,679	355

The decline in the two most recent years, when supervisory staffing was on a part-time basis, was substantially less than in either of the two preceding years, when full-time staffing was provided.

For the tenth consecutive year, the Library displayed Books on Exhibit's annual collection of new library books of the year in the fall and in the spring. Books of interest on the elementary and secondary levels were shown separately. The fall exhibit, October 11-22 and November 1-12, featured 1001 new books. The spring exhibit, February 7-18 and February 28-March 10, featured 645 books. In addition to books of interest to children, each exhibit had an added section of professional books in the field of education. Invitations were sent to over 50 teachers, librarians, administrators and others interested in children's literature.

Weeding and updating of the collection continued throughout the year, and the staff prepared a location guide to the collection to facilitate retrieval of materials.

C. Periodicals and Reserves

During the year 38 new journal subscriptions were added, while 178
old subscriptions were cancelled, for a net reduction in paid subscriptions
of 140. Despite this reduction of about 12% in the subscription list,
total expenditures for periodicals were nearly 10% higher than in the
previous year because of a continuing high rate of inflation. Subscription
statistics are as follows:

New subscriptions (1971/72)	38
Cancellations	178
Total paid subscriptions (8/31/72)	1,111
Gift subscriptions	86
PL 480	27
Total (8/31/72)	1,224

Following a period of training and experiment with the binding equipment acquired in Summer 1971, the student staff now produces excellent
bindings at a cost of about $5.00 per volume less than a commercial binder
would charge. Off-shelf time for journals being bound is about four weeks
less than it would be with a commercial binder, and patron access to current
journal literature is accordingly much better than in the past. Volumes
bound in 1971/72 came to 1,086.

The storage collection of journals (16,000 vols.) was put in good shelf
order during the year. Previously the physical arrangement of this collection
had been so chaotic that retrieval of a large portion of our journal holdings
could not be accomplished on demand, and frequent resort to interlibrary loan
was necessary to obtain journal articles actually owned by the Library.

The physical layout of the Reserve Collection was changed in 1971/72
to make possible the following:

1. Open access to the collection of bound journals on stack
    level 1;

2. Open access to Reserve books on 2- and 48-hour loan;

3. Closing of the outside entrance to the Periodicals/Reserve
    Room, and elimination of the exit-check station.

The result of this rearrangement is improved access to the collections

for our patrons, and a sharp reduction in student labor required to staff

the operation--about 7,000 hours less per year than formerly required

(3 1/2 FTE positions).

Count of Items Placed on Reserve

	1970/71			1971/72		
	Books	Articles	Total	Books	Articles	Total
Fall	785	320	1,105	858	424	1,282
Interim	31	33	64	807	349	1,156
Spring	527	215	742	887	695	1,582
Summer	48	37	85	100	39	139
Totals:	1,391	605	1,996	2,652	1,507	4,159

D. Reference Department

In August, 1972, free-standing stacks were placed in the north end of

the Reference Room, adding about 516 lineal ft. of shelf capacity and reducing

load factors from about 90% to a comfortable 60%, permitting addition of new

volumes over the next several years without major reshifts. No seating

capacity was lost by adding the stacks, but there is now a feeling of con-

gestion about the room that is not conducive to concentrated study.

All the large oak study tables were refinished during the summer, and

special atlas shelving was constructed to improve maintenance and appearance

of the atlas collection.

The intern concept of reference staffing has withstood well the test

of time. For a period of about four months in 1972 we were able to schedule

two interns in the Reference Room, but continuing budget retrenchment re-

quired transferring one position to the Circulation Department, with piecemeal staff backup provided in the Reference Room from other departments when possible.

Interlibrary Loans. This service, provided by the Reference staff, continued at a brisk pace. In the course of the year 3,442 items were obtained for our patrons on interloan, and we delivered 1,017 items to other libraries. Most of the work is done by student staff, who are trained and supervised by the Bibliographical Intern.

In 1970/71 we provided our own courier service to the University of Minnesota Libraries, since the CLIC system did not at that time include the University. CLIC later gained access to the University collections (through MINITEX) and we were thus able to abandon the courier service in 1971/72. CLIC performance improved dramatically throughout 1971/72, when the Union Catalog became fully operational and access to the University's collection was provided. Many procedural and technical problems were overcome in the course of the first full year of operation, and the system now functions at peak efficiency. Current success rates of the CLIC interloan system are in the eighty to ninety percent range, a performance level that is indeed outstanding, and unsurpassed by any other such network in the country.

Interloan Statistics

Items Obtained for Macalester Patrons

	1970/71			1971/72		
Source	Requests	Filled	%	Requests	Filled	%
Courier	4,198	2,715	65	-	-	-
CLIC	1,445	513	35	4,824	3,316	69
Others	242	171	71	231	126	55
Totals	5,885	3,399	58%	5,055	3,442	68%

Items Sent to Other Libraries

	1970/71			1971/72		
Source	Requests	Filled	%	Requests	Filled	%
CLIC	848	424	51	1,711	1,007	59
Others	20	14	70	10	10	100
Totals	868	438	51%	1,721	1,017	59%

E. Audio-Visual Department

With the resignation of Mr. Ivan Hernandez as Director of the Audio-Visual Center in December 1971, the Center ceased to be an independent unit and became a department of the Library, with Mr. Wynn Lee as its acting head. The merger has worked well, and Mr. Lee and his staff did a commendable job in making a smooth transition to the new arrangement and keeping productivity at the previous high levels, while regular staff complement was being reduced about 30%.

The statistical evidence appended to this report demonstrates clearly that Audio-Visual equipment is being used widely and frequently throughout the College. Tape recorders, particularly cassette models, registered high use rates because of an increase in independent oral projects--interviews, language training, etc. New darkroom facilities in the department vastly expanded the variety and amount of photographic work that could be handled in house: developing, printing, enlarging in all but the largest formats. The high quality of copy stand work created a strong demand for 35mm slides produced from illustrations in books. Indeed slides were probably the most commonly used visual medium on campus last year: slide projectors had a high circulation rate, and more sophisticated slide presentations involving dissolve units and synchronized sound tracks became more frequent as classroom presentations were offered in lieu of traditional term papers. The Audio-Visual Department provided technical assistance as well as machinery to students producing these shows. Further use of slides in the classroom was facilitated at the end of the year by the acquisition of four 35mm cameras which could be loaned on a short-term basis. Initial use rates suggest that the cameras will be frequently used.

Audio-Visual has become an increasingly important element in the College this year because it has broadened its operations to include not only traditional classroom activities (film projections and the like) but independent projects which involve the student directly. Audio-Visual is thus becoming a more audible and more visible presence in the College community as a whole.

REPORT ON USAGE OF AUDIO-VISUAL FACILITIES
1971-72

Equipment Used	Fall	Interim	Spring	Summer	To
Our Films Used	237	32	96	26	3
Motion Picture Projectors	341	99	325	218	9
Overheads Booked	131	2	65	87	2
Screens Booked	88	4	64	84	2
Slide Projectors Booked	68	20	150	173	4
Portable Address	11	3	9	67	
Public Address	30	6	12	3	
Filmstrip Projectors	18	1	40	9	
Opaque Projectors	21	23	38	33	1
Tape Recorders	222	51	278	215	7
Video Tape Recorders (portable)	31	12	52	10	1
Video Tape Recorders (studio)	56	0	93	4	1
Phonographs	55	13	48	58	1
Totals	1,309	266	1,270	987	3,8
Services Used					
Films Booked - Feature Films	180	1	126	159	4
Slides (copied, developed, etc.)	687	78	1,937	2,148	4,8
Tapes Dubbed	202	0	95	22	3
Clear Acetates and Transparencies	548	19	273	67	9
Ditto Masters	863	217	78	175	1,3
Posters and Signs	185	0	264	0	4
Average Daily Phone Calls	163	33	170	31	
35mm Cameras				85	
Totals	2,828	348	2,943	2,687	8,8

F. Olin Science Library

Circulation statistics are as follows:

	1970/71	1971/72
Books and Periodicals	1,816	1,385
Reserves	1,005	1,114

Normally the Olin Reserve Collection contains about a hundred items
or less; it will be noted that they account for nearly as much loan activity
as the books and journals in the general collection, which number about
9,000 volumes. The use rate of the Olin general collection is about 1/3
that of the general library, and unit service costs are accordingly quite
high.

Shelfload factors in Olin have become critical. At some time in the
year ahead, following consultation with academic departments involved,
transfer of portions of the collection for storage will have to be undertaken.

V. THE COLLECTIONS

During 1971/72 13,335 volumes (or bibliographic items) were added to
the collections, bringing the total count (as established by the
August 29, 1972 census) to 230,873 items. The analysis of additions, and
holdings as of September 1, 1972, is as follows:

Added 1971/72

	Volumes (or bibliographic items)
Books	11,474
Bound periodicals and abstracts	1,086
Newspaper and periodical indexes	170
Microfilm reels	329
Microfiche	241
Records and tapes	35
Total	13,335

Total Resources September 1, 1972

	Volumes (or bibliographic items)
Books	198,705
Bound periodicals and abstracts	25,281
Newspaper and periodical indexes	337
Microfilm reels	2,524
Microfiche	1,489
Records and tapes	2,537
Total	230,873

Subscriptions in Force, September 1, 1972

Newspapers	60
Journals	1,224
Other Serials	437
Total	1,721

A chart showing collection growth from 1885, with projections through
1980, is on the following page.

VI. <u>PHYSICAL PLANT</u>

Renovations and repairs costing about $16,000 (as estimated in
Vice President McLarnan's report of January 17, 1973) are needed in the
Weyerhaeuser Library. Carpet runners on the stack stairways are urgently
needed, and have been requested several times during the last two years.
Tiles on the stair treads are worn, cracked, and slick, presenting an obvious
safety hazard along a route that receives heavy daily use.

Following removal of stacks from the main floor, south wing, in
March, 1971, the progressive cracking of the concrete floor appears to have
halted.

An airconditioning unit and humidifier were installed in the Rare Book
Room in Spring, 1972, to provide climate control needed to protect the books
in that room.

Custodial services continue to be quite satisfactory.

Building security control was significantly improved by closing off
access to ground level areas except through the main lobby/stack stairway
route.

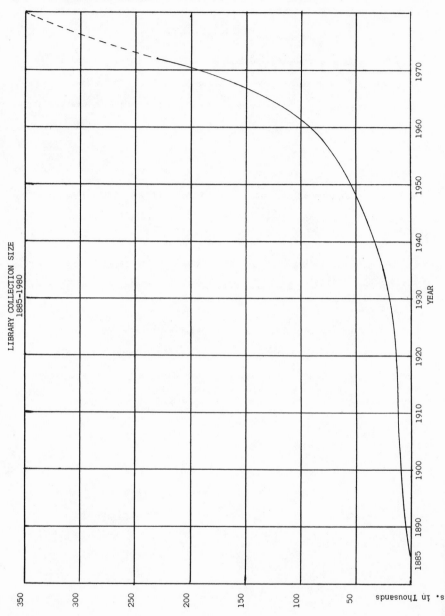

LIBRARY COLLECTION SIZE
1885-1980

YEAR

s. in Thousands

VII. STAFF ACTIVITIES

Mrs. Jean Archibald served as Chairman of the Academic Division of
the Minnesota Library Association during 1971/72, and also served on the
MLA Board of Directors. She was Secretary/Treasurer of the Macalester
College Council of Educational Administrators and Professionals, and
served on the President's Supporting Staff Advisory Council and the Planning and Priorities Committee.

Mr. Gore served on the Editorial Board of the Minnesota Library
Association, on the CLIC Board of Directors, on the College's Curriculum
Committee and Educational Resources Advisory Council, and as Chairman of
the College's Bookstore Committee, and was elected President of the
Macalester College Council of Educational Administrators and Professionals
for 1972/73. Mr. Gore also served as Treasurer and board member of
International Conferences.

Mr. Ondercin offered an Interim course in bibliography, and Mr. Lee
offered a course in French literature during the Spring session.

Mr. Dickinson received the Ph.D. degree in Anthropology, University
of Minnesota, at the Spring Commencement.

The Library was host to two Hill Fellows from October 17 through
November 5, 1971: Mrs. Vivian Jeffries, Texas College, Tyler, Texas; and
Miss Miriam E. Penn, Virginia Union University, Richmond, Virginia. During
that period they observed and participated in the various operations of the
Library.

The Library hosted a two-day conference on campus (sponsored by
International Conferences) entitled "Cost-Saving Techniques for the Library
of the 'Seventies." Mrs. Archibald, Mr. Cramer, Mrs. Kellar, Mrs. Nelson,
Mrs. Newcomb, Mr. Ondercin, and Mrs. Stenger conducted workshop sessions for

the Conference, which was attended by seventy librarians from a six-state region. A copy of the Conference program is appended.

Publications, Speeches, etc.

Gore, Daniel. "In Hot Pursuit of a Fast Cat," paper presented to the Academic Libraries Section, North Dakota Library Association, Fargo, N. D., October 22, 1971; and to the Conference on Cost-Saving Techniques, January 13, 1972.

"Books vs. Janitors; or, Where Do You Want to Spend Library Funds in the Twenty-First Century?" paper presented to the general session of the North Dakota Library Association's Annual Convention, October 23, 1971.

"Alfred the Great and the Reserve Book: Blame it on the Vikings," American Libraries, Vol. 3, No. 4 (April, 1972), 405-408.

Economics of Approval Plans, edited by Peter Spyers-Duran and Daniel Gore. Westport, Conn., Greenwood Press, 1972.

"Adopting an Approval Plan for a College Library: The Macalester College Experience," in Economics of Approval Plans, pp. 24-35.

"The Case for Compact Shelving," paper presented to the Conference on Cost-Saving Techniques, January 13, 1972.

"Approval Plans for the Small Library," paper presented to the Conference on Cost-Saving Techniques, January 14, 1972.

"Increasing the Usefulness of Library Buildings: An Experiment Proposed for the Macalester College Library." (A grant proposal) 20 pp.

VIII.   <u>PROBLEMS PRESENT AND DISTANT</u>

Library salary schedules will experience some urgently needed improvements in 1972/73, but will still fall well below schedules for comparable positions at the University of Minnesota Libraries. Further adjustments should be made for 1973/74, to bring them up to average levels
observed at the University.

Staff complement will be further reduced in 1972/73, in anticipation
of further budget retrenchments, to keep the acquisitions budget at
current levels. To accomplish the reductions without curtailing services,
further modifications of operating procedures will be required, as will
reassignment of some staff positions.

Inadequate shelf space for a growing collection continues to be a
critical problem. In the long run only a new building will provide long-
term relief for that and other space problems (especially the acute
shortage of special group study, seminar, and AV viewing rooms). In the
meantime a compact shelving installation in Weyerhaeuser, costing about
$45,000, will be required within the next 18 months at the outside. Grant
funding for this equipment is being actively sought at this writing.

The Library on this campus--as on many others--has unfortunately been
long regarded as merely another support unit, tangential to the main educational mission of the College. To help counteract this fundamentally
mistaken view, and to bring librarians into more active involvement in
student and faculty affairs, steps are being taken to place staff members
in formal teaching assignments as circumstances permit. In Spring, 1972, the
Curriculum Committee approved a regular-session course, "Introduction to
Bibliography," to be offered twice each year by Library staff (beginning

Fall, 1972). A regular session course in the literature of government documents will be proposed for 1973/74. During fiscal 1972/73 library staff will be offering courses in bibliography, anthropology, cinema, French literature, and history, in addition to their usual library assignments. Although the educational role of the Library goes far beyond the offering of this handful of formal courses, the teaching of these courses by librarians may bring into clear focus a fact that should be obvious to all but rarely is: that the people who make and manage libraries well know what the educational enterprise is about, and do play an active and creative role in carrying out its mission, both in the classroom and in the library.

IX.   A TRIBUTE TO THE LIBRARY STAFF

The fact that the Library continues to maintain a healthy acquisitions program despite repeated cuts in the total budget is solely the result of the staff's extraordinary ability, and willingness, to maintain outstanding performance levels in the face of repeated and substantial reductions in staff positions. The dollar value of position cuts (as of September, 1973) will approximate the dollar value of the entire book budget. When library budget cuts are made elsewhere, they typically occur first, and deepest, in the book budget. Macalester College is unusually fortunate in having a library staff so talented and adaptable as to keep the book budget intact, and service levels at an all-time high, during a prolonged period of budget retrenchment. It remains a distinct pleasure to be held accountable for their performance.

———

Individual reports of the various Library departments are on file and available for inspection in the Library Office. These reports account in full detail for all aspects of the Library's operations.

Fenix....It is unique: it is unparalleled in the whole world. The Bestiary; a book of beasts

CONFERENCE ON COST-SAVING TECHNIQUES FOR THE LIBRARY OF THE 'SEVENTIES

JANUARY 13-14, 1972
MACALESTER COLLEGE

General Sessions - Theatre, Janet Wallace Fine Arts Center   Workshop Sessions

January 13

8:30 - 9:00 a.m.   Coffee & Registration in the Lobby

9:00 - 10:30 a.m.   Welcoming Remarks
Kenneth Goodrich, Vice-President and Provost, Macalester College

"The Cataloging Frontlog"
Marvin Scilken

"In Hot Pursuit of a Fastcat"
Daniel Gore

2:00 - 2:45   "Dividing a Catalog" (slide show)
Peter Spyers-Duran

"The Case for Compact Shelving"
Daniel Gore & Clifford Brown

January 14

9:00 - 10:30 a.m.   "Approval Plans for the Small Library"
Daniel Gore & Dealer Representatives

2:00 - ?   A Free-for-All, with Peter Spyers-Duran as Referee

....

Program Chairman, Daniel Gore
Master of Ceremonies, Peter Spyers-Duran
Production Stage Manager, Marymina Stenger

Thursday 10:30-Noon

Circulation Systems - Humanities 203
Bro-Dart Company

Frontlogs and Fastcats - Humanities 109
Jean Archibald and Marvin Scilken

Thursday 3:30-5:30

Interloans via Courier - Humanities 203
David Ondercin

Reclassification Procedures - Humanities 109
Marymina Stenger

Reserve Room Procedures - Humanities 107
Jean Archibald

Friday 10:30-Noon

Acquisitions Programs (Computer-Based)-Humanities 208
Peter Spyers-Duran and Dealers Representatives

Public Library Special Topics - Humanities 107
Marvin Scilken

L.C. Classification: Problems - Humanities 109
Marymina Stenger

Demonstrations

Minolta Retrieval of Catalog Copy - Ruth Newcomb
Catalog Card Production - Corinne Kellar & Lois Nelson
In-House Periodical Binding - Robert Cramer
Compact Shelving - Clifford Brown

Macalester College

Annual Report of the Library 1972/73

St. Paul, Minnesota

MACALESTER COLLEGE
SAINT PAUL, MINNESOTA 55105

■ WEYERHAEUSER LIBRARY

January 25, 1974

Mr. John M. Dozier
Vice President and Treasurer
Macalester College
St. Paul, Minnesota 55105

Dear John:

Here are fifteen thousand words telling how we handled in fiscal 1972/73 the twenty-five billion words that make up the Macalester College Library.

Brevity may be the soul of wit, but justice requires that the outstanding accomplishments of our staff be set forth with a fullness that matches my esteem for their extraordinary contributions to the College. Whoever wishes to assess directly the worth of their labors will find ample material for doing so in the pages that follow.

As Treasurer of the College you will particularly want to know just what we did with the third of a million dollars we spent from the College treasury last year. Every dollar has been accounted for, I believe; and I hope you will find that each dollar spent yielded at least a dollar's worth of educational benefits.

Knowing that your interests go far beyond the bare bones of fiscal matters, I have gone far beyond the mere reporting of statistical data to explain the educational motives and goals out of which the data emerged. Since this is my first report to you in your new capacity as general overseer of library affairs, let me express here my full satisfaction in the new relationship, and my great appreciation for your precise grasp and generous support of the library's mission.

Sincerely,

Daniel Gore
Director

DG:db

CONTENTS

I. INTRODUCTION

The formidable task of re-organizing library procedures and services
stands virtually complete today, after three years of concentrated effort
to find the best ways to use the human, bibliographical, and diminishing
financial resources available to us.

Staff complement has been reduced about forty percent; but while
that was happening we took on and substantially completed a major reclassification project, so for the first time in seven years the collection is
organized by one subject classification scheme rather than two.

New books reach the library on or shortly after official publication
date, and are available for loan the day after we receive them, instead
of waiting the traditional four to six months in the cataloging workroom
to be processed.

Today we have ready access to some three million books in the libraries of St. Paul and Minneapolis; three years ago we were largely re-
stricted to the holdings in our own collection.

Control of loans has become precise and effective, and books returned from loan are at long last being promptly reshelved.

After repeated shiftings the collections are in good shelf order and
evenly distributed over the available shelving, which, though scant, will
take us comfortably over the period of several years required to fund,
plan, and construct a new library building.

Planning for a new building is well underway, and fund raising has
begun in earnest.

Students at Macalester are now offered formal instruction in using
the library's complex resources instead of being abandoned to the (usually)

unproductive devices of their own untutored imaginings.

A library of any size is like the universe itself: alive, intricate, always changing, and more than a little perplexing to anyone (librarians included) who considers the thing closely. A complete accounting of one year in the life of a library would go far beyond what is offered here.

But the following pages tell as much as most readers will care to know about the many steps taken during fiscal 1972/73 to continue improving library services while lowering the costs of providing them. Anyone who desires to know more is invited to consult the detailed individual reports of the library's various departments. These reports are on file in the Library Office, and always available for inspection.

II.   STAFF

A.   Technical Services Department

In September 1972 Mr. Richard Higginbotham was employed to fill a part-time position vacated by Mrs. Elli Sorensen. He also devoted a substantial part of his time to supervisory work at the Circulation Desk. Mrs. Kellar, whose regular assignment was in cataloging, gave about half her time to Reserve Desk duties.

B.   Circulation Department

Mr. Ondercin resigned his post as head of the department in February 1973, and was replaced by Ms. Jean Francis, who also continued to carry out her existing supervisory duties in periodicals, reserves, and gifts.

Mr. Haberkorn left the staff in December 1972, and was not replaced.

C. Other Departments: No personnel changes.

D. Summary of Staff Reductions

Library Staff Roster (excluding AV)

Fall 1970	Fall 1971	Fall 1972	Fall 1973
Gore	Gore	Gore	Gore
Archibald	Archibald	Archibald	Archibald
Adamson	Barnes	Barnes	Barnes
Barnes	Cobb	Crouse	Crouse
Buggs	Cramer	Dickinson	Dickinson
Cobb	Crouse	Francis (3/4)	Francis
Cramer	Francis (1/2)	Haberkorn (1/2)	Hampl
Crouse	Haberkorn (1/2)	Hampl	Higginbotham (1/2)
Francis	Hampl	Higginbotham (1/2)	Kellar
Hampl	Kellar	Kellar	Nelson
Harri (1/2)	Leonard	Nelson	Newcomb
Kellar	Nelson	Newcomb	Oliver (1/2)
Kerr	Newcomb	Oliver (1/2)	Rude
Kiscaden	Oliver (1/2)	Ondercin	Salscheider
Leonard	Ondercin	Rude	Shin (1/2)
Meyn	Rude	Salscheider	Stenger
Nelson	Salscheider	Shin (1/2)	
Newcomb	Shin (1/2)	Stenger	14 1/2 FTE
Oliver (1/2)	Sorensen (1/2)		
Pressman	Stenger	15 3/4 FTE	
Rude			
Salscheider	17 1/2 FTE		
Shin (1/2)			
Sorensen (1/2)			
Stenger			
MICROFICHE CATALOGING DEVICE			
(in exchange for one staff position)			
24 FTE			

AV Staff Roster

1971	1972	1973
Hernandez	Lee	Lee
Jackson (3/4)	Jackson (3/4)	Jackson (3/4)
Derks	Browne (1/2)	Browne (1/2)
Hakala (1/2)		
3 1/4 FTE	2 1/4 FTE	2 1/4 FTE

E. Student Staff

Total hours of student work (all units except AV) came to 22,245, essentially the same as reported for the previous year.

Hours of student work in the AV Department came to 7,118, about the same as in the previous year. (Through oversight last year's report omitted 981 hours worked in the summer session.)

In fiscal 1972/73 student staff contributed 47% of the total hours worked in the library (including AV). This percentage is abnormally high in comparison with the average of 31% among a group of 40 other comparable college libraries. It underscores the unusual degree to which we rely upon student workers to keep the library operating. And it bears out our conviction that working in a library is a valuable educational experience in itself, and that students should be given the widest possible opportunities to obtain that experience.

From the mere standpoint of economics, it would probably be cheaper to hire full time clerical staff to take over most of the work done by students. Not that their work is inefficiently done—far from it—but that so much staff time must be devoted each year to training and supervising a large staff of student workers, many of whom are newcomers to the library. At various times during the year we have some 160 different students working for the library, or about ten students (average) for each regular FTE staff position. Since each student works an average of only 180 hours per year, an extraordinary amount of staff time must be given over to training, supervision, and scheduling. But it is worth it, in our opinion, in terms of what the students learn about libraries, and about working harmoniously, productively, and responsibly with other people in an enterprise that serves the common good.

F. Staff Organization

The organizational methods outlined in the 1970/71 Report (pp. 5-7) continue to yield good results and were not modified.

G. General Appraisal of the Staff

Morale and productivity remained high throughout the year. With a mid-year reduction of an additional 1.5 FTE staff positions, it became necessary to schedule more people for occasional evening work than in the past. While few people will seek evening work as a matter of preference, the new schedules were well accepted as a matter of necessity. And, since evening hours are often our busiest, the staff have become more generally involved in the public services of the library, and thus better acquainted with its primary mission: service to students and faculty. Their performance in this, as in other areas, is outstanding.

III.   THE 1972/73 BUDGET

A. Library (excluding the AV Department)

The budget for 1972/73 was set at $253,000, excluding student help.
A detailed analysis of budget results appears on the following page.
Expenditures by major categories over the past three years are as follows:

Title	1970/71	1971/72	1972/73
Salaries and wages	$149,638	$127,826	$121,137
Acquisitions and binding	101,158	105,579	123,163
Operations (net)	13,463	9,402	8,400
Totals	$264,259	$242,807	$252,700

Expenditures for salaries and wages in 1972/73 fell $8,563 below the
budgeted level of $129,700, from termination of 1.5 FTE staff positions
early in the fiscal year. The total for acquisitions and binding includes
an accrual figure of $9,800 from the previous year's budget, making the
total substantially higher than the sum of $114,000 budgeted for this cate-
gory. The accrual resulted from the library's discontinuing its former
practice of closing its annual book purchase accounts on July 31 (as di-
rected by the provost) rather than August 31. This sum is not distributed
in the analysis of departmental book expenditures, which accordingly shows
a total expenditure for books $9,800 less than that shown on the following
page.

Primarily as a result of the under-expenditure in salaries of $8,563,
and the over-expenditure on books from the accrual account, the total budget
came out essentially on balance, showing a net under-expenditure of $300.

Library Budget 1972/73

Actual Expenditures

Title		Expenditures
1. <u>Salaries and Wages</u>		$ 121,137
2. <u>Acquisitions and Binding</u>		123,163

Books	$101,154*	
Periodicals	21,001	
Binding	1,008	

3. <u>Operations</u> (Net; expenses less income)   8,400

<u>Expenses</u>

Supplies	5,127
Telephone	282
Postage	482
Printing	872
Travel	156
Equipment purchase	2,661
Equipment repair	503
Photocopying	4,871
Membership (CLIC)	1,916
Interlibrary loans	524
	17,394

<u>Income</u>

Overdue fees	6,184
Picture rentals	23
Lost Books	49
Photocopying	2,738
	8,994

Grand Total: $252,700

Budgeted Total: $253,000

*Includes $9,800 accrual noted on previous page.

The "Supplies" account shows an increase of about $1,700 over the previous year's. The increase is wholly attributable to new costs associated with the microfilm circulation control system installed in February 1973. (On a full-year basis, these costs will run about $2,800.) By shifting to the new system (described more fully elsewhere in this report), we were able to eliminate staff positions costing about $12,000 annually, and substantially increase income from overdue fees by virtue of significant improvements in recording loans. The added cost in supplies is therefore returned many times over elsewhere in the budget.

Major items of equipment purchased during the year were two microfilm circulation control units ($800 each), one microfilm reader (not associated with the circulation control system), and three cassette playback units for use in the main reading room.

B. AV Department

The authorized budget was $45,626, excluding student help. (This figure is $1,700 greater than shown on the budget worksheet, owing to a one-time transfer into the Repair account of a portion of the money released by cancellation of a library staff position--a transfer authorized after the worksheet figure was approved.) Gross expenditures came to $41,140, and income from services and sales was $8,749, for a net expenditure of $32,391.

Expenditures by Categories

Title		Amount
Salaries and Wages		$25,616
Operations (net)		6,775
Office supplies	$6,698	
Other supplies	1,344	
Dues	10	
Subscriptions	30	
Freight	11	
Telephone	13	
AV	857	
Postage	322	
Printing	171	
Travel	14	
Equipment purchase	2,177	
Repair	3,877	
Gross:	$15,524	
Operating Income:	8,749	

Total net expenditures: $32,391

The "Repair" account appears abnormally large in relation to the previous year's, but is accounted for by the expenditure of $1,700 on a contract that covered overhaul of TV studio equipment and training of personnel to maintain and operate it. This expense should not recur in 1973/74.

IV. DEPARTMENTAL ACTIVITIES

A. Technical Services

1. Acquisitions

The computer-based profile acquisitions program functioned well throughout the year. Notice slips generated by the jobber's computer dropped from 14,834 titles in 1971/72 to 11,738 in 1972/73, a reduction of about 21% that came about not through any major changes in our profile, or cutbacks in the publishing industry, but rather through more intensive selection on the jobber's part of books to be profiled initially.

Statistical results of the profile program in 1972/73 are the following:

	Number	Dollars	Average
Notice slips from the Abel Co.	11,738	$120,297	$10.25
"Buy" slips from faculty	5,441	55,493	10.20
"Don't Buy" slips from faculty	7,764	80,166	10.35
Total slips from faculty	13,205	135,659	10.30
Acceptance rate	41%	41%	
Rejection rate	59%	59%	

If one should wonder how the faculty returned some 1,500 more slips than the Abel Company sent us in 1972/73, the explanation is that many of the returns were from slips sent to the faculty for review in the previous year. The acceptance rate of 41% is exactly one percentage point lower than in the previous year.

The average price of an accepted title rose to $10.20 from the previous year's $9.00--an increase of 13% which, coupled with a projected increase of at least that amount in 1973/74, and a $6,000 reduction in

available acquisitions funds, requires us to abandon the laissez-faire
approach to profile buying, and develop departmental allocation formulas
for 1973/74.

The price increase also stimulated us to seek another book jobber.
Beginning in January 1974, our profile program will be serviced by the
Baker & Taylor Company, which recently developed a service virtually identical to Abel's, with a guaranteed discount of 15% on all purchases--
roughly double the discount offered by Abel. Assuming that we continue
to acquire five or six thousand new titles annually through this program
the discount improvement will yield a savings of four or five thousand
dollars a year.

Expenditures by departments from college funds (excluding the $9,800
accrual sum mentioned on p. 6) for profile and other book purchases, and
for journal subscriptions appear on the following page.

The total college expenditures on library acquisitions came to
$122,154 (including the accrual item and $1,865 from a Kellogg Foundation
grant). An additional $7,500 was expended from a Federal grant awarded to
Cooperating Libraries in Consortium, and $1,008 was spent on binding, bring-
ing the total expenditure on library materials to $130,663.

With few exceptions the hundred thousand dollars spent on book purchases brought to the library single copies of titles new to the collection.
Duplication of titles has been routinely avoided in the past so book funds
will bring in the maximum possible number of different titles to the collection. This practice has the warrant of universal custom among academic
libraries, although it has little merit today from the standpoint of reason.

For it is well known that demand on individual titles in a library may

Departmental Book and Periodical Expenditures 1972-73

| Division | Expenditure by Division | | Total |
	Books	Periodicals	
1. Social Sciences			
Geography	2,970.58	348.35	3,318.93
Political Science	7,400.68	1,406.05	8,806.73
Psychology	2,898.77	1,962.25	4,861.02
Sociology & Anthropology	5,645.45	586.30	6,231.75
Totals	18,915.48	4,302.95	23,218.43
2. Business and Economics	2,851.27	994.15	3,845.42
3. Education	4,328.28	452.00	4,780.28
4. Fine Arts			
Art	1,521.59	304.04	1,825.63
Journalism	254.04	94.00	348.04
Music	2,071.99	129.35	2,201.34
Totals	3,847.62	527.39	4,375.01
5. Humanities			
Classics	1,532.04	73.20	1,605.24
English	11,700.29	675.25	12,375.54
Foreign Languages			
French	1,878.58	110.97	1,989.55
German	3,495.69	327.46	3,823.15
Russian	1,014.23	138.60	1,152.83
Spanish	632.37	119.00	751.37
History	19,849.49	483.91	20,333.40
Language (General)		159.60	159.60
Philosophy	2,158.35	371.58	2,529.93
Religion	2,166.16	356.62	2,522.78
Speech & Theatre	1,171.11	146.40	1,317.51
Totals	45,598.31	2,962.59	48,560.90
6. Physical Education	273.36	174.30	447.66
7. Science and Mathematics			
General		118.00	118.00
Biology	3,036.45	3,931.00	6,967.45
Chemistry	3,025.58	1,219.03	4,244.61
Geology	1,033.39	767.67	1,801.06
Math	958.63	1,469.60	2,428.23
Physics	1,287.46	1,656.30	2,943.76
Totals	9,341.51	9,161.60	18,503.11
8. Library and Miscellaneous	6,197.98	2,424.63	8,622.61
Grand Totals	91,353.81	20,999.61	112,353.42

vary by factors as great as a thousand to one. Some books will be called for only once in a century, or less, while others may be wanted ten times (or more) in one year. Yet academic libraries have customarily provided the same number of copies of both categories of books: one. The inevitable result of such an acquisitions policy is that books in heavy demand are often not available when you want them: somebody else got there first.

Recent statistical inquiries into this phenomenon yield the melancholy prediction that 50% of the searches for books owned by an academic library will end in (at least temporary) failure. Half the books you want to borrow from an academic library are likely to be on loan to someone else at the time you want them. Hence the common belief among college students that library theft rates are staggeringly high. Although the book census we made last year indicates a theft rate at Macalester at near-zero level. our clientele have assumed we were being systematically robbed. How else explain the dismal phenomenon of being thwarted every time you tried to borrow our sole copy of Yeats's Collected Poems?

Looking for an explanation, and knowing that theft was not it, we came upon a series of remarkable statistical studies of library collection use, conducted in recent years by Dr. R. W. Trueswell, now chairman of the Industrial Engineering Department of the University of Massachusetts. What these studies conclusively show is that a very small percentage of the titles in any academic library account for a very high percentage of actual use. And if you do not provide multiple copies of the high-demand items, you thereby guarantee a very high rate of disappointment and frustration to your borrowers.

The characteristic response to expressions of such frustration has been this: the library director seeks large sums of new money for the book budget, and, when he gets it, proceeds to spend it all on single copies of more titles new to the collection until the money runs out. But when the money is all spent, the frustration continues unabated, for nothing was spent on what was really needed: multiple copies of high-demand titles. (During the last two decades of rapidly rising college enrollments, the average tenure of academic library directors equalled in brevity that of college presidents.)

In a rational attempt to lower the disappointment rate among users of the Macalester Library, we sought and obtained support from the Library Committee to devote a portion of the 1973/74 book budget to buying multiple copies of books known to be in high demand. Using Dr. Trueswell's statistical criteria for identifying these books, we are at this writing selectively duplicating them as they are returned from loan to the Circulation Desk. Over the next ten years we may add about 10,000 such volumes, with the statistically predictable goal in view of drastically reducing the current disappointment rate, which, as noted, we have good reason to assume now runs at the fifty percent level.

Three years ago we inaugurated a program of delivering to Macalester readers, within 48 hours, any book they wanted from the University Library's two-million title collection. That program has proved decidedly beneficial, and is much esteemed by our clientele, especially faculty in quest of uncommon research materials. But it does little to relieve the general frustration level among student borrowers. For what any two students are likely to need at any one time is not ready access to two million different books, but prompt availability of two copies of the same book. Offering them two

million other books is no help in that situation. Buying a second copy is.
To put the matter another way: we could spend twenty million dollars buying two million more titles for the Macalester Library, and still maintain
a disappointment rate of fifty percent. Or we can spend a hundred thousand
dollars over the next ten years on ten thousand copies of certain titles already in the collection, with some assurance of bringing the disappointment
rate down to a tolerable level of, say, ten percent or less.

In short, we can never afford to rival the University Library in the vast range
of titles it places at a reader's disposal. But we can afford to do what
it does not: provide sufficient copies of heavily used titles to guarantee
that one copy will ordinarily be available whenever you want to read it.
And with the fast interloan service provided by the University Libraries,
we can enjoy the best of both worlds at relatively little cost: prompt
access to millions of little-used books, and prompt access to the several
thousand books that are always in heavy demand.

GIFTS AND GRANTS

In 1972/73, CLIC received a Federal grant of $50,000 for the joint
purchase of expensive and commonly needed publications. The grant guidelines indicated that a major portion of the materials purchased should be
related to the study of the disadvantaged. Each CLIC library examined its
needs and compiled a list of priority items totalling $7,500 per library.
The Macalester Library selected and acquired the following titles, which
are also available for use by students and faculty of the CLIC colleges.

* Cumulated Subject Index to Psychological Abstracts.
    First supplement, 1961-65. $295.00
    Second supplement, 1966-68. 2 vols.   390.00
      Boston, G. K. Hall, 1968-71.

* Cumulated Author Index to Psychological Abstracts.
    Second supplement, 1964-68   275.00
      Boston, G. K. Hall, 1970. 2 vols.

* Index to Periodical Articles By and About Negroes.
    Cumulation, 1950-1959; 1960-1970.   90.00

Africa South of the Sahara: Index to Periodical
    Literature, 1900-1970.   325.00
    Boston, G. K. Hall, 1971. 4 vols.

Biographical and Historical Index of American Indians   705.00
    and Persons Involved in Indian Affairs.
    Boston, G. K. Hall, 1966. 8 vols.

Schomburg "Starter" Collection.   925.60
    St. Paul, Minn., 3M International Microfilm Press.
    (32 full and 5 partial microfilm reels of basic titles
    from the New York Public Library's Schomburg Collection
    of American Negro history and culture)

History of the French Revolution, by Jules Michelet.   270.00
    9 vols. Translated by Keith Bokford. Wynnewood,
    Pa., Kolokol Press, 1972.

Civilisation, by Kenneth Clark. 2 volume set. (Each   250.00
    volume contains 8 filmstrips and 8 LP records)

* The New York Times - Microfilm. 1932-1945.   4,132.00

The four starred titles extend indexes and microfilm holdings already

in Macalester's collections.

   In April 1971, the W. K. Kellogg Foundation awarded a grant of $5,000

to the College to be expended over a three year period on College Resources

for Environmental Studies.

   During the period from May 1972 - April 1973, the following amounts

were spent from the CRES grant:

              Books $363.66
              Periodical Subscriptions 109.50
              Abstracts & Indexes   387.00
              Films   1,005.00
                                      $1,865.16

Summary of Kellogg grant purchases through April 1973:

1971/72		$1,397.18
1972/73		1,865.16
	Total spent	$3,262.32

Balance for 1973/74 purchases $1,737.66

In the summer of 1973, the Longyear Company of Minneapolis gave us its entire library. This collection consists chiefly of items related to mining geology and engineering--a total of about 5,453 books, periodicals, government documents, and maps. The estimated value of this collection is $11,000. It greatly augments the library's resources in the field of geology.

Various other gifts from alumni and friends of the College totalled 2,261 items during 1972/73, with a total estimated value of $3,806.46

Other notable acquisitions during 1972/73 purchased from the library budget are:

Encyclopedia Americana. 1973. 30 vols.

Encyclopedia Canadiana. 1972. 10 vols.

Halkett & Laing. Dictionary of Anonymous and Pseudonymous English Literature. 7 vols.

Schlesinger Library on the History of Women in America. Radcliffe College. 3 vols.

1970 Census of Population.

1970 Census of Housing.

2. Cataloging and Reclassification

Statistics for the last four years are these:

	1969/70	1970/71	1971/72	1972/73
Volumes reclassed	1,908	25,923	26,778	24,891
Volumes cataloged	10,909	11,094	8,298	10,911
Volumes withdrawn (includes lost and stolen)	3,331	3,524	2,062	665
Total units processed	16,148	40,541	37,138	36,467

From September 1970, when the major reclass project got underway, through August 1973, 79,500 volumes were converted from the Dewey to the Library of Congress (LC) system. The conversion process involves a good deal more than identifying the proper LC call number for each book and labeling it on the spine. A new set of catalog cards bearing the LC call number must be created and filed, and the old set withdrawn. Each book requires an average of about 6 catalog cards, or 500,000 new cards for the 79,500 volumes reclassed through August 1973. Cards can be ordered commercially (for about 7 cents each, including staff handling costs), but ours were made by the staff on a Xerox machine at a total cost (including labor) of about 1.5 cents each, or $7,500 for 500,000 of them--about $27,000 less than we would have spent with a commercial supplier.

In addition to the labeling and card work, a substantial amount of shelving work has also gone into the project: 79,500 volumes were unshelved to be reclassed, and the same number were reshelved at the end of the process. Moreover, the entire collection of 200,000 books has been shifted several times to take up space vacated by reclassed Dewey volumes and thus create space elsewhere, in the proper sequences, as books return to the shelves with new LC numbers.

The average cost of reclassing one volume has been estimated by other libraries to be at least $2.00. On that basis our staff completed about $160,000 worth of reclass work over the past three years. But since

instead of adding staff to handle a major new project, we have in fact
reduced processing staff positions nearly 50% since the project began,
no new budget money was required to cover the labor costs of the enterprise.

The only money spent on this project that would not have been spent
without it paid for supplies and meter charges to produce catalog cards
on the Xerox machine--about $5,000 for 500,000 cards.

Getting $160,000 worth of work done for $5,000 vividly underscores
the outstanding achievement of the processing staff in developing and
carrying out routines of vastly improved efficiency. Since accomplishments of that magnitude merit full public notice, I will name here the
persons most directly involved in the reclass work: Mrs. Marymina Stenger,
who has supervised the project from its beginning, and set in motion the
myriad revisions in procedure required to make it run; Mrs. Mary Hampl,
Mrs. Corinne Kellar, Mrs. Lois Nelson, and Mrs. Ruth Newcomb. Thanks to
their steady, expert attention to what seemed an endless task at the beginning, the Macalester Library has, for the first time in seven years,
virtually all its books in one classification scheme. (Some 1,500 volumes
remain to be reclassed at this writing.) And the frustration to scholars
of searching two different class areas in the library for books on the
same subject is finally at an end--and about 20 years sooner than might
have been possible had new budget money been required to underwrite the
costs of a conventionally handled reclass project.

> The heart can think of no devotion
> Greater than being shore to the ocean;
> Holding the curve of one position
> Counting an endless repetition.
>   --R. Frost

Had the poet ever devoted himself to reclass work, his heart would have thought of something else, especially in Minnesota.

FASTCAT

The FASTCAT system of temporarily cataloging new books was developed at this library three years ago, and has been continuously employed since then. Certain refinements have been added along the way, but its cardinal virtue remains its capacity to make new books available for circulation the day after they are received in the library. (Conventional cataloging approaches result in an average four months' delay before a new book leaves the cataloging workroom, and many books will be held up a year or longer, waiting for the Library of Congress to produce cataloging copy.)

Macalester's FASTCAT method was described in the Library Journal of September 1, 1972 and has since been adopted by a number of libraries elsewhere, among them being those of

> The University of Alberta (Canada)
> Brandon University (Canada)
> Red Deer College (Canada)
> The University of Windsor (Canada)
> Universidad del Valle de Guatemala
> Universidad de San Carlos de Guatemala
>   (where it is called "CAT-RAP," for
>   Catalogacion Rapida)
> Manhattan College (N.Y.)
> Lake Forest College (Ill.)
> Wesleyan University (Conn.)
> Veterans Memorial Public Library (Bismarck, N.D.)
> Lansing Community College (Michigan)
> Field Museum of Natural History (Chicago)
> Temple University (Philadelphia)
> Bradley University (Ill.)
> Boise State College (Idaho)
> Medford Public Library (Mass.)
> University of Missouri (St. Louis)
> The Universities Center (Jackson, Miss.)
> Anderson College (Ind.)
> Mt. Pleasant Public Library (Mich.)
> Bir Zeit College (Israel)
> Duke University

A "Best-Seller" category was added to our FASTCAT collection during the year, and proved popular enough to be continued as a regular offering of the library.

B. Circulation Department

Ms. Jean Francis was named head of the department in February 1973, and since that time she has brought about broad-scale improvements in its organization, operation, and services. For the first time in memory, books returned from loan are normally reshelved within 24 hours, and thus available to other borrowers. The need for minimal turn-around times is plainly implied in the statistical evidence that 70% of the books borrowed on any given day will have been borrowed at least once in the previous 12 months. Books returned from loan are _ipso facto_ high-demand titles,[*] and should be made accessible for subsequent loan in the least time possible.

Also, for the first time in memory, the file of loan records is in near-perfect order, something that was impossible of achievement under the former system of hand-made, hand-sorted, and hand-filed borrowers' records. Overdue records are also in excellent shape, and the many ambiguities and uncertainties about who returned what, and when, have been virtually eliminated under the new system. Collection of overdue fees has accordingly increased, and we believe that as borrowers become better acquainted with the effectiveness of the system, the rate of overdues will drop from its traditionally and unsatisfactorily high levels.

The central feature of the new record-keeping system is the use of microfilm equipment to record photographically both the item borrowed and the I.D. card of the person borrowing it. Positive identification of the

---

[*]The average use rate of books in this library is once every four years.

two key elements in each transaction is thus invariably achieved by this method. Time required to complete a transaction, and to discharge a returned book, is drastically reduced, and sort-and-file operations are totally eliminated. Savings in staff time are such that 1.5 FTE staff positions could be dropped when the microfilm system was acquired in February 1973.

Maintaining loan records on microfilm has been a common practice among public libraries for years, simply because it is both the cheapest and most effective way to control tens of thousands of loans. But while it is a very simple matter to identify all overdue items through this system (we use the College's computer to identify transaction numbers of overdue items, and then retrieve hard copy from the microfilm of transaction records bearing those numbers) it is exceedingly difficult (though not impossible) to identify the borrower of any given title while it is still on loan. Re-call capability therefore does not exist in any practical sense.

For that reason academic libraries have made little (perhaps no) use of "transaction" charging systems. They want to be able to re-call a book on demand, and that is easily done with the type system we abandoned.

However, while it was always easy for us to re-call a book on loan, it was usually very difficult or impossible actually <u>to get it back</u> before the loan period expired. So difficult, in fact, that even while we had the old system, if asked to re-call a book we would simply borrow it from another CLIC library, or buy another copy, whichever was quicker or seemed more reasonable. This approach proved to be far more effective than conventional re-call, so we could dispense with re-call capability in considering any alternative to the former control system.

By enabling us to eliminate 1.5 FTE staff positions the new system effectually reduced net library operating costs by at least $10,000 per year--money that would otherwise have had to be taken from the book budget. On that basis we are now able to buy five times as many books as we were ever asked to re-call in the past. And as noted above, our loan records are for the first time in near-perfect order, the control of loans and overdues is precise, and books returned from loan are for the first time being promptly re-shelved.

RECORDED LIBRARY USE

Total recorded circulation (all categories) came to 77,134 in 1972/73, a drop of 11,352, or 13% from the previous year. Since loans were counted in the same way in both years, this difference represents an actual decline in use, the first in three years.

The decline can be explained in part by the fact that enrollment in 1972/73 was about 7% less than in the previous year. The rest of the decline may be attributed to substantial increases in the use of audio-visual services over the past three years, which may very well have displaced some of the demand for printed materials.

Circulation statistics by categories appear on the following page.

Overdue statistics for the year are these:

	Notices	covering	Books
First	4,151		8,652
Second	2,174		4,157
Third	894		1,650
Fourth	347		641

These figures indicate that 19% of all 4-week loans fell overdue, an

Circulation Statistics, 1972/73

Category	Weyerhaeuser Students	Faculty	Olin Students	Faculty
Books (general)	45,481	2,998	1,113	211
Curriculum Lab	1,058	150		
College Cat. and Pam.	85	9		
Paperbacks & Mysteries	349	110		
Cassettes	458 (students and faculty)			
Government Documents	92	13		
FASTCAT	2,165	764	56	46
Juvenile	2,420	471		
Phono Records	1,869	82		
Art Rentals	31	1		
Periodicals	2,796 (Students and faculty)		132	25
Storage	587 (Students and faculty)			
Reserve	12,235 (Students and faculty)		1,327	
Totals:	69,626	4,598	2,628	282
Combined:	74,224		2,910	
Both Libraries:	77,134			

apparently substantial increase over the 10% overdue rate reported in 1971/72. It is reasonable to assume, however, that there was no real change in the actual overdue rate: what changed was our effectiveness in identifying and processing overdues with the new microfilm charging system.

SHELVING CAPACITY OF LIBRARIES

A precise inventory of our shelving was taken on August 24, 1973, and the following results were obtained:

Building	Shelf Feet	Book Feet	Load Factor
Weyerhaeuser	26,733	18,619	70%
Olin	1,479	1,321	88%
Storage	6,930	3,938	57%
Totals	35,142	23,878	68%

A library is conventionally held to be loaded to full efficient capacity when the shelfload factor reaches 75%. Beyond that level so little space is left vacant on each shelf that extensive shifting of the collections is required when space must be opened for the addition of, say, a newly acquired ten-volume set. Libraries can in fact be operated at levels beyond the 75% limit, but very precise management of space is required even before that point is reached, and one must be both exact and lucky thereafter to avoid excessive use of shelving labor. Empty shelf space is to the librarian what altitude is to the pilot. We can keep operating perhaps to the 90% load factor level, but it is like flying a plane cross-country at 100 foot altitudes: there is no margin

for error, and one's attention must never lapse, or things will swiftly
go to pieces.

At the 90% level we will have 31,500 feet of usable shelf space, or
7,622 feet more shelving than was occupied by books on August 24, 1973.
Since one foot of shelf space holds an average ten volumes, and we are
adding about 12,000 new volumes each year, we will reach the 90% level about
six years hence.

If, however, we should in the meantime acquire and install compact
shelving in the ground-floor periodicals room of Weyerhaeuser, this would
increase gross shelf footage by about 6,000 feet, bringing the total to
about 41,000 feet.

On that basis, a 75% (optimum) load factor would yield 30,600 feet
of usable space, or roughly 7,000 feet more than is now occupied by books.
At current intake rates we would reach 75% load about six years hence by
using compact shelving or, as noted above, a 90% level over the same period
if we do not acquire compact shelving.

In either case we therefore have ample lead time for planning and constructing a new building. However, since the proposal for a new building
contemplates a shift to compact shelving around the 25th year of its life,
it would be prudent to test its acceptability while we are still in our
present quarters, especially so since the additional shelf space would also
greatly improve shelving efficiency and lower the costs of routine shelf-
work.

Load factors in the Olin Science Library are now so high (88%) that
in the course of 1973/74 the library, in consultation with the science
faculty, must devise some modified strategy for providing library services
in that branch.

THE CURRICULUM LABORATORY

Circulation activity in this collection declined again in 1972/73, as it did in each of the four preceding years:

Year	Loans	Dropped	%
1967/68	4,627		
1968/69	3,841	986	21
1969/70	2,655	1,182	31
1970/71	2,034	625	23
1971/72	1,679	355	17
1972/73	1,208	471	28

C. Periodicals

Subscription statistics as of August 31 for each of the last two fiscal years are as follows:

	1972	1973
Subscriptions added (previous 12 mos.)	38	21
Subscriptions dropped	178	73
Subscriptions in force	1,111*	1,059
(Non-gift subscriptions:	998	914)

During the year 1,041 periodical volumes were bound on the library's equipment, at a total cash outlay of $1,008. A commercial bindery would have charged about five thousand dollars more to do the same job, and kept the issues being bound off the shelves an average five weeks longer time.

---

*Erroneously reported as 1,224 in the 1971/72 Annual Report, through double-count of gift subscriptions.

D. Reserve Desk

During the year the reserve operation was moved in toto from the
ground floor Periodicals Room to the Main Floor Reading Room. In its
new location it is far more convenient for student access, and also much
easier to staff, being in close proximity both to the Circulation Desk
and to the library workrooms. Of the numerous changes made over the last
three years to improve the services and operating efficiency of the library,
this is the one change that had the miraculous effect of making everyone
immediately happy with it. Everything else required a measure of rational
discourse, which the staff have unfailingly and cheerfully provided to
puzzled patrons.

Count of Items Placed on Reserve

		Books	Articles	Total
Fall	1970/71	785	320	1,105
	1971/72	858	424	1,282
	1972/73	769	392	1,161
Interim	1970/71	31	33	64
	1971/72	80	346	426
	1972/73	142	85	227
Spring	1970/71	527	215	742
	1971/72	887	695	1,582
	1972/73	1,184	824	2,008
Summer	1970/71	48	37	85
	1971/72	100	39	139
	1972/73	420	232	652

E. Reference Department

In addition to their usual tasks of developing the reference collection and providing bibliographical assistance to hundreds of students
every week, the reference staff have initiated regular course offerings
in bibliographical methods. Mr. Dickinson taught the "Introduction to
Bibliography" course in fall and spring sessions, and Mrs. Archibald
taught "Research Methods in Government Publications" as an Interim course.
Both courses will be offered hereafter in each regular session provided
there is sufficient demand. Macalester is one of the few colleges in
the country that not only provide an excellent library for their students,
but will also teach them to become proficient in using it.

"What Thoreau got from Harvard," says his biographer Henry Seidel Canby,
"was something quite indispensable. He was disciplined in the exactness,
the accuracy, and the care for meaning which is the essence of scholarship.
And, more important still, he learned to use a library." What Thoreau got
from Harvard, any student who wants it can certainly get from Macalester
today.

                          INTERLIBRARY LOANS

The success rate for items borrowed from other libraries has risen
from 58% in 1970/71 to 78% in 1972/73, as a result of steady improvements
in the CLIC operation. No interloan network anywhere reports results significantly better than 78%; most are far worse.

Total requests fell about 20% below the previous year's, while total
deliveries fell only 11%, thanks to the improved success rate. The reduced
level of requests reflects in part a reduced enrollment figure. Also, with

more students now taking the inter-college bus to other campuses, it is probable that direct borrowing from the other libraries siphoned off some demand that was previously satisfied by interloan services.

Interloan Statistics
Items Obtained for Macalester Patrons

Source	1970/71			1971/72			1972/73		
	Requests	Filled	%	Requests	Filled	%	Requests	Filled	%
Courier	4,198	2,715	65						
CLIC	1,445	513	35	4,824	3,316	69	3,765	2,949	78
Others	242	171	71	321	126	55	198	92	46
Totals	5,885	3,399	58%	5,145	3,442	68%	3,963	3,041	77%

Items Sent To Other Libraries

Source	1970/71			1971/72			1972/73		
	Requests	Filled	%	Requests	Filled	%	Requests	Filled	%
CLIC	848	424	51	1,711	1,007	59	1,532	975	64
Others	20	14	70	10	10	100	17	8	47
Totals	868	438	51%	1,721	1,017	59%	1,549	983	64%

F. Audio-Visual Department

Summary statistics on the following page reveal a continuing upward trend in demand for AV services. Loans of equipment were up by about 20%

AV SERVICES

COMPARATIVE TOTALS

Equipment Used	1971/72	1972/73
Motion Picture Projector	973	920
Overhead Projectors	285	284
Screens	241	263
Slide Projectors	393	524
Portable Public Address	90	29
Public Address	51	32
Filmstrip Projectors	65	160
Opaque Projectors	117	147
Tape Recorders	794	1,143
Phonographs	125	150
Video Tape Recorders (Portable)	90	120
Video Tape Recorders (Studio)	151	59
Cameras	-	184
Totals:	3,375	4,015

Services Used		
Our Films Used	391	475
Films Booked	476	305
Slides and b/w prints	4,850	3,327
Film - sold	-	939
Tapes - sold/dubbed	415	1,121
Transparencies	906	856
Ditto Masters	2,038	1,869
Signs	449	470
Totals:	9,525	9,362

from the previous year. In some categories, such as slide projectors, filmstrip projectors, and tape recorders, demand increased by 40% or more.

Use of studio videotape facilities is notable in its decline, caused by a drop in secondary education enrollment, and the unreliability of obsolete studio equipment. Portable videotape equipment, on the other hand, was used with increasing frequency, since it often substituted for studio equipment and also took up the overflow from other departments, notably Psychology and Speech and Theatre, where demand for their own VTR equipment sometimes exceeds supply.

Production services continued at about the previous year's level. Two special large-scale production projects were carried out during the summer months. Fifty-three Calligraffiti were mounted and matted for a November Library exhibit; and some 600 phonodiscs were transferred to cassette format for a new circulating collection to be offered by the library in 1973/74.

V.   THE COLLECTIONS

During the year 14,072 volumes (or bibliographic items) were added to the collections, bringing the total count to 244,280 items, of which 235,000 are bound volumes of books and journals. The median collection size of all colleges having similar programs and enrollment is 90,000 volumes.

Added 1972/73

Categories	Volumes (or units)
Books	10,358
Bound periodicals and abstracts	1,041
Newspapers and periodical indexes	11
Microfilm reels	1,013
Microfiche	921
Records and tapes	728
Total:	14,072
Withdrawals:	665
Net Increase:	13,407

Total Resources September 1, 1973

Categories	Volumes (or units)
Books	208,398
Bound periodicals and abstracts	26,322
Newspapers and periodical indexes	348
Microfilm reels	3,537
Microfiche	2,410
Records and tapes	3,265
Total:	244,280

Subscriptions in Force September 1, 1973

Newspapers	56
Journals	1,059
Other serials	470

VI.   PHYSICAL PLANT

Exterior woodwork on the Weyerhaeuser Library was painted during the
summer of 1973.

Carpet runners on the stack stairways have not yet been provided, but
are definitely needed. Tiles on the stair treads are worn, cracked, and
slick, and present a serious safety hazard along a route that receives
heavy daily use.

The floor of the Word Library was carpeted in the fall of 1972, and
shelving was installed to accommodate the nucleus collection of the Word
Library, bought with a portion of the funds donated for this purpose to
the College several years ago by Mr. Charles W. Ferguson of Mt. Kisco,
New York.

Cracking of the concrete floor of the main reading room, south wing,
appears to have ceased.

VII.   PLANNING FOR A NEW BUILDING

A. Basic Considerations

During the decade of the 1960's, library construction flourished in
this country as never before, thanks mainly to the availability of federal
funding on an unprecedented scale. In that one decade some four billion
dollars' worth of new libraries were built on college and university campuses
around the country. And when the boom ended, there was scarcely a college
of any distinction that could not boast of its fine new library building.

Macalester College was among the few exceptions, for it had made
an addition to its old building in 1960 that everyone believed would be adequate to the College's needs for at least another twenty years. But with
the rapid development and expansion of its academic program in the 1960's,
as the College swiftly moved into the first rank of the nation's liberal
arts institutions, the library's collections expanded at a rate no one had
foreseen in 1960, and by 1968 the building was overflowing with books and
students. Its life span was reached twelve years sooner than anyone had
reason to expect, and Macalester today finds itself with a library building
seriously inadequate to the scope and quality of its educational program.

In the Macalester College Comprehensive Campus Plan of 1968, it was
recommended that a new building be constructed to house the library and related educational functions. The report stated furthermore that the existing structure did not constitute a facility "appropriate to a first-class
academic institution concerned with total education." In 1971 the faculty
passed a document on Long-Range Institutional Planning which stated: "The
needs of the College with respect to physical facilities are varied. We
do not attempt to identify them here, with one exception: The library is
an essential element in teaching and learning at Macalester and the maintenance of a strong library program is a matter of great and continuing
concern...We believe that among competing demands for new or improved
physical facilities on campus, a new building for housing the library and
other learning resources holds first priority."

Despite the present adversity posed by a long overdue new building
for the library, Macalester now stands ready to benefit handsomely and
uniquely from all that was learned elsewhere over the last ten years about

what to seek, and what to avoid in a new building. Drawing upon the rich and varied experience of others, Macalester proposes to construct a library building that will be, like its academic program, a model of excellence, a hallmark of what a library should be, and a visible testament to the College's deep and abiding faith in the life of the mind.

THE LIBRARY BUILDING: DESIGN AND FUNCTION

The building will be sited at the center of the campus, in an area that will become the formal entrance to the College, to indicate symbolically that the route to learning leads directly through the doors of a fine library. The placement of the building will signify to visitors and regulars alike the College's central commitment to the worth and values of a life strengthened and illuminated by humane learning.

Because of its imposing size (100,000 square feet) and central location, this building must be, in its external design, an elegant, harmonious, and inviting structure, to symbolize Macalester's deep concern for the excellent things of the human spirit, and to proclaim its invitation to all who see the building to enter and share that concern.

To design the library, the College will therefore commission an architect noted for his genius in producing work of outstanding aesthetic quality, without sacrificing functional efficiency. The building must be comfortable, beautiful and appealing in its interior design and furnishings, so those who enter will be tempted to remain, and take pleasure in the aesthetic as well as the intellectual offerings of the library. The building must also not consume any more energy for heating and lighting than the building it replaces and, hopefully, less than presently used.

A building of such excellent quality will cost about $50.00 per square foot, or about five million dollars for construction.

In addition to housing the collection, the proposed library building would have at least the following special features:

> Seminar rooms, where classes can be held in close proximity to book collections.
>
> Group study rooms, for the many students who like to discuss books and ideas with each other in the library.
>
> Comfortable, good looking furnishings, and carpeting throughout the building, not only for reduced noise level but also so students will feel good about being in the library, and want to come to it.
>
> A coffee shop, as a common informal meeting ground for staff and students and faculty from all disciplines. (Nothing of the sort now exists anywhere on campus.)
>
> Lounges where patrons can relax from their studies and have their spirits refreshed by the beauty of their surroundings.
>
> A photography lab and darkroom large enough for class instruction.
>
> A fully equipped multi-media auditorium (about 200 seats) both for media presentations and instruction, and special lectures, poetry readings, etc.
>
> Facilities for viewing cassette television.
>
> Individual sound carrels for listening to music and spoken recordings.

A specially equipped room for reading microfilm.

Computer terminal installations, both for individual
    and group instruction.

Fully equipped audio-visual service and production
    facilities.

A manual printing press, and craft bindery, where students
    can learn the typographical arts, and make their own
    fine books.

Equipment and facilities for the College's printing and
    information services.

Above all, space: space for growing collections that have
    nearly trebled in size since the present building was
    added to in 1960; and for students who find cramped,
    unpleasant quarters wherever they turn in this badly
    over-crowded building.

THE CONSTANT VOLUME LIBRARY

Unlike other academic library buildings, the proposed new library will
never be outgrown, nor will it require construction of additions.

Librarians have been greatly troubled by the problem of rapid collection
growth ever since the invention of printing in the 15th century vastly expanded man's capacity to produce books.

The problem became especially acute in the 20th century when academic
libraries began to double in size every 15 to 20 years. (The doubling time
had been 50 to 100 years in the 19th century, and even that low rate caused
trouble.) The unavoidable consequence of this accelerated geometrical growth

pattern has been an embarassingly and burdensomely frequent replacement, or expansion, of library buildings.

Common sense tells us this process must eventually be halted by rational means, or else grind to a disruptive halt of its own inertia.

In its proposed new library building, Macalester College is committed to finding a rational means to achieve a constant-volume collection, so the building will never have to be added to, nor ever replaced by another so long as it is structurally sound.

The approach Macalester is taking is three-pronged, and in its totality, without precedent: it involves a combination of (1) the use of compact steel shelving; (2) the replacement of certain bound volumes with micro-equivalents when the originals are no longer under copyright restriction; and (3) the employment of recently developed statistical criteria for weeding books whose predictable use levels will be zero, or close to it.

(1) The building will be designed to hold 500,000 volumes using conventional bookstacks. That capacity would theoretically be reached around the year 2000. However, instead of expanding or replacing the building as the collection grows, we will gradually introduce compact drawer-type shelving, which doubles the shelving capacity per square foot of floor space it occupies. Book capacity of the building is thus expanded to 1,000,000 volumes, a size that will be reached around mid-21st century.

(2) By that time 50% or more of the collection will have aged enough to pass out of copyright restriction, and much that is worth retaining can be replaced with commercially available micro-equivalents, which essentially require zero space. Every year thereafter, about 2% of the collection (or 20,000 volumes) will pass into the public domain. Such volumes as do not

then become available in microform will very likely prove to be excellent candidates for weeding.

(3) At the million-volume level, by weeding only 1.5% of the collection (15,000 volumes) each year, we would achieve a constant-volume collection, assuming intake still approximates the present rate of 15,000 volumes/year. (This rate will never alter significantly, unless enrollment size does: for academic library expenditures always remain a very steady percentage of total institutional expenditures.) Recent statistical studies by Dr. R. W. Trueswell (Chairman of the Industrial Engineering Department of the University of Massachusetts) conclusively establish that weeding (using objective statistical criteria) at the 1.5% level will have zero effect on demand-availability of books that students and faculty will want to use in any academic library.

Employing techniques (2) and (3) simultaneously, there can be no reasonable doubt that, at the million volume level, Macalester will achieve a constant-volume library, by keeping outflow equal to intake. And by shifting to compact shelving, we will reach that level with only half the floor space traditionally required.

We can confidently predict at this point that Macalester's new library building will thus become a trailblazer for other academic libraries throughout the country: the first in library history to commit itself rationally to a future where zero collection growth will be attained, and where the unceasing process of replacing or adding to library buildings will finally cease.

B. Chronology of Planning Work

On the 13th of November 1972, and again on March 6, 1973, the library director met with the Education Committee of the Board of Trustees and placed before them various data indicating the College's need for a new library building, and what the size and life span of such a building might be.

At the second meeting the Education Committee authorized planning for a new building to begin, with the very general understanding that the con-templated capacity would be about 500,000 volumes (assuming conventional shelving); that it would provide seating for about 500 readers; that its book capacity would be reached some 25 to 30 years hence; and that the total project cost would be in the range of four to six million dollars.

On March 7, 1973 the president appointed the Library Planning Advisory Committee, with the following membership: Daniel Gore, Chairman; Jean Archibald (Associate Library Director); John Schue and Jeremiah Reedy (faculty); John Dozier and Arthur Heuer (administration); Joanne Ruby and Michael Lee (students); and David Nicholson and Cargill MacMillan, Jr. (trustees).

The Committee met for the first time on March 20, 1973, and subse-quently met on April 5, April 26, June 13, and August 1. (Minutes are on file in the library office.) At its first meeting the Committee was in-vited to submit to the president the names of three candidates for the post of building consultant. This was done, and after credentials were obtained for the two candidates who expressed interest in the post, the president with the concurrence of the library director invited Dr. Ellsworth Mason, Director of the University of Colorado Libraries, to serve as building

consultant. Dr. Mason has served as consultant on 85 library building
projects to date, and is nationally recognized as the leading practitioner
in the field. On May 14 Dr. Mason accepted the invitation, and made his
first visit to the campus July 31-August 1.

C. Accomplishments

At the request of the Committee, the Office of Educational Research
conducted two questionnaire surveys of the College community, to ascertain
preferences with respect to building site, and specific services, facilities,
etc. to be provided in the new building.

From this survey emerged a general preference that the building be
located somewhere in the Old Main/Carnegie/Weyerhaeuser elbow. A notable
division exists between faculty and student preference for the field between
Humanities and the gym as a building site: faculty ranked this area as
first preference (on a scale of ten) while students ranked it eighth. While
the Committee has not yet taken a formal position on the question, its feeling, both before and after the survey, has been that the ideal site is in
the approximate locale of Old Main.

The purpose of the first survey was to elicit unstructured expressions
of general interest, from which specific questions could be formulated by
the Committee for inclusion in the second questionnaire survey. Survey
results conform in most respects to Committee anticipations. In some instances where expression of interest is relatively weak, the Committee believes careful interpretation is required. To cite one example, the
apparently low average level of interest in a curriculum lab probably implies zero interest among those persons whose program makes no use of the

lab, and high interest among those whose program does. In this instance, and others like it, the Committee will take into account factors other than the raw statistical results. (Copies of the OER's survey report are available in the Library Office.)

On July 31 the consultant met with the president and the library director, and on the following day met with the library committee. In these meetings, and extended conversations with the library director, the consultant made the following observations and recommendations:

1. That the need for a new building is self-evident; Macalester College is virtually unique among outstanding liberal arts colleges in the inferior quality and overcrowding of its library building;

2. That a new building will both enhance the College's educational mission, and its efforts to recruit new students and top calibre faculty;

3. That the library director, in consultation with the Committee, begin drafting a building program, to be reviewed and critiqued by the consultant as it is in progress;

4. That an architect should be commissioned as soon as a building program is drawn up;

5. That the architects be given ample time (nine months or longer) to perfect their planning, to avoid the serious flaws that typically result from overhasty design work;

6. That negotiations with the architect be centralized

in one body, preferably the Committee, to avoid con-
flict and confusion arising from overlapping authority;

7. That interior design is a prime factor in the overall
   appeal of a building; and a first rate interior design consultant should be engaged by the College if
   the architect's staff does not include one;

8. That collection capacity should be in the range of 500,000
   volumes, and seating capacity about 1/4 of enrollment, or
   500 seats.

9. That the ideal site is in the Old Main/Carnegie area.

D. The Building Program

To ensure that no legitimate interest is overlooked in developing the
program, the Committee will invite written submissions of specific interests
from all parties who hold them, and will conduct hearings on those interests
where appropriate.

The Committee has invited each department head (faculty and administrative) to develop and submit written statements of special departmental requirements and desires, with estimates of square footage needs and specifi-
cation of any required special equipment.

The program will be carefully reviewed by the Committee as it develops,
and analyzed and critiqued by the consultant as it advances from draft to
final form. Copies of each draft stage will be submitted for review and recommendation by the president, and the finished program will then be trans-
mitted for his approval and the Trustees'.

VIII.   STAFF ACTIVITIES

Mrs. Jean Archibald completed her term as Chairman of the Academic
Division of the Minnesota Library Association in 1972/73, and as a mem-
ber of the MLA Board. In Interim 1973 she taught a course entitled
"Methods of Research in Government Publications." On March 26-27, 1973,
Mrs. Archibald conducted a workshop on journal binding at the Conference
on Management Problems in Serials Work, held at Florida Atlantic University.
She served as a member of the Grants Committee of Cooperating Libraries in
Consortium throughout the year.

Mr. Dickinson offered an Interim Course, "Archaeological Laboratory
Techniques," and taught the "Introduction to Bibliography" course in the
fall and spring sessions.

Mr. Higginbotham received the master's degree in library science at
the University of Minnesota.

Mr. Lee taught a course in French Cinema during Interim, and taught
Humanities "The Modern World--II" in the spring session.

Mr. Gore served on the Editorial Board of the Minnesota Library
Association; on the College's Curriculum Committee, Library Committee,
Library Planning Advisory Committee (as chairman) and Staff Advisory Council,
and served as president of the Macalester College Council of Educational
Administrators and Professionals. He presented a paper on serials problems
at the Conference on Management Problems in Serials Work, and at the Annual
Meeting of New England College Librarians, Providence, R. I., May 18, 1973.
Mr. Gore also served as a consultant to the libraries of Knox College,
Monmouth College, Carl Sandburg Junior College, and Florida Atlantic

University.

Mr. Ondercin taught an Interim course, "Studies in Women's History."

PUBLICATIONS, SPEECHES, ETC.

Archibald, Jean and Dickinson, Dennis.

Guide to Periodical Indexes and Abstracts. St. Paul, Macalester
    College, 1973.

Gore, Daniel.

"In Hot Pursuit of FASTCAT," Library Journal, Vol. 97, No. 15
    (Sept. 1, 1972), 2693-95.

Economics of Approval Plans, edited by Peter Spyers-Duran and
    Daniel Gore. Westport, Conn.: Greenwood Press, 1972.

"Adopting an Approval Plan for a College Library: The Macalester
    College Experience," in Economics of Approval Plans, pp. 24-35.

"Sawing Off the Horns of a Dilemma: Or, How to Cut Subscription
    Lists and Expand Access to Journal Literature," paper presented
    at the Conference on Management Problems in Serials Work,
    Florida Atlantic University, March 27, 1973; and at the New
    England College Librarians' Annual Meeting, Providence College,
    May 18, 1973.

IX.   PROBLEMS PRESENT AND DISTANT

With the end of a major reclass project in sight during 1973/74, and

a consequent reduction in technical services staff requirements in the off-

ing, a general re-organization of library staff will be required. Reclass

staff are being trained to perform a variety of tasks in the public service

areas (reserves, periodicals, circulation, and reference), and reassigned

gradually to those areas as the reclass project nears its conclusion.

College funds for books and journals in 1973/74 will be about $6,000 less than in 1972/73. Inflation will further reduce buying power at least 10%, creating a total potential drop of $17,000 in buying capacity. Response to a voluntary approach to balancing the budget by cutting journal subscriptions proved unpromising. The Library Committee therefore concluded that the laissez faire approach to book buying over the last three years must be given up.

Comparing Macalester's acquisitions budget with those of the other ACM libraries, the Committee found it to be the largest of the group, and 2.5 times greater than the average. On that basis the Committee felt there is nothing wrong with the budget as a whole. Still it is not enough to go around on the random distribution basis of the last three years.

The Committee will therefore allocate 1973/74 book and journal funds by department, using as its basic criterion the average pattern of expenditures by department over the last three years--the only period for which data are available. The Committee assume that each department will develop internal policies and procedures to ensure optimum use of its allocation.

(At this writing the allocation procedure has been in effect for five months, and appears to be functioning quite well.)

Library space for people and collections will be an abiding problem until a new library is built. As noted elsewhere in this report, the space problem in the Olin branch has reached the critical stage, and must be resolved before the year is out.

Obtaining sufficient hours of student work has been a constant problem for the past three years. Although total requirements have been reduced some 30% over that period through various improvements in library operations, we still experience continuing difficulties in obtaining student staff even at that reduced level. With regular staff positions cut by 40%, maintaining adequate student staff becomes a critical concern. If the many students who wish to do so could work more than the average seven hours per week allotted, the problem would be substantially solved, and the difficulties of training, scheduling, and supervising would be greatly alleviated.

The broad-scale problem caused by insufficient copies of high-demand titles in the collection has been with us for many years. But now that it is clearly understood and the long-term process of systematically identifying and duplicating these titles has begun, this problem will gradually abate. Within ten years it should be virtually eliminated, assuming funds are available each year for dealing with it.

When the Office of the Provost was absorbed by the Office of the President in July 1973, the Library, which had formerly reported to the Provost, was transferred to the Office of the Vice-President and Treasurer-- Mr. John Dozier. While such an alignment for an academic library is admittedly unusual, and might be imagined for that reason to portend certain novel organizational problems, none has developed nor are any anticipated. Since the new arrangement results in one Tar Heel reporting to another, what might normally be construed as a problem became instead an opportunity, from which the Library has benefited substantially during the first half-year of the new relationship.

X. A TRIBUTE TO THE STAFF

Since the fall of 1970 ten staff positions have been terminated, amounting to a reduction of about forty percent. During the same period a major reclass project was added to the usual duties of the staff, and that project is now virtually complete. Adding duties while reducing staff required total revision of every aspect of the library's operations, to bring about large increases in operating efficiency. Old ways of doing things had to be given up, and many new ways quickly learned. Stress runs high among people involved in sudden, total change, but this staff has weathered well the prolonged turmoil of transition. They understood and accepted the need for it from the outset, and got on with the work that had to be done in a spirit of good will and common dedication without which all the procedural reforms might have come to nothing.

As just one measure of what has been accomplished, suffice it to say that the reduction of ten positions frees up each year approximately the sum of money required to fund the book budget. In that respect, our excellent showing in comparison with similar libraries may be viewed as a direct result of outstanding staff performance. Had it been merely average, positions could not have been reduced and the book budget would accordingly have suffered drastic cuts.

To Mrs. Jean Archibald, Associate Director of the Library, and Mrs. Dorothy Barnes, Library Secretary, I acknowledge an enormous debt of gratitude for doing what only they could have done so well: keep communications among the whole staff wide open, relaxed, and reliable; see that everything was done when it had to be done, and in the way it ought to be done; and advise their boss firmly and well to the contrary whenever he was about to make some wrong-headed decision. The work of this wonderful wordhouse never went waywardly under their careful watch.

To be held personally accountable for the many activities of a library staff is a responsibility that becomes a pleasure when their work is so cheerfully and ably done. They have my full gratitude for making the weight of that responsibility seem so comfortable to carry, during a time of swift and fundamental change.

Macalester College

Annual Report
of the
Library
1973/74

St· Paul, Minnesota

■ WEYERHAEUSER LIBRARY

February 3, 1975

Dr. A. Truman Schwartz
Dean of the Faculty
Macalester College
St. Paul, Minnesota 55105

Dear Truman:

Pursuing the familiar theme of our convivial discourse, I'm pleased to submit in this <u>Annual Report</u> yet another piece of weighty evidence (if more were needed) that something is amiss with the Second Law of Thermodynamics.

For here is the record of an organization that continues to run briskly uphill, against the entropic tug of inflation and budgetary retrenchment, when logic, economics, and the Second Law all say it should be running down to a standstill. Was it Von Weizsäcker who theorized that human intelligence could prove to be a countervailing force to the dire imperatives of the Second Law? He might be cheered, as I am, and as I desire that you will be (both as Dean and Thermodynamicist) to behold how our Library staff have given substance to his optimistic vision.

While the evidence in this <u>Report</u> consists mostly of colorless statistical summaries, I know you will be mindful of the fact that it is nonetheless a record of purposeful, fruitful human activity, and a testament to the diligence and dedication of a talented staff.

They join me in wishing you success and all happiness in your new post as Dean of the Faculty.

By the way, the calligraphy and illustrations in this <u>Report</u> were provided by our sibylline friend Judy Duncan, who characteristically declines to offer any clue as to what the illustrations mean. Something full of wit and portent, I suspect, if a man were deep enough to puzzle it out. Let's talk about that-- and thermodynamics too--at our next convivial occasion.

Sincerely,

Daniel Gore
Director

DG:db

CONTENTS

I. INTRODUCTION

Economics of Academic Libraries is the title of a recent, grim prophetic
work commissioned by the American Council on Education, and written by two
economists who believe that the cost of operating academic libraries must continue to rise, as it has in the past, at a rate far steeper than the inflationary rise in the consumer price index. Their reasons for this gloomy forecast
are varied and complex, but underlying them is the familiar claim that "As in
higher education generally, the quality of service provided by a library depends on human activity, much of which does not lend itself to cost-reducing
technological innovation. Thus, 'productivity' in library operations is much
more difficult to increase than it is, say, in manufacturing or agriculture."
So the authors predict that libraries will either price themselves out of
society's reach, or cut costs by cutting essential services, unless automation
of library operations some day turns the cost curve downward.

The results cited in this Annual Report of the Macalester Library, and the
three preceding ones, go far to dispel the economists' gloom. Over the last
four years individual productivity of library staff has essentially doubled, the
amount of useful work done increasing somewhat, while staff complement diminished by nearly fifty percent. And for the most part that gain depended on practically nothing in the way of technological innovation. It depended on the willingness of an able staff to abandon cumbersome, outmoded ways of doing things,
and to take up new ways when better ones could be found. It depended on a
readiness to learn new tasks and, when those were learned, to learn some more.
Above all, it depended on a faith that the work of a library is not only well
worth doing, but worth doing supremely well.

The results attest to the strength of that faith:

- A major reclass project (82,000 volumes) begun and completed while positions were being cut.
- Average costs of processing new books cut by 70 percent.
- Average time for acquiring and processing new books cut by 90 percent.
- Journal binding costs cut 80 percent.
- Interlibrary loan deliveries increased ten-fold.
- Book budget unscathed, and hours of opening during regular sessions unreduced.
- Library staff offering for the first time formal course work in bibliography.

The pages ahead chronicle in generous detail the concluding steps in the four-year reorganization of the Library. Those who wish to see details in superfluity are invited to consult the more voluminous annual, weekly, monthly, and quarterly reports of the Library's several departments, all on file in the Library Office.

II.   STAFF

A.   Audio-Visual Department

   Mr. Wynn Lee, Acting Head of the Department since January 1972, vacated
the post in August 1974, and Dr. Dennis Dickinson succeeded him as Head of
the Department. Mr. Tom Browne resigned his post as part-time Technical Assistant to work full time in the Language Laboratory, and was replaced by Mr.
Duane Vigeant, beginning in the Fall Term of 1974.

   Mrs. Lois Nelson was assigned to the Department on a half-time basis
beginning Fall 1974, to assist in the expanded taping projects of the unit.

B.   Circulation Department

   Mr. Richard Higginbotham left his part-time position to resume graduate studies, and was replaced by Mr. Michael Keller. Mrs. Bernice Oliver was
transferred from Periodicals to Circulation, replacing Mrs. Salscheider, whose
new assignments are noted below.

C.   Curriculum Lab and Olin Library

   Under Mrs. Stenger's supervision, Mrs. Rosemary Salscheider oversees the
routine activities of these units, also giving some time to the work of the
Technical Services Department.

D.   Periodicals Department

   Mrs. Mary Hampl was named Periodicals Supervisor.

E. Reference and Interlibrary Loan Department

Dr. Dickinson left his post as Bibliographical Intern to become Head
of the AV Department, September 1974. His former duties are now shared by
Mrs. Archibald, Mrs. Stenger, and himself when AV schedules permit.

F. Reserve Department

Mrs. Corinne Kellar became Reserves Supervisor.

G. Technical Services Department

Mrs. Marymina Stenger, Head of the Department, was given additional supervisory responsibilities for interlibrary loans, the Olin Library, and the
Curriculum Lab.

Mrs. Peggy Rude transferred from Olin to Technical Services Fall 1973,
and Mr. Higginbotham moved from Technical Services to Circulation. Upon completion of the reclass project Mrs. Corinne Kellar and Mrs. Mary Hampl concluded their assignments in Technical Services, Mrs. Kellar then being appointed Reserves Supervisor, and Mrs. Hampl Periodicals Supervisor.

H. Staff Roster 1970-1974

Library

Fall 1970	Fall 1971	Fall 1972	Fall 1973	Fall 1974
Gore	Gore	Gore	Gore	Gore
Archibald	Archibald	Archibald	Archibald	Archibald
Adamson	Barnes	Barnes	Barnes	Barnes
Barnes	Cobb	Crouse	Crouse	Crouse
Buggs	Cramer	Dickinson	Dickinson	Francis
Cobb	Crouse	Francis (3/4)	Francis	Hampl
Cramer	Francis (1/2)	Haberkorn (1/2)	Hampl	Kellar
Crouse	Haberkorn (1/2)	Hampl	Higginbotham (1/2)	Keller (1/2)
Francis	Hampl	Higginbotham (1/2)	Kellar	Nelson (1/2)
Hampl	Kellar	Kellar	Nelson	Newcomb
Harri (1/2)	Leonard	Nelson	Newcomb	Oliver (1/2)
Kellar	Nelson	Newcomb	Oliver (1/2)	Rude
Kerr	Newcomb	Oliver (1/2)	Rude	Salscheider
Kiscaden	Oliver (1/2)	Ondercin	Salscheider	Shin (1/2)
Leonard	Ondercin	Rude	Shin (1/2)	Stenger
Meyn	Rude	Salscheider	Stenger	
Nelson	Salscheider	Shin (1/2)		13 FTE
Newcomb	Shin (1/2)	Stenger	14 1/2 FTE	
Oliver (1/2)	Sorensen (1/2)			
Pressman	Stenger	15 3/4 FTE		
Rude				
Salscheider	17 1/2 FTE			
Shin (1/2)				
Sorensen (1/2)				
Stenger				

MICROFICHE CATALOGING DEVICE
(in exchange for one staff position)

24 FTE

Audio-Visual

1971	1972	1973	1974
Hernandez	Lee	Lee	Dickinson
Jackson (3/4)	Jackson (3/4)	Jackson (3/4)	Jackson (3/4)
Derks	Browne (1/2)	Browne (1/2)	Vigeant (1/2)
Hakala (1/2)			Nelson (1/2)
	2 1/4 FTE	2 1/4 FTE	
3 1/4 FTE			2 3/4 FTE

I. Student Staff

In the course of the year some 200 different students worked for the
Library or its Audio-Visual Department. With more than 10% of the College's
total enrollment employed at various times during the year, the Library partici-
pates to an unusual degree in the training and guidance of Macalester students.
Many of their assignments require substantial training, skill, and intelligence.
All of them require responsible, punctual, courteous performance, and provide
an excellent opportunity for students to cultivate the virtues of reliability
and amiability that the world will demand of them when their Macalester days
are over. The hiring, training, scheduling, and supervision of so large a
part-time staff comprise a major portion of the regular staff's duties, the
ratio of student to other staff being on the order of ten to one. As I have
noted in previous Reports, while this may not be the most economical pattern
of staffing a library, it certainly maximizes the opportunities for students
to learn about libraries, and to master the indispensable art of working harmoniously with other people. On that basis the educational benefits are well
worth the costs of some modest reductions in overall efficiency.

Total student hours worked in 1973/74 came to 22,029 for the Library,
and 5,115 for its AV Department. Totals for the last four years are as follows:

	Library	AV Department
1970/71	29,387	–
1971/72	22,622	6,685
1972/73	22,245	7,118
1973/74	22,029	5,115

Assuming regular staff complement remains fairly constant in the future, our minimal requirements for student help in the Library and AV will remain in the 28,000 hours per year range. While this prediction can be made with confidence and ease, we have not yet found any routine, systematic way to obtain delivery of the requisite hours through the College's Financial Aid Office, which oversees the placement of all student aides. Repeatedly having to make last-minute, piecemeal solutions to the student staffing problem is wearisome and frustrating to the regular staff, and a constant distraction from other pressing duties. A rational and reliable routine method of obtaining requisite hours of student help would yield substantial benefits in the Library's operations. To cite only one example, shelfreading of the collections to keep books in correct order often falls far behind schedule, when student staff complement intermittently falls below authorized levels. With sufficient student staff, shelfreading would not be interrupted, the collections would always be in good order, and books could be found where they are supposed to be shelved.

J. General Appraisal of the Staff

With the completion in February 1974 of a major reclass project, which involved the labors of five regular staff members during its peak phase, a major reassignment of positions became necessary, the details of which are recorded above. Since total staff complement had been reduced from 24 to 13 FTE positions during the 3 1/2 year span of the reclass project, no staff layoffs were required at its termination. Substantial gains in operating efficiency made it possible to add this sizeable project in 1970 without adding staff, and routine attrition permitted gradual reduction of staff complement as the project gradually approached completion. The staff who remain have adjusted well to the numerous changes in assignment that were necessary to avoid lay-off situations. The varied experience they gained by working in several departments of the Library gives them a more comprehensive grasp of the Library's total services than one commonly finds among library staffs. Accordingly, they can and do provide much better guidance to the oft-bewildered library patron than one receives from librarians whose experience is confined, as it normally is, to the activities of a single department.

With the reorganization of services and collections now complete, staff assignments should remain fairly constant in the year ahead.

III. THE 1973/74 BUDGET

A. Library (excluding AV Department)

The budget for 1973/74 was set at $251,900,excluding student help. A detailed analysis of budget results appears on the following page. Expenditures by major categories over the past four years are as follows:

Title	1970/71	1971/72	1972/73	1973/74
Salaries and wages	$149,638	$127,826	$121,137	$126,829
Acquisitions and binding	101,158	105,579	123,163	113,238
Operations (net)	13,463	9,402	8,400	8,072
Totals	$264,259	$242,807	$252,700	$248,139

Expenditures for acquisitions and binding in 1973/74 were slightly higher than in the previous year, although they appear from the above figures to be nearly $10,000 less. That is because the 1972/73 figure includes an accrual sum of $9,800, actually spent not in that year but in the two previous years, but not reported in those years because, at the former provost's direction, the Library's acquisitions accounts were closed on August 1 rather than September 1. Acquisitions expenditures over the past three years have thus remained fairly constant, in the range of $110 - 113,000 per year.

Student help expenditures are not included in the above figures because the Library's authorized operating budget makes no line-item provision for such expenditures. They are however a significant part of the cost of operating the Library, amounting to about $41,000 in 1973/74. The average rate of compensation in that year comes to about $1.85 per hour, and will be about 10% higher in 1974/75.

Library Budget 1973/74

Actual Expenditures

Title		Expenditures
Salaries and Wages		$ 126,829
Acquisitions and Binding		113,238
Books	$85,577	
Periodicals	26,174	
Binding	1,487	
Operations (Net; expenses less income)		8,072

Expenses

Supplies	$4,896
Telephone	229
Postage	515
Travel	699
Equipment purchases	1,807
Equipment repair	448
Photocopying	5,762
Membership (CLIC)	1,682
Interlibrary loans	676
	$16,714

Income

Overdue fees	4,805
Book sales	80
Lost books	140
Picture rentals	50
Photocopying	3,567
	$ 8,642

Grand total:	$248,139
Budgeted total:	$251,900

B. AV Department

   The authorized budget was a net figure of $33,750, comprised of $27,750
for salaries and wages (excluding student help) and $6,000 for net operating
expenditures (gross less income from services, sales, etc.). This was the
first fiscal year in which an AV budget was formulated on a net basis. The
decision to do that was based on the extreme difficulty of predicting the
quantity of supplies, tape, equipment, etc. the department might sell in the
course of a year. The results of net budgeting in 1973/74 are reassuring: net
operating expenses came to $5,147, against a net budgeted figure of $6,000.
Since the same net figure of $6,000 is set for 1974/75, the differential will
offset inflationary effects in the course of the year.

   Total gross operating expenditures (excluding salaries, wages, and student
help) were $23,026 in 1973/74, and $15,524 in 1972/73. The net figures are
$5,147 in 1973/74, and $6,775 in 1972/73. Thus while the gross figure increased by $7,502 from the previous year, the net declined by $1,628. These results
underscore the desirability of continuing net budgeting for AV to maintain a
realistic picture of actual operating needs and costs.

   An analysis of expenditures appears below. Student help is excluded,
since the line-item budget makes no provision for it. College expenditures for
student help in AV were about $9,322 in 1973/74, at an average rate of $1.83
per hour.

   Following a theft of equipment from the department in the course of the
year, Comptroller William Halloran authorized a special expenditure of $3,400
for replacements, against an anticipated reimbursement of at least that amount
from insurance. In the analysis below that sum is treated as an item of income.

AV Budget 1973/74

Actual Expenditures

Title   Expenditures

Salaries and Wages $26,745

Operations (Net; Expenses less income)   5,147

Expenses

Supplies	$11,686
Dues	10
Subscriptions	28
Freight	19
Telephone	202
AV	2,150
Postage	360
Printing	191
Equipment Purchase	7,337
Equipment Repair	1,042
	$23,026

Income

Services and supplies	$13,145
Insurance	3,400
Library tape purchases	1,334
	$17,879

Grand total:	$31,892
Budgeted total:	$33,750

IV.   DEPARTMENTAL ACTIVITIES

A. Technical Services

    1. Acquisitions

    Beginning in February 1974 the computer-based profile acquisitions pro-
gram previously serviced by the Richard Abel Company was placed with the
Baker & Taylor Company, which offered a substantially better guaranteed discount on new books. Although Baker & Taylor supplied new books to the Library
for only six months of fiscal 1973/74, the average per-volume cost of books
acquired throughout the year dropped by four percent, from $10.20 to $9.80
per volume. Delivery schedules and billing procedures are also substantially
better with the new jobber.

    Statistical results of the profile program in 1973/74 are as follows:

	Number	Dollars	Average
Notice slips from the jobbers	13,932	$141,000	$10.20
"Buy" slips from faculty	3,733	36,400	9.80
"Don't Buy" slips from faculty	8,587	89,300	10.40
Total slips from faculty	12,820	125,700	10.20
Acceptance rate	29%		
Rejection rate	61%		

    The acceptance rate of 29% falls far below the 41% level of the two pre-
vious years. The drop may be attributed to the fact that in 1973/74, for
the first time in many years, expenditures of each academic department were
limited to a fixed sum allocated by the Faculty Library Committee.

    Expenditures by departments from College funds for profile and other book
purchases, and for journal subscriptions, appear on the following page.

    Total College expenditures on acquisitions came to $111,752. An addition-

Departmental Book and Periodical Expenditures 1973/74

Division	Expenditure by Division Books	Periodicals	Total
1. Social Sciences			
Geography	$ 2,221.37	$ 385.40	$ 2,606.77
Political Science	5,712.40	1,204.60	6,917.00
Psychology	3,284.44	2,266.45	5,550.89
Sociology & Anthropology	5,422.80	621.55	6,044.35
Totals	16,641.01	4,478.00	21,119.01
2. Business and Economics	3,545.09	1,372.25	4,917.34
3. Education	1,567.75	376.50	1,944.25
4. Fine Arts			
Art	1,801.66	311.00	2,112.66
Journalism	333.12	100.65	433.77
Music	1,961.10	144.60	2,105.70
Speech	778.24	159.45	937.69
Totals	4,874.12	715.70	5,589.82
5. Humanities			
Classics	1,188.69	113.50	1,302.19
English	12,651.42	520.30	13,171.72
Foreign Languages			
French	1,625.88	232.93	1,858.81
German	2,849.56	307.46	3,157.02
Russian	2,563.99	115.50	2,679.49
Spanish	1,111.22	161.00	1,272.22
History	11,622.71	329.75	11,952.46
Philosophy	2,411.15	888.90	3,300.05
Religion	3,597.09	267.75	3,864.84
Totals	39,621.71	2,937.09	42,558.80
6. Physical Education	715.02	184.98	900.00
7. Science and Mathematics			
Biology	3,062.34	5,288.10	8,350.44
Chemistry	1,677.15	3,807.64	5,484.79
Geology	885.38	827.15	1,712.53
Math	1,066.71	1,204.48	2,271.19
Physics	1,015.93	1,875.13	2,891.08
Totals	7,707.51	13,002.52	20,710.03
8. Library and Miscellaneous	10,905.26	3,107.10	14,012.36
Grand Totals	$85,577.47	$26,174.14	$111,751.61

al $5,000 was spent from a Federal grant to the College, $6,143 from a CLIC
Federal grant, $1,738 from a Kellogg grant, and $1,487 was spent on binding.
The value of gift books added was $5,000, bringing the total value of new
acquisitions during 1973/74 to $131,120.

Duplication Policy

With the approval of the Faculty Library Committee, the Library inaugurated in 1973/74 a program of systematically acquiring added copies of all boo
whose loan records indicated the demand for them exceeded the supply of copies
available. In the course of the year more than nine hundred such volumes were
bought, at a total cost of $5,862. A complete list of these high-demand title
is on file in the Library office. It is one of the most interesting bibliographies the Library owns, for it pictures precisely the principal reading in
terests of Macalester students -- not what someone thinks they ought to be
reading, but what in fact they are reading.

The reasons for the duplication program are spelled out on pages 198-202
last year's Report. The cardinal reason is that one copy of a high-demand
title is not enough to satisfy the reasonable expectations of a community of
2,000 readers. Last spring the Library made a survey to determine how often
books it owns are not on the shelf when readers want to borrow them. The fail
ure rate turned out to be 42%, which seems intolerably high, although about
what we expected from the published findings of the several other academic
libraries that have made similar surveys. The duplication program, together
with a reduction of the general loan period from five weeks to three, should
bring about significant reductions in the average failure rate.

GIFTS, GRANTS, AND NOTABLE ACQUISITIONS

An HEW grant of $5,000 was expended in 1973/74 to acquire resources in
black and other ethnic studies, in environmental, ecological, and urban
studies, and in the field of drug abuse. Most of the grant was devoted to
the purchase of the following films:

> Black Anger
> Harvest of Shame
> Black and White in South Africa
> Introducing the Indian Viewpoint
> The Village
> To Make the Balance
> To Find Our Life: The Peyote Hunt of the Hichols of Mexico
> The Tenement
> Henry, Boy of the Barrio
> Black History: Lost, Stolen or Strayed?
> Black Music in America: Then Till Now
> The Toughest Game in Town
> People, Power and Change
> Losing Just the Same
> Civil Disorder: The Kerner Report I & II
> Civil Disorder: The Kerner Report III
> I am Joaquin

In 1973/74, CLIC received a Federal grant of $50,000 for the joint pur-
chase of expensive and commonly needed publications. The grant guidelines indicate that a portion of the materials ordered should be related to the study
of the disadvantaged. Each CLIC library examined its needs and compiled a list
of priority items totalling approximately $6,143 per library. The Macalester
Library selected and acquired the following titles, which are also available
for use by students and faculty of the CLIC colleges.

> *Africa South of the Sahara: Index to Periodical Literature.
>   First Supplement. Boston, G. K. Hall, 1973
>
> African Authors. V. 1, 1900-1973. Detroit, Gale Research Co., 1973.
>
> Afro-American Encyclopedia. 10 vols. Educational Book Pubs., 1973.
>
> American Statistics Index. Washington, D. C., Congressional Informa-
>   tion Service, 1973.

Afro-American Artists: A Bio-bibliographical Directory.
    Boston, Boston Public Library, 1973.

American Black Women in the Arts and Social Sciences: A Biblio-
    graphic Survey. Scarecrow, 1973.

The Chinese Classics. 7 vols. Wynnewood, Pa., Kolokol Press,
    1973-

Great Soviet Encyclopedia. 3rd ed. 30 vol. set.

*New York Times. Microfilm. 1914-1929.

The starred titles extend existing collections.

During the past three years, the Library has been vitally enriched with a

variety of materials related to environmental studies, acquired through a

$5,000 grant from the Kellogg Foundation. A committee of librarians and facul-

ty members selected outstanding books, periodical subscriptions, abstracts, in-

dexes, government documents and maps, and films presenting many aspects of en-

vironmental problems. All films were reviewed before purchase, and during the

past year, extensive use was made of these films by the geology, geography and

biology classes. In future years, urban geography classes will actively use

the numerous topographic maps of Minnesota, acquired with grant funds, in their

field trips for the study of environmental problems and planning.

All materials purchased through the Kellogg Grant will help sustain the new

environmental studies program at Macalester College. They will be especially

useful in the senior seminar in environmental studies which will be offered for

the first time at Macalester in 1974/75.

During the period from May 1973-April 1974, the following amounts were

spent from the grant:

Books	$395.95
Periodical Subscriptions	96.50
Abstracts & indexes	405.00
Films	640.74
Maps	200.00
	$1,738.19

Summary of Kellogg Grant Expenditures, 1971/72-1973/74

Total by year:

May 1971-April 1972	$1,397.18
May 1972-April 1973	1,865.16
May 1973-April 1974	1,738.19
Total:	$5,000.53

Total by category:

Books	$1,871.20
Periodical Subscriptions	291.49
Abstracts and indexes	967.00
Government documents	25.10
Films	1,645.74
Maps	200.00
Total:	$5,000.53

Gifts from alumni and friends of the College totalled 3,798 items during 1973/74, of which 1,577 items were added to the collections, having an estimated value of $5,000.

Other notable acquisitions during 1973/74 purchased from the Library budget are:

Encyclopedia Britannica. 1974. 30 vols.

Monographic series reprinted by Arno Press:

Mass violence in America. 27 vols.

Medicine in Society. 45 vols.

Religion in America. 30 vols.

Russia Observed. 84 vols.

Women in America. 31 vols.

Calligraffiti Collection

Over the past two years the Library acquired some eighty pieces of the calligraphic work of Judith Anne Duncan, with funds given to the Library by our generous old friend Charles W. Ferguson, of Mt. Kisco, N.Y. On November 4, 1973, the Library opened a special exhibit of the collection. The show attracted much favorable attention among students, faculty, and townspeople during the six months it enlivened the walls of the main reading room. A permanent memorial of the exhibit is the text that Miss Duncan painted on the paneling of the lobby on opening day:

Mene
Mene
Tekel
Upharsin

(Bible readers will recognize this passage as the original "handwriting on the wall," from Daniel 5:25.) The letters were made four inches high, that he (or she) may run that readeth it (Habakkuk 2:2), or they who run may read.

The brochure of the show is bound in following this page.

Calligraffiti

An Exhibit of
The Wall-Writing Art
of Judith Anne Duncan
in the

Weyerhaeuser Library
of Macalester College
November 4-17, 1973

Of the billions of words a library contains, the few that are boldly displayed always turn out to be flatly admonitory ("Silence, Please"), coldly commanding ("Show ID Card to Borrow Books"), or drearily functional ("Washrooms on the Third Floor"). You would think librarians have no reverence for the word when they display only that sort of thing. And the lettering style usually seems better suited to a supermarket or a discount house, than to a building whose reason for being is to preserve and propagate and celebrate the recorded word.

To adorn the blank spaces on library walls, librarians commonly exhibit pictures instead of words, sometimes in such profusion one feels he may have entered an art museum by mistake. Yet proper words properly written make beautiful pictures, and not to the mind's eye alone.

Why not enliven library walls with beautiful words instead of pictures? Writing on walls is, after all, an ancient and widely practiced mode of communication, and not always disreputable: consider, for example, the monumental lettering in the Jefferson Memorial, or the classical quotations Montaigne inscribed on the walls of his tower study. You find graffiti everywhere: in subway stations, on the bark of trees, in vespasiennes — but never on the walls of libraries, where of all places they have a proper claim to be.

Yielding to an irresistible impulse to write on library walls, but lacking the rare talent to make the beautiful letters we wanted to see there, we commissioned Miss Judith Duncan to do our wall writing for us. Miss Duncan is a librarian at the University of Minnesota, and an expert calligrapher (literally "maker of beautiful letters"). Since the graffiti she has made are beautiful both to behold and to read — qualities rarely found in your ordinary wall writing — we needed another name than graffiti to indicate the distinction, and so coined the word calligraffiti to convey their special nature: "beautiful wall writings."

The letter shapes Miss Duncan uses are mainly derived from the two great scribal bookhands of the Middle Ages, the Carolingian minuscule (800-1300 A.D.) and the Gothic, a 14th century evolutionary development of the Carolingian. And occasionally Miss Duncan employs hands of her own devising, to reflect some special character of the text — as in Herrick's poem "On Julia's Clothes."

Our celebration of the beauty of the word, in its visual as well as its intellectual aspects, will be a permanent offering of the library: an inducement for readers to form an acquaintance with authors new to them, and a perpetual reminder to all that lettering — the most practical and widely practiced of all the arts — is indeed the art of arts.

(Calligraffiti in the show were purchased by
the library with a portion of the funds generously
provided by Mr. Charles E. Ferguson for the
establishment of Macalester's Word Library.
None of the items in the show is for sale ❧)

The text of this brochure ❧
was composed by Daniel Gore
& calligraphed by Judith Duncan
during the tenth month of 1973,
for the joy of doing ❧

EVALUATION OF THE CURRENT ACQUISITIONS (PROFILE) PROGRAM

"To the mind as to the eye," said the redoubtable Dr. Johnson, "it is difficult to compare objects vast in their extent, or various in their parts." So when it comes to comparing and judging libraries, practically everyone ignores their parts, and judges them by their bulk: the bigger the better. The assumption is not wholly unreasonable, for the more books you buy, the better the chance you will acquire the necessary good books along with the masses of mediocre ones. But sheer bulk is no sure sign of quality in a library, any more than it is in a lady. It can indeed mean just the opposite, especially where the prompt acquisition of notable new books is concerned.

Qualitative evaluation of retrospective holdings -- books, say, more than ten years old -- is a fairly simple matter. You simply check your holdings against standard, critical bibliographies of relevant subject areas to discover what percentage of their listings the library owns.

Evaluating current acquisitions is more difficult, since no standard guides are available. One therefore usually ignores the problem, or approaches it impressionistically.

In a quarter of a century of reading book reviews in The New Yorker, I have observed an editorial practice that is possibly unique with that journal. Only books likely to appeal to a highly literate, cultured audience are chosen for review, and rarely is a book panned. It is not because the reviewers are irresponsibly charitable, or mindless, that so few books are condemned; but rather that The New Yorker uses its reviews not to warn readers away from books but to attract them to the very few (about one in a hundred) the editors think worthy of an intelligent, sophisticated reader's attention. The fact that a book is chosen for review in The New Yorker is a distinction in itself.

If one is willing, as I am, to accept The New Yorker reviews as a gauge of a library's coverage of notable new books, then it is possible to go beyond mere impressionism in judging the adequacy of a current acquisitions program. Although not a comprehensive criterion, The New Yorker appears useful as a weather vane, to indicate directions and general tendencies.

Why be concerned with the acquisition of significant new books, when in the course of time they will all become old books, and thus susceptible of more reliable evaluation?

The answer is that demand for books is usually at its peak when they are new. At Macalester some 20% of faculty loans are of books from the FASTCAT shelves, books whose average age is about one year. Yet that collection represents only 3.5% of total holdings, so demand for them is six times greater than the average. For an academic clientele, having new books available when they are new is a significant measure of a library's quality, no matter what its size may be.

For a comparative measure of the adequacy of our current acquisitions program, I have used recent New Yorker reviews to test not only our own holdings, but also those of the University of Minnesota and three neighboring college libraries (designated as Library A, B, and C). To get some indication of the relative speed with which new books are acquired, I have used two different runs of New Yorker reviews.

One run consists of all titles reviewed in calendar 1973, excluding mystery and detective novels, and insignificant works of fiction. In this group there are 252 titles, most of them published from one to two years prior to the time I checked them in the catalogs of the five libraries (mid-June 1974).

The other run consists of all titles (with the same exceptions) reviewed in the January-March 1974 issues of The New Yorker -- books that for the most part were three to twelve months old when the holdings check was made.

Here are the results of the holdings checks in the catalogs of 5 libraries:

TITLES FROM 1973 NEW YORKER REVIEWS

	Mac	U of M	A	B	C
Holds	151 60%	169 67%	139 55%	81 32%	8 3%
Lacks	101 40%	83 33%	113 45%	171 68%	244 97%
	252	252	252	252	252

TITLES FROM JAN.-MARCH 1974 NEW YORKER REVIEWS

	Mac	U of M	A	B	C
Holds	30 46%	16 25%	20 31%	10 15%	0
Lacks	35 54%	49 75%	45 69%	55 85%	65 100%
	65	65	65	65	65

Observations and Comment

No library holds such a high percentage of the sample as to suggest it may be using New Yorker reviews as a selection guide. The Macalester Library definitely does not, except as a backup to the profile program, and in the present instance, after the survey was made. If any library were using The New Yorker as a buying guide, our sample here could not be an unbiased criterion for comparing acquisitions performance.

The Macalester Library is the only one of the five that uses a profile acquisitions program.

Macalester, the University, and Library A all use some form of temporary catalog entry to signal promptly the availability of new books. Libraries B and C do not. For purposes of this survey a title is counted as not held when there is no entry for it in the public catalog. Whether it was on order or being processed is immaterial, since it would not normally be available to the public.

For titles reviewed in the 1973 New Yorker, Macalester shows up slightly worse than the University, and slightly better than Library A. Libraries B and C are far behind the other three.

For titles reviewed in the 1974 New Yorker, Macalester scores nearly twice as high as the University, fifty percent higher than Library A, and many times higher than Libraries B and C.

On this comparative showing the coverage of notable new books provided by Macalester's profile approach is quite good. The promptness with which new books are made available is not approached by any of the other four libraries.

Although our comparative standing is excellent, there are lapses in our selection that should spare us from complacency. For example, it is not easy to understand how we could have missed such obvious books as Kafka's Letters to Felice, D. H. Lawrence's John Thomas and Lady Jane, Joan Noble's Recollections of Virginia Woolf, Ezra Pound's Selected Prose, Whitney Seymour's Why Justice Fails, or C. L. Sulzberger's Age of Mediocrity. (All have since been ordered, of course.) The percentage of such failures is at least small enough that one might expect them to be remedied eventually by haphazard. But nothing will compensate for the fact that those books were not available when they were brand new -- except of course that many of them could have been borrowed for our readers through the CLIC interloan network.

Of the 317 titles checked, 26 were available only at Macalester; 22 were available only at the University; 17 at Library A; 6 at Library B; and none at Library C. Overall, 22% of the titles were unique to the library holding them, whereas 16% were held by none of the five libraries.

The results of this comparative qualitative analysis corroborate the general impression I have received from random faculty comments:that the Profile/ FASTCAT combination accomplishes the one thing they have always most wanted from a library -- swift delivery of notable new books.

(The survey list of 317 titles is on file in the Library office.)

Collection Statistics

During the year 11,330 volumes (or other units) were added to the collections, bringing the total to 255,610 items, of which 244,254 are bound volumes of books and journals. The median collection size of all colleges having similar programs and enrollment is about 100,000 volumes.

Items Added 1973/74

Category	Volumes (or units)
Books	8,885
Bound periodicals and abstracts	796
Newspaper and periodical indexes	11
Microfilm reels	628
Microfiche	0
Records and tapes	1,516
Total:	11,836
Book witdrawals:	506
Net increase	11,330

Total Resources September 1, 1974

Category	Volumes (or units)
Books	216,777
Bound periodicals and abstracts	27,118
Newspaper and periodical indexes	359
Microfilm reels	4,165
Microfiche	2,410
Records and tapes	4,781
Total:	255,610

<u>Subscriptions in Force September 1, 1974</u>

Newspapers	50
Journals	899
Other serials	491

2. <u>Cataloging and Reclassification</u>

In February 1974 we concluded the 3 1/2 year long project of reclassify-
ing the collections from the Dewey to the Library of Congress (LC) system. The
LC system has been applied to all books acquired since 1968, the change being
made simply because it costs about a dollar less per book to use LC than Dewey.
Whether LC is the intellectually better system is a moot question, for as the
distinguished Argentine author and librarian Jorge Luis Borges avers, "There is
no classification of the universe that is not arbitrary and conjectural. The
reason is very simple: we do not know what the universe is." But we do know
what the comparative costs of classification are, and they point decisively to
LC as the system of choice.

Converting pre-1968 collections from Dewey to LC was a task formidable in
scope, swift in pace. Some 82,000 volumes in all were reclassed during the
3 1/2 year period. But instead of adding processing staff to handle this extraordinary additional workload, we reduced the complement from 7 to 2.75 FTE
positions as the project moved along. Substantial gains in operating efficiency made possible the simultaneous reduction in staff and increase in production.

Cataloging statistics for the last five years are as follow:

	1969/70	1970/71	1971/72	1972/73	1973/74
Volumes reclassed	1,908	25,923	26,778	24,891	4,303
Volumes cataloged	10,909	11,094	8,298	10,911	11,565
Volumes withdrawn	3,331	3,524	2,062	665	506
Total units processed	16,148	40,541	37,138	36,467	16,374

B. Circulation Department

Total recorded circulation for the year comes to 80,860, an increase over the previous year of about 4% while enrollment dropped 7%. FASTCAT loans increased more than 50% over previous years, although size and composition of the collection remained fairly constant. In fall of 1973, at the suggestion of Steve Olson, a Macalester student, we began leaving dust wrappers on new books during their FASTCAT phase, and this practice may have stimulated much of the increased interest in FASTCATs. Reserve loans rose 16% from improved service and record keeping under Mrs. Kellar's full-time supervision. Cassette loans increased eight-fold, after the formation last fall of a sizeable new collection of music and spoken recordings on tape. Loans of curriculum materials declined for the sixth successive year by about 30%. Use of that collection is about 1/6 of what it was in 1967/68.

Circulation Statistics 1973/74

Category	Weyerhaeuser		Olin	
	Students	Faculty	Students	Faculty
Books (general)	44,846	3,854	929	189
FASTCAT	3,704	1,016	44	55
Curriculum Lab	810	31		
College catalogs & pamphlets	21	1		
Paperbacks & mysteries	214	108		
Cassettes	3,387 (students and faculty)			
Government documents	97	6		
Juvenile	1,769	346		
Phonodiscs	1,089	82		
Art Rentals		28		
Periodicals	2,679 (students and faculty)			
Storage	479 (students and faculty)		60	29
Reserve	14,134		853	
Totals:	73,229	5,472	1,886	273
Combined:	78,701		2,159	
Both libraries:	80,860			

Per capita use of the Macalester Library is substantially higher than that of neighboring institutions. The comparative data on the following page bear out the common belief that Macalester students pursue their academic work with most uncommon vigor.

CIRCULATION STATISTICS FOR THE FIVE COLLEGE CONSORTIUM, 1973/74*

College	Enrollment Fall 1973	Books	Journals	Audio Visual	Reserves	Other	Interlibrary Loans	Total Loans	Loans per capita
Augsburg	1,703	20,392	3,231	111	9,104	-	1,137	33,975	19.9
Hamline	1,327	18,769	4,908	218	7,940	1,230	2,822	35,887	27.0
Macalester	1,876	55,247	2,790	3,093	16,452	3,248	3,448	84,278	44.8
St. Catherine	1,688	38,853	7,431	2,598	4,103	2,970	1,313	57,268	33.9
St. Thomas	1,928	22,787	501	no record	17,257	-	2,102	42,647	22.1

*Data supplied by Andrea Honebrink, CLIC Coordinator

Analysis of FASTCAT Collection Use

Since FASTCAT books are in much higher relative demand than any others, and since the collection is relatively small, we recently made a study of the use of that collection to see how well the selection of new books conformed to current reader interests.

On October 24, 1974, there were 7,710 volumes in the FASTCAT collection, of which 6,101 were on the shelves, and 1,609 on loan.

With rare exceptions these 7,710 volumes represent profile orders. The time period during which the books were received by the Library and first shelved runs generally from January 1972 through October 24, 1974. The average shelf age of a book in FASTCAT is thus about 11 months, but the average varies from one subject class to another owing to variances in the proportion of books removed from each class for permanent cataloging and transfer to the general collections. The median shelf age of all books is about twelve months.

In the academic year 1973/74, there were 4,819 recorded loans of FASTCAT books, and 48,700 recorded loans of books from the general collections. FAST-CATs thus accounted for 9% of all regular book loans, although the FASTCAT collection represents only 3.5% of the total collection of 216,777 books. On that showing it appears that the average demand rate for FASTCATs is nearly triple that for the general collection.

Faculty loans of FASTCATs were 20.5% of total faculty book loans in 1973/74, indicating a demand rate for FASTCATs nearly six times that for the general collection. Faculty interest in new books is vividly illuminated by their heavy borrowing of FASTCATs.

Just as in the general collections, demand on the FASTCAT collection is very unevenly distributed. Of the 7,710 volumes in the collection, 4,396 have not circulated once since they were acquired. The number of books not circulated thus averages 57% overall, but the average varies widely from one subject grouping to another. Among Best Sellers, 5% have not circulated once; of the Russian collection, 89% show no recorded use. The figure for Psychology is 25%, for History 70%, for English 64%, and for Spanish 85%. (Data for all areas are presented on the chart on page 276.)

The percentage of FASTCATs on loan on October 24, 1974, when the survey was made, also merits attention. Of the 7,710 volume collection, 1,609, or 22%, were on loan. This compares with 3,300 volumes on loan at the same time from the 209,000 volume general collections, representing 1.6% of the total.

Distribution of FASTCATs currently on loan varies widely from subject to subject. Thus 46% of Psychology FASTCATs are on loan, 9% of History, 16% of English, 7% of Russian, 1% of Spanish, 33% of French, and 50% of Art. There is a positive (though uneven) correlation between the percent of books on loan in a subject area, and the percent that have circulated at least once. This correlation confirms the typical dilemma that books in relatively high demand are also those least likely to be available when one wants to borrow them. Spanish, with only 1% of its books currently on loan, has had only 15% of its collection borrowed at least once; and Psychology, with 46% of its FASTCATs on loan, has had 75% of its books borrowed at least once. The relatively low (38%) on-loan figure for Best Sellers, which have the highest use (95%) results from a special loan period of one week for those books, as compared with the three week period for all other FASTCATs.

FASTCAT volumes, like those in the general collections, are systematically duplicated as use levels warrant. FASTCATs on extended faculty loan are usually duplicated only when a patron requests it, since they return from loan too seldom to generate a loan record evidencing heavy use.

The predictable future demand for books that do not circulate once during their first year on the shelf is so low as to raise some doubt about the College's need to own them. Those that remain two years or more unused on the

FASTCAT shelves have near-zero probability of ever being borrowed.

Notes on FASTCAT Procedures

When a new book is ordered by the Library, it is assigned an order number consisting of two elements: a letter code (derived from the Library of Congress classification outline) designating the academic department initiating the order, and a serial number indicating the book is the nth volume purchased by the department for the FASTCAT Collection. Thus the 1,000th volume ordered by the English Department has the order number PR 1000. The order number QA 25 indicates the 25th volume ordered by the Math Department.

When the order is placed with the jobber, a copy of the order slip is filed in the TITLE section (only) of the card catalog.

When the book arrives, its order number is typed on a label and attached to the spine, where it becomes the book's call number during its FASTCAT phase. Normally the book is shelved in FASTCAT within 24 hours after the Library receives it.

A tape is attached to the order slip in the TITLE catalog, stating the book is available on FASTCAT. Since the order slip bears the book's order number, its call number is thus available to readers.

A FASTCAT ordinarily remains in the FASTCAT collection for 18 to 24 months before it is removed for permanent cataloging. By then Library of Congress catalog copy is available more than 95% of the time, and the FASTCAT remains in the catalog work room only two or three days while metamorphosing into a general collection item. When LC copy is not available, the book is immediately returned to the FASTCAT shelf and allowed to wait another year for permanent cataloging.

SUBJECT ANALYSIS OF FASTCAT USE

FASTCAT CLASS	Vols. in Class	Vols. on Shelf	Vols. on Loan	% on Loan	Vols. on Shelf Borrowed at Least Once	Total Vols. Borrowed at Least Once	% Borrowed at Least Once	Median Shelf Age of Volumes	% Adjustment for 12 mo. Median	Adjusted % Borrowed at Least Once in 12 mos.
B - Philosophy	188	134	54	28.9	52	106	56.4	11 mos.	+ 9	62.5
BF - Psychology	323	174	149	46.2	92	241	74.6	9.5	+26	93.8
BL - Religion	302	246	56	18.5	86	142	47.0	11	+ 9	51.2
D - History	1,268	1,159	109	8.6	273	382	30.1	12	0	30.1
G - Geography	234	178	56	23.0	71	127	54.3	10.5	+14	62.0
GV - Phys. Ed.	65	45	20	30.9	24	44	67.7	5.5	+118	100
HB - Economics	272	170	102	37.7	63	165	60.7	13	-8	55.9
HM - Sociology	569	363	206	36.3	101	307	54.0	9	+33	72.0
J - Pol. Sci.	624	488	136	21.8	120	256	41.0	12.2	-2	40.2
L - Education	219	173	46	21.0	44	90	41.1	11	+9	44.8
M - Music	130	97	33	25.4	18	51	39.2	8.3	+45	57.0
N - Art	79	39	40	51.0	19	59	74.7	14.5	-17	62.0
PA - Classics	99	70	29	29.4	19	48	48.5	8.8	+36	66.0
PG - Russian	217	202	15	6.9	21	36	10.6	11	+9	11.5
PN - Speech/Theatre	196	171	25	12.8	75	100	51.0	13	-8	46.9
PNA - Journalism	47	37	10	21.2	17	27	57.4	9	+33	76.5
PQ - French	141	94	47	33.3	20	67	67.1	6.8	+76	100
PQA - Spanish	227	225	2	1.0	33	35	15.4	9	+33	20.4
PR - English	1,422	1,197	225	15.8	286	511	35.9	12.2	-2	35.2
PT - German	264	215	49	18.6	17	66	25.0	9.8	+22	30.4
QA - Mathematics	88	64	24	27.3	21	45	51.1	8.2	+46	74.7
QC - Physics	66	42	24	36.5	12	36	54.5	14.5	-17	45.2
QD - Chemistry	139	108	31	22.3	38	69	49.6	15.8	-24	37.6
QE - Geology	141	130	11	7.8	32	43	30.5	17	-29	21.5
QH - Biology	269	202	67	24.9	86	153	56.9	12.2	-2	55.8
X - Miscellaneous	17	8	9	53.0	0	9	52.9	1.2	+1000	100
Y - Best Sellers	104	70	34	32.7	65	99	95.2	5	+230	100
Totals:	7,710	6,101	1,609	21.9%	1,705	3,314	43.2%			

Median figure in this column is 55.9%

The size of the FASTCAT collection remains fairly constant, even though four or five thousand volumes are added to it each year. As new FASTCATs are added, the oldest ones are removed and permanently cataloged for the general collections.

FASTCAT is exclusively a collection of new books. Books acquired when more than a year or so old bypass the FASTCAT collection and are permanently cataloged on receipt.

Shelving Capacity of Libraries

A precise inventory of shelving was taken on August 24, 1973 and the results reported in last year's Annual Report. The estimated condition as of September 1974 is this:

Building	Shelf Feet	Book Feet	Load Factor
Weyerhaeuser	26,733	19,500	73%
Olin	1,479	1,400	95%
Storage	6,930	4,000	58%

While the space situation in Weyerhaeuser is still tolerable, the Olin Library is fully loaded and some decision must be taken shortly regarding future housing of that collection.

Background of the Olin Space Problem

The Olin Library opened in 1965, equipped with 1,479 linear feet of book shelving. No architectural provision was made for future expansion of shelving capacity, nor is there any material in the library files indicating any

strategy for dealing with the problem that would arise when shelfload reached
100% capacity.

In recent years the Olin collection has grown at a rate of about 100 to
150 ft. per year. Assuming the acquisitions budget continues at its present
level, the growth rate will decline somewhat as a result of inflation, but
will still be substantial in relation to total shelving capacity.

The Olin Library is now at 100% capacity. Within the next ten years the
collection will probably double in size.

There being no possibility of doubling the space in Olin for library purposes, the remaining options for accommodating future growth are these:

(1) Create a no-growth collection by removing to storage each year as
     many linear feet of books and journals as are added each year.

(2) Expand present shelf capacity of Olin by replacing conventional
     stacks with compact stacks.

The No-Growth Solution

The Library Committee met twice with the Olin Department chairmen in
1973/74 to discuss possible solutions to the growth problem.

At the first meeting I suggested the simplest first step would be to follow the approach taken at Weyerhaeuser in the fall of 1970, when it became
necessary suddenly to remove some 10,000 volumes because of a progressive
structural failure on the main floor of the Library. The decision taken at
that time was to remove to storage virtually all journal volumes published
more than five years ago.

The reasons for that approach are two:

(1) It is well known that demand levels on journal literature approach

zero after the fifth year of its life. (At the U. of Chicago, for example, the average demand for a serial volume is once every 300 years.)

This journal demand phenomenon thus provides a straightforward, easily applied statistical criterion for identifying items that can be removed to storage with little inconvenience to users of the library.

(2) Removing journal volumes to storage requires minimal changing of inventory and cataloging records. One simply announces that, with stated exceptions, all journal volumes beyond a certain date are shelved in storage.

Of the **thousand** or so journal titles then shelved in Weyerhaeuser, only twelve were initially retained in their entire runs in Weyerhaeuser, because demand for them was known to be particularly great (New Yorker, Time, Newsweek, and suchlike journals). Subsequent experience indicated that about half a dozen other titles should have been kept intact, and their backruns were then returned from storage.

The decision to remove journal backruns has withstood well the test of experience. Average demand rate on the storage collection is about 1/10 the rate for the general collection, and user dissatisfaction has accordingly been extremely low. Only one complaint has come to my office in the four years since the decision had to be made, and that one came in the shock of the immediate aftermath of having some 10,000 volumes suddenly vanish from a convenient and familiar location.

The Olin chairmen tentatively agreed that a similar approach might be best for the space problem in the Olin Library, and were invited to study the situation and propose a cutoff date criterion, plus a list of titles to be kept in Olin in their entire runs. From that data the library staff would then measure the space that would thus be freed up, so we would all know to what extent these measures would solve the problem.

At our second meeting one chairman raised another possibility, that the journal overflow be distributed among various departmental storage rooms in Olin, so Olin faculty would have ready access to these volumes. I demurred to this suggestion for the following reasons:

(1) The available space as described probably would not absorb more than a one or two year growth of the library, which would amount only to a brief postponement of the problem. (Subsequent inspection of that space has confirmed its deficiency as to capacity.)

(2) Dispersal of the collection in this manner would make it exceedingly difficult of use to all except those who possessed keys to the respective storage areas, and impossible for the library to administer.

As another alternative to our central storage area under the Dining Commons, we then agreed to investigate the possibility of using the Rice Hall storage area jointly with the Housing Office, which now utilizes that space to store dorm furniture, etc. The three chairmen and I inspected the area, and the reaction was mainly negative, with one chairman suggesting the area had "possibilities." The problem is not space, which is ample, but other things, among them:

(a) Though under a common roof with Olin, the area is quite remote and difficult of access. For those who frequently eat at the Dining Commons, the storage collection there is more convenient.

(b) The Housing Office is unwilling to distribute keys to their storage area, so access would be possible only when the area was staffed with library personnel. Open hours for Dining Commons storage are 10 hours per week; half that would probably suffice for an ancillary storage area.

(c) The area is generally forbidding in appearance, and, as one chairman noted, "depressing."

While no option is foreclosed at this moment, the Rice Hall possibility now seems generally unappealing, so I asked the three chairmen to propose criteria acceptable to them if the Dining Commons option were followed.

They did so, as follows:

(1) Journal volumes more than 10 years old to be removed to storage.

(2) Of the (approximately) 67 titles currently subscribed to, all but 13 shall be kept in their entire runs in Olin.

Measurements were made based on these specifications, and the result of applying them today would be to remove to storage about 125 linear feet of journals, and about 10 ft. per year each year hereafter.

Since the collection is growing at about 150 ft. per year, the problem will not be solved by this approach. Other related possibilities to consider are these:

(1) Reduce the cutoff date criterion;

(2) Reduce the number of journal titles kept in entire runs;

(3) Develop criteria for removing monographs to storage;

(4) Add conventional shelving units in the library, and thus postpone the problem for a couple of years, perhaps with some sacrifice of seating capacity;

(5) Replace all journal backruns with microfilm where available; potentially very costly unless we could find a buyer for our backruns.

(6) Some combination of the above.

The Compact-Stack Solution

This option, if exercised, would at least double present shelf capacity without curtailing seating capacity, and thus accommodate growth for another decade, after which it appears the no-growth option would have to be exercised.

Because of the dense load it carries, compact shelving must be supported on floors having 160 lb/sq. ft. live load capacity. Mr. Asuncion advises that the building may possibly have the requisite structural capacity. If the College is minded to consider this option further, a structural engineer should be consulted for a precise evaluation.

3,000 linear feet of compact shelving would double present shelving capacity, and cost about $20,000 installed. Then ten years hence it will be loaded to capacity, and the College will face the shelving problem again.

Up to this point I have not thought compact shelving a realistic option, as I have tried for four years, without success, to obtain funds for compact shelving in Weyerhaeuser.

C. Reserves

Total activity was nearly 50% greater than in 1972/73, partly because loans of certain non-reserve items (best sellers and cassette tapes) were added to the unit's responsibilities. Improved services and record-keeping under Mrs. Kellar's full-time supervision are also reflected in the statistical leap.

Count of Items Placed on Reserve

		Books	Articles	Tapes	Total
Fall	1970/71	785	320		1,105
	1971/72	858	424		1,282
	1972/73	769	392		1,161
	1973/74	948	745	56	1,749
Interim	1970/71	31	33		64
	1971/72	80	346		426
	1972/73	142	85		227
	1973/74	96	21		117
Spring	1970/71	527	215		742
	1971/72	887	695		1,582
	1972/73	1,184	824		2,008
	1973/74	946	806	56	1,808
Summer	1970/71	48	37		85
	1971/72	100	39		139
	1972/73	420	232		652
	1973/74	193	32		225

D. Periodicals

Subscription statistics as of August 31 for each of the last three fiscal years are as follows:

	1971/72	1972/73	1973/74
Subscriptions added (previous 12 mos.)	38	21	49
Subscriptions dropped	178	73	153
Subscriptions in force	1,055	1,003	899
Paid			748
Gift			151

During the year 796 journal volumes were bound by library staff.

E. Reference Department

　　Besides providing the usual range of reference services, the staff also taught formal courses in general bibliography and in the bibliography of government documents. Both courses were offered in fall and spring terms.

Interlibrary Loans

Items Delivered to Macalester Patrons

Source	1970/71 Number	1970/71 % of Requests	1971/72 Number	1971/72 % of Requests	1972/73 Number	1972/73 % of Requests	1973/74 Number	1973/74 % of Requests
Cour-ier	2,715	65						
CLIC	513	35	3,316	69	2,949	78	3,287	82
Others	171	71	126	55	92	46	48	50
Totals	3,399	58%	3,442	68%	3,041	77%	3,335	82%

　　The rate of non-delivery of interloan requests has dropped from 42% to 18% over the last four years. In 1973/74 the Library satisfied 95% of all requests for journal articles through interloan, and 71% of all book requests. Our CLIC interloan network presently gives access to some 3,000,000 different books, and 30,000 journals in the Twin Cities. Most requests are filled within 48 hours, at no cost to the patron, whether student or faculty.

Items Loaned to Other Libraries

	1970/71 Number	1970/71 % of Requests	1971/72 Number	1971/72 % of Requests	1972/73 Number	1972/73 % of Requests	1973/74 Number	1973/74 % of Requests
CLIC	424	51	1,007	59	975	64	1,260	71
Others	14	70	10	100	8	47	230	99
Totals	438	51%	1,017	59%	983	64%	1,490	74%

Loan of items to other libraries more than tripled over the last four years, while the satisfaction rate climbed from 51% to 74%. Of the 230 items lent to non-CLIC libraries in 1973/74, 210 were copies of the Library's Annual Reports.

F. Audio Visual Department

The statistical summary on the following page indicates a steep decline --nearly 40%--in the loan of AV equipment for classroom and other use. What appears to cause the drop is the increasing number of departments and students who buy their own AV equipment. When, for example, a sociology class of 100 students learns that the course requires repeated use of a portable cassette recorder, many students will buy their own rather than compete with classmates, and the rest of the College, for the 20 units available for loan from AV. Our staff devoted much time during the year helping individuals and departments select and buy their own equipment.

Production and other services showed an increase of 15%, practically all of it in the making of ditto masters. Use of darkroom facilities shows a steady decline since they were first provided three years ago. According to the previous head of the AV Department, this results from the creation, or reactivation, of other darkrooms on campus "in imitation of the facility in Audio-Visual."

Film continues to be the leading AV medium in the classroom, and much staff time is spent searching catalogs and scheduling and controlling rentals. Our own film collection grew by several dozen items, most notably the Kenneth Clark Civilisation series (held jointly with CLIC), plus films treating minority groups and ecological issues.

A descriptive catalog of our film holdings was prepared during the year, and recently distributed.

In addition to its usual services, the department continued to be the production arm of the Library's cassette recording project. During the year 600 musical and 112 spoken records were taped for loan at the Library's Reserve Desk.

AV Loans and Services

Equipment Loans	1971/72	1972/73	1973/74
Motion Picure Projector	973	920	921
Slide projectors	393	524	317
Filmstrip projectors	65	160	59
Overhead projectors	285	284	146
Opaque projectors	117	147	101
Screens	241	263	129
Tape recorders	794	1,143	571
Phonographs	125	150	80
Cameras	-	184	47
Portable VTR	90	120	32
Studio VTR	151	59	64
Portable Public Address	90	120	32
Public Address Systems	51	32	10
	3,375	4,015	2,509

Services			
Our films booked	391	475	505
Other films booked	476	305	319
Slides and b/w prints	4,850	3,327	2,889
Rolls film sold	-	939	1,533
Tapes - sold and dubbed	415	1,121	1,080
Transparencies made	906	856	494
Ditto masters made	2,038	1,869	3,530
Signs made	449	470	380
	9,525	9,362	10,730

V. PLANNING FOR A NEW BUILDING

Pending some progress in raising funds, planning is being held in abeyance.

VI. STAFF ACTIVITIES

Mrs. Archibald taught the course "Methods of Research in Government Publications" in the fall and spring terms. She served as Secretary of the Government Documents Round Table of the Minnesota Library Association, and participated in the Federal Documents Regional Workshop in Chicago. Throughout the year she was a member of the CLIC Grants Committee. In April 1973 Mrs. Archibald addressed the Women's Book Club of Macalester, speaking on "Sinclair Lewis in the Twin Cities" and on the Library's collection of Lewisiana.

Mrs. Archibald supervised an Interim project in government documents undertaken by Natalie Swit, a Macalester freshman. As part of the project Miss Swit developed a bibliography of significant documents on contemporary issues -- energy crisis, consumer problems, environment, health care, etc. -- and then acquired 150 of them as gifts to the Library, through correspondence with nineteen U. S. Representatives and Senators.

Dr. Dickinson was awarded the Master's degree in Library Science at the University of Minnesota. He taught the "Introduction to Bibliography" course in the fall and spring terms, and during Interim supervised eight interns in archaeology at the Minnesota Historical Society, and one independent in library science. During the summer he attended a week-long Workshop in Photographic Techniques sponsored by the University of Minnesota.

Ms. Francis learned to operate the computerized segment of the Library's circulation system, and during the summer enrolled in Math 15 to develop the added expertise that enabled her to improve the existing computer program.

Mr. Gore served on the Staff Advisory Council, the Library Committee, the Curriculum Committee, and the Executive Board of CLIC. In the spring term he taught a course in Anglo-Saxon language and literature. The following items by Mr. Gore were published or presented during the year:

> Bibliography for Beginners. 2nd ed. New York: Appleton-
> Century-Crofts, 1973.
>
> Management Problems in Serials Work. Edited with Peter Spyers-Duran.
> Westport, Conn.: Greenwood Press, 1974.
>
> "Sawing Off the Horns of a Dilemma," in Management Problems in
> Serials Work, pp. 104-114.
>
> "The Destruction of the Book by Oversewn Binding--And How to
> Prevent It," in Management Problems in Serials Work,
> pp. 121-128.
>
> "Let Them Eat Cake While Reading Catalog Cards; An Essay on the
> Availability Problem," paper presented to a meeting of the
> Association of College and Research Libraries, Chatham
> College, Pittsburgh, April 27, 1974.

During the year Mrs. Salscheider completed two courses in Library Science at the College of St. Catherine.

VII. PROBLEMS PRESENT AND DISTANT

Securing adequate hours of student help is our only present problem of much consequence. Having no authority to mandate solutions to it, we repeatedly appeal to others for help with it, and the ensuing temporary relief enables us to move on from one crisis to the next. Knowing this problem besets other units on campus, and believing better remedies are possible than those thus far devised, we call again upon the College's administration to develop a lasting cure for this chronic ailment.

Such problems of building space as we now have can be satisfactorily resolved for at least four more years without a new building, and without any

bold departures from conventional library practice. But if the fund raising
effort does not mature and flourish within that period, Macalester, like many
other colleges around the nation, may be obliged to revise fundamentally its
concept of what an academic library should be.

This problems-list is as brief, as my Reports have been long over the
past four years, enumerating the scores of problems taken on and swiftly solved
by the combined endeavors of the Library staff. I know that many people at the
College share my abiding gratitude for the quality and amplitude of their
accomplishments, and for the amiable but resolute spirit in which their work is
done. I admire the industry of this staff, their talents, and their faithfulness to their vocation; and I applaud their achievements.

Macalester College

Annual Report of the Library
1974·1975

St. Paul, Minnesota

■ WEYERHAEUSER LIBRARY

February 14, 1976

Dr. A. Truman Schwartz
Dean of the Faculty
Macalester College
St. Paul, Minnesota

Dear Truman:

My library reports are like the tropical lightning: they are
liable to strike any time. This summing up of library accomplishments in the academic year 1974/75 was meant to reach you
by last Thanksgiving, but a disc and a nerve conspired behind
my back to turn an Annual Report into a Valentine. And it may
be so read, as a testament of the Library staff's good will to
all at the College who benefit from their collective labors.
As you reflect upon this chronicle of a year's work, I think
you will conclude, as I have done, that a great measure of good
will must have been superadded to the abundant talent and energy
which the people of the Library have applied to a task that,
five years ago, required twice their number to get it done.

The calligraphy and illustrations are again this year the work
of our sybilline friend Judith Anne Duncan, who will tell us no
more of their hermetic import than that the drawings depict
"the Four Benevolent Beasts of Chinese mythology." The press-
work was done by Jerry Johnston and the Department of Printology,
a group that always turns out fine printing for us on amazingly
short schedules.

Some people cannot hold a job; others can't keep a boss. The
Library has reported to four different people since 1970. With
your incumbency we had particularly hoped that a season of continuity in administrative relationships had begun. Good luck
in bosses can't last forever. We keenly regret your recently
announced decision to give up administration next fall for the
cooler ambience of thermodynamics, but wish you serenity and
success in that energetic concern.

Sincerely,

Daniel Gore
Library Director

CONTENTS

I.   INTRODUCTION

In case no one but David White has noticed--I had lost sight of the fact
myself until he recently discovered it and graciously re-awakened me to it--
the Library concluded in 1974/75 a long revolution without a revolt. It began
five years earlier, and as it ran its course every library function was radically
altered, and useless (but costly) activities were simply dropped, such as the
compilation and distribution of monthly accessions lists.

Some changes were highly visible: the creation of FASTCAT; the transfer
of the card catalogs to the Reference Room, and of the Reserve Desk to the main
floor; the relocation of the Circulation Desk and the two-step reduction of the
general loan period from a full semester to three weeks. Some changes were less
noticeable: the reclassification of 82,000 volumes (when that large project was
nearly done, a student wrote us to ask when it would begin); the shifting of
practically every volume in Weyerhaeuser to make more efficient use of scarce
shelf space; and the reduction of staff positions from 24 to 11. Still other
changes were practically invisible: a steep decline in operating costs; much
improved availability of books we own; and a ten-fold increase in interlibrary
loan services. The full account of the whole revolution is spread through this
and each Annual Report of the four preceding years.

Few people really enjoy change, even when they understand it is necessary
and believe that it may prove beneficial. Risks must be taken when necessity
dictates revolutionary change, and sometimes we feared being figuratively hoist
on our own petard--or literally crushed beneath our own card catalog. In the
night that followed the day the catalog was moved to the Reference Room, I awoke

with the unsatisfactory realization that I had failed to ask the campus engineer whether the floor would carry the heavy load. I had been used to working in newer buildings with floors designed to carry anything you might think to put on them. Inspection of Weyerhaeuser by the engineer early the next morning--and all subsequent experience--confirmed that the catalog would not make an unplanned descent to the ground floor. No crashes, no explosions, no loud noises.

Most of the changes, but certainly not all of them, were well received at the outset. Some of them gradually won general favor among our patrons after a scratchy trial period; and one or two are here and there still cordially despised, despite our recurring effort to explain their obscure virtues. Our microfilm circulation control system occasionally stirs warm passions because one cannot tell (as one could with its unholy manual predecessor) just who has a given book on loan, unless and until it falls overdue. Re-calling books from loan is therefore not possible. With the previous system it was--though the books rarely or never came back anyhow. When we realized that our average success was much greater in acquiring a wanted book through interloan than through re-calling it from loan, we decided to shift to the microfilm system, simply because it provides far more accurate and dependable control than a manual file, and does it at a staff cost about $15,000 less per year than we had been paying for a system that mainly yielded chaos--and the occasional spiritual comfort of at least knowing who had borrowed an urgently needed book, though he would not return it. Some day we expect to have a fully automated circulation system, and it will do everything that anyone could reasonably hope for, except reduce the cost of circulation control.

We are true believers in the maxim, "When it is not necessary to change,

it is necessary not to change." Change for its own sake is a bad joke on everyone, for it produces nothing but frustration and apprehension. Few changes were
made last year for few were needed. But refinements continued to be made in a
complex pattern of operations that is still rather new to us, with the notable
result that staff positions could be reduced by a further 15 percent at the beginning of the 1975/76 academic year.

The pages that follow tell as much as most people will care to know about
the year's work of the Library. Those who wish to know more are invited to
consult the far more detailed reports of the Library's several departments, on
file in the Library Office and available for inspection on request. What none
of these documents can properly convey is the abiding determination of the people
who do the Library's work to make it as useful as may be to the large numbers of
people who call upon its resources many thousands of times each year. To find
that out you should come to the Library, as Prof. White regularly does, and
see for yourself.

II. STAFF

At the onset of the College's fiscal troubles in the fall of 1970, we initiated a program of drastically reducing the number of staff positions through normal attrition, hoping in this way to spare everyone the emotional and financial hardship of being laid off. By this approach the number of FTE library positions was cut from 24 in fall 1970 to 13 in fall 1974, and the painful prospect of having to terminate anyone's position seemed to be averted. But in spring of 1975 we were instructed to remove yet another 2.5 FTE positions, and this could be done only through ending the employment of three persons.

As part of the ensuing rearrangements, Mr. Duane Vigeant was named head of the AV Department, succeeding Dr. Dennis Dickinson, who accepted a post with the University of Chicago Library. Mrs. Stenger's supervisory responsibilities were expanded to include interlibrary loans and the Periodicals Department. Mrs. Nelson, who had been working part-time in AV, returned to her full-time assignment in Technical Services.

Mrs. Jean Francis resigned as head of the Circulation Department to join her husband in Dubuque, and was succeeded by Mrs. Pamela Cameron, who came to us from the Lansing Public Library.

Mr. Un Chol Shin resigned to accept a teaching appointment at Carleton College. Miss Dorothy Ward and Mr. Wesley Boomgaarden, both graduate students at the University of Minnesota Library School, were employed as part-time circulation assistants beginning September 1975.

Most of the Library's regular staff have been with the College five years or longer, giving a continuity and stability to the operation from which we all-- students, faculty, and staff--draw large benefits.

Staff rosters for the Library and its AV Department appear on the following pages.

LIBRARY

Fall 1970	Fall 1971	Fall 1972	Fall 1973	Fall 1974	Fall 1975
Gore	Gore	Gore	Gore	Gore	Gore
Archibald	Archibald	Archibald	Archibald	Archibald	Archibald
Adamson	Barnes	Barnes	Barnes	Barnes	Barnes
Barnes	Cobb	Crouse	Crouse	Crouse	Boomgaarden (1/3)
Buggs	Cramer	Dickinson	Dickinson	Francis	Cameron
Cobb	Crouse	Francis (3/4)	Francis	Hampl	Crouse
Cramer	Francis (1/2)	Haberkorn (1/2)	Hampl	Kellar	Kellar
Crouse	Haberkorn (1/2)	Hampl	Higginbotham (1/2)	Keller (1/2)	Nelson
Francis	Hampl	Higginbotham (1/2)	Kellar	Nelson (1/2)	Newcomb
Hampl	Kellar	Kellar	Nelson	Newcomb	Oliver (1/2)
Harri (1/2)	Leonard	Nelson	Newcomb	Oliver (1/2)	Salscheider
Kellar	Nelson	Newcomb	Oliver (1/2)	Rude	Stenger
Kerr	Newcomb	Oliver (1/2)	Rude	Salscheider	Ward (1/3)
Kiscaden	Oliver (1/2)	Ondercin	Salscheider	Shin (1/2)	
Leonard	Ondercin	Rude	Shin (1/2)	Stenger	
Meyn	Rude	Salscheider	Stenger		
Nelson	Salscheider	Shin (1/2)			
Newcomb	Shin (1/2)	Stenger			
Oliver (1/2)	Sorensen (1/2)				
Pressman	Stenger				
Rude					
Salscheider					
Shin (1/2)					
Sorensen (1/2)					
Stenger					
MICROFICHE CATALOGING DEVICE	17 1/2 FTE	15 3/4 FTE	14 1/2 FTE	13 FTE	11 1/6 FTE
(in exchange for one staff position)					
24 FTE					

AV Department

Fall 1971	Fall 1972	Fall 1973	Fall 1974	Fall 1975
Hernandez	Lee	Lee	Dickinson	Vigeant
Jackson (3/4)	Jackson (3/4)	Jackson (3/4)	Jackson (3/4)	Jackson (3/4)
Derks	Browne (1/2)	Browne (1/2)	Vigeant (1/2)	
Hakala (1/2)			Nelson (1/2)	1 3/4 FTE
3 1/4 FTE	2 1/4 FTE	2 1/4 FTE	2 3/4 FTE	

Student Staff

As I have noted in previous Reports, the Library relies to an unusual degree upon student help in carrying out its work. In 1974/75 students contributed 40% of the total hours worked in the Library, and 50% of the total in its AV Department. Those ratios are at least double what one typically finds in an academic library, and they attest to the strength of our conviction that library work offers young people an invaluable opportunity for intellectual and personal growth. Nearly 200 different students work with us in the course of a year, or an average of about 15 students per regular staff member. Staff must obviously spend a great deal of their time in training and overseeing the work of students, but everyone prospers under the arrangement: all staff are in close personal touch with large numbers of Macalester students, and no one feels any sense of isolation from the central purpose and end result of our common enterprise--the education of young people. Being thus fully integrated in their work and actively witnessing its outcome in the maturing of young minds and spirits, our staff find much personal satisfaction in their labors, while the work itself thrives and flourishes.

Total student hours worked in 1974/75 came to 18,985 for the Library, plus 5,455 for its AV Department. Totals for the last five years are:

	Library	AV Department
1970/71	29,387	No data
1971/72	22,622	6,685
1972/73	22,245	7,118
1973/74	22,029	5,115
1974/75	18,985 hours	5,455 hours

The perennial, ever-vexing problem of obtaining promptly a sufficient number
of student workers for the Library was swiftly solved at the outset of the fall
(1975) term through the benign genius of Mrs. Tanis Yonkers and Mr. Duane Elvin,
of the Personnel Office. Our sense of relief and gratitude for this timely wonder
are as large as our five year frustration with this Gordian knot was prolonged and
intense.

Over the past five years, as a result of gains in operating efficiency,
regular staff positions in the Library have been reduced by about 54%, and student
staff hours by about 35%. For those who wish to know what such things mean in
their plain pecuniary aspect, they mean a reduction in operating costs of about
$120,000 each year, or, say, the normal income from an endowment of two million
dollars--which the people working in the Library, through their varied talents
and joint faithfulness to their calling have given to the College.

III. THE 1974/75 BUDGET

Library (excluding AV)

The sum budgeted was $242,030; the net sum spent was $224,944. Neither figure takes into account student help, which came to $38,439, but does not appear as a regular budget line item. The five-year record of library expenditures (from College funds only) is as follows:

	Salaries	Acquisitions	Operations (Net)	Total Spent	Total Budgeted
1970/71	$149,638	$101,158	$13,463	$264,259	$292,500
1971/72	127,826	105,579	9,402	242,807	255,000
1972/73	121,137	123,163	8,400	252,700	253,000
1973/74	126,829	113,238	8,072	248,139	251,900
1974/75	124,572	94,773	5,599	224,944	242,030
1975/76					194,193

A detailed analysis of 1974/75 expenditures appears on the following page. The Library's portion of the Educational and General budget has fallen from 5.7% in 1967/68 to 3.0% in 1975/76. While it is not yet time to announce that the sky is falling, a glance upward will confirm that it is lowering.

Indeed it is much lower than those figures suggest, for a dollar in 1975/76 is worth only 2/3 of the 1970/71 dollar. Taking that home truth into account, the sum budgeted for the Library in 1975/76 is 55 percent less than the figure budgeted in 1970/71.

Library Budget 1974/75

Actual Expenditures (College Funds Only)

Category		Expenditures
Salaries and Wages		$ 124,572
Acquisitions and Binding		94,773

Books	$67,411	
Periodicals	25,639	
Binding	1,723	

Operations (Net; expense less income)   5,599

Expenses

Supplies		5,297
Telephone		322
Postage		611
Printing		1,485
Travel		737
Equipment purchases		1,571
Equipment repair		410
Photocopying		5,545
Membership (CLIC)		2,048
Interlibrary loans		511
	Total:	$18,537

Income

Fines and fees		8,019
Photocopying		3,963
Other		956
	Total:	$12,938

Grand Total:	$ 224,944
Budgeted Total:	$ 242,030

AV Department

    The authorized budget was a net figure of $27,680, comprised of $21,680 for salaries and wages (excluding student help) and $6,000 for net operating expenditures (gross less income from services, sales, etc.).

    Although not a line item in the budget, College expenditures for AV student help in 1974/75 came to about $11,000, for 5,455 hours of work.

Actual Expenditures, 1974/75

Category	Amount
Salaries and wages	$19,830
Operations (Net)	3,575

Expenses

Supplies	$6,337
Dues	10
Subscriptions	15
Freight	7
Telephone	64
AV	2,445
Postage	410
Printing	581
Equipment purchases	2,134
Equipment repair	1,726
Travel	106
Total:	$13,835
Income:	$10,260

Grand Total (net):	$23,405
Budgeted total (net):	$27,680

IV. DEPARTMENTAL ACTIVITIES

Technical Services: Acquisitions

The computer-based profile acquisitions program provided by the Baker and
Taylor Company functioned well throughout the year. Average cost of a volume
thus acquired was $9.60. In the previous year it was $9.80, and the year before
that $10.20. The reduction in cost, when one would have expected an increase,
came about as a result of more favorable discounts obtained when we dropped our
previous book jobber in mid-1973/74. The average cost will undoubtedly rise
however, in 1975/76, as a result of inflation.

Statistical results of the profile program in 1974/75 are these:

	Number
Notice slips from the jobber	14,077
"Buy" slips from faculty	3,492
"Don't Buy" slips from faculty	8,580
Total slips	12,072
Acceptance rate	29%
Rejection rate	71%

The acceptance and rejection rates are exactly what they were in the previous
year. Each year about 15% of slips routed to faculty are not returned, so the
true rejection rate is somewhat higher than indicated above.

Expenditures by departments from College funds for profile and other book
purchases (including added copies), and for journal subscriptions, appear on the
following page.

Total College expenditures on acquisitions came to $93,050. An additional
$4,235 was expended (mainly on films) from a Federal grant, $2,890 from a Hill
Foundation grant for materials on urban affairs, and $1,723 was spent on binding

Departmental Book and Periodical Expenditures 1974/75

		Expenditure by Division		
Division		Books	Periodicals	Total
1.	Social Sciences			
	Geography	$1,838.46	$ 479.29	$2,317.75
	Political Science	6,644.89	1,498.99	8,143.88
	Psychology	3,365.12	2,212.87	5,577.99
	Sociology & Anthropology	4,335.23	752.96	5,088.19
	Totals	$16,183.70	$4,944.11	$21,127.81
2.	Business and Economics	1,557.32	1,526.12	3,083.44
3.	Education	2,602.72	391.80	2,994.52
4.	Fine Arts			
	Art	2,553.26	448.15	3,001.41
	Journalism	284.64	117.52	402.16
	Music	1,609.08	134.72	1,743.80
	Speech	736.25	203.76	940.01
	Totals	$5,183.23	$ 904.15	$6,087.38
5.	Humanities			
	Classics	845.00	126.53	971.53
	English	9,626.70	677.36	10,304.06
	Foreign Languages			
	French	1,106.67	265.85	1,372.52
	German	1,562.80	365.49	1,928.29
	Russian	600.63	103.21	703.84
	Scandinavian	571.40	36.35	607.75
	Spanish	647.51	151.77	799.28
	History	10,272.93	613.84	10,886.77
	Linguistics	466.82		466.82
	Philosophy	1,712.22	773.99	2,486.21
	Religion	1,925.92	292.20	2,218.12
	Totals	$29,338.60	$3,406.59	$32,745.19
6.	Physical Education	530.89	196.54	727.43
7.	Science and Mathematics			
	Biology	2,544.87	3,304.35	5,849.22
	Chemistry	1,164.41	3,970.46	5,134.87
	Geology	539.44	671.21	1,210.65
	Math	800.57	1,442.06	2,242.63
	Physics	257.67	2,241.36	2,499.03
	Totals	$5,306.96	$11,629.44	$16,936.40
8.	Library and Miscellaneous	6,707.73	2,640.43	9,348.16
	Grand Totals	$67,411.15	$25,639.18	$93,050.33

The value of gift books added to the collections was $2,690, bringing the total value of new acquisitions during 1974/75 to $104,588.

Value of new acquisitions for each of the last five years is:

1970/71	$108,658
1971/72	130,388
1972/73	134,469
1973/74	131,120
1974/75	104,588

Duplication Program

A systematic program of buying added copies of high-demand titles was init: ated in 1973/74, when a survey we conducted indicated that our patrons fail 42% of the time to find on the shelves the books we own that they want to borrow. Somebody else had already borrowed the book. A second survey, conducted April 1975, showed that the failure rate had fallen to 30%, presumably a result of the duplication program and a reduction of the general loan period from five weeks three.

In 1974/75 some 1,400 added copies were acquired, at a cost of about $8,50(A complete list of these high-demand titles is available on request at the Library Office. It is one of the most interesting bibliographies we own, for it accurately depicts the principal reading interests of Macalester students.

Those interested in the complete rationale for the program, and the way it is conducted, may obtain from us for the asking a copy of Daniel Gore's "Let The Eat Cake While Reading Catalog Cards: An Essay on the Availability Problem" (Library Journal, Jan. 15, 1975, pp. 93-98).

GIFTS AND GRANTS

In addition to the Federal and Hill Foundation grants mentioned above, two anonymous donors pledged to the Library the sum of $15,000 towards the formation of a special collection of the world's finest literature. A substantial nucleus collection will be in place by Fall Opening, 1976. The area designated for this new collection is the entire south wing of the main reading room, which will be fully carpeted and handsomely furnished, as a special inducement to lead young readers to discover the great authors.

The idea for the collection arose several years ago, when we were stirred to thought by the unpleasing realization that the worth of libraries, like the worth of banks, is usually measured by the size of their holdings. Books become abstracted into mere numbers because of their great quantity, and librarians are tempted to regard them as all being exactly equal in value, like dollar bills. Does your library own a million books? Excellent! Then it is ten times a better library than the one down the road with only a hundred thousand. Spend ten million dollars to add another million books to it, and it will be twice as good a library as it used to be--and twenty times better than the one down the road.

Competition among libraries inevitably drifts into a rivalry of mere size. Quantity signifies quality, more is synonymous with better, and most is best-- as if the Astrodome were a better building than the Parthenon.

Librarians see the folly of quantitative values as clearly as other persons. They make no claim that a thousand murder mysteries are better than one Hamlet, a hundred volumes of Harper's Magazine more precious than one "Ode on a Grecian Urn." But the values of sheer quantity become inescapable for librarians--and those who judge their efforts--in a world that has already produced fifty million books, and adds five hundred thousand new ones to the heap each year. A librarian who aspires to build a small library excites no more applause than a mountain climber who scales a foothill. The conditions of his calling compel him to think big.

For the welfare of his patrons, it would be well if, in the midst of superfluity, he could also think small. Especially so if his patrons are college
students, making their first tentative explorations in the forest of books. A
moderate-sized library of several hundred thousand books, even if perfectly cataloged and staffed by amiable experts to guide the perplexed, is still a bewildering maze for the beginner. Where do you start in a library that already holds
more books than you can read in a thousand years, and each year adds more than
a lifetime's new reading?

Well, a college student starts where his professors tell him to start, and
that's that. The college library is only an adjunct to the classroom. It is
the kitchen, and the faculty furnish the recipes for all the intellectual cookery
that goes on in it.

The picture is plausible, orderly, reassuring, and wrong. A careful investi
gation of the actual reading habits of students discloses the startling fact that
nearly half the books they borrow from the library may have nothing to do with
the courses they are taking.* The library for them is no kitchen, but the site
of the self-made uncoerced curriculum, where each decides for himself how he
shall stretch his mind, what intellectual itch he will scratch next, what beckoning curiosity he will heed today, and what tomorrow, and tomorrow, and tomorrow.
The library is the place for the unfettered exuberant intellectual growth of the
young. It is a region for spontaneous exploration and discovery, and a lot of
it is going on, as we know from the observed reading habits of undergraduates--
and from our recollection of what our own intellectual excitements were like in
our youth.

But in a library of hundreds of thousands of books, the discovery of "the

---

*Irene A. Braden, The Undergraduate Library (Chicago: American Library
Association, 1970), p. 56.

best that has been thought and said in the world" can be a disheartening task
for the novice. It is like trying to find two grains of wheat hid in two
bushels of chaff. The card catalog gives no help in distinguishing wheat from
chaff, being merely a record of what is there, not an indicator of its value.
Nor is there help from the subject classification of books, which simply
arranges them on the shelves by type without disclosing anything of their relative merit. A student gazing at a collection of five thousand novels will be
hard put to discover for himself the dozen or so of the calibre of Tom Jones or
The Brothers Karamazov. If he is not a literature major he may never discover
them, although he is seeking just such books, and they lie right before his eyes.
If he is not a biology major, he will miss Fabré's classic work on insects, just
as the biologist is likely to miss Plato's Republic, or the philosopher to miss
Plutarch's Lives.

Do people really want to be plainly told what the great books are, and then
go on to read them? The financial success of such enormous publishing ventures
as the "Great Books of the Western World" proclaims emphatically that they do.
People will spend large sums of money to possess such sets, even though the editorial work be unsatisfactory, the typography inferior, and the bindings unlovely.

People want to be shown the great authors. But librarians, prompted by
worthy motives of neutrality, instead show them everything. The giants fade from
view amid a swarm of pygmies.

Librarians lose sight of the giants too. Pressed as they are to keep up
with the tens of thousands of new books coming out each year, it is no cause for
scandal if they lose sight of the fact that there is not one good reading edition
of Keats in the library, not enough copies of War and Peace to satisfy the demand, and no copy at all of the Upanishads. Glaring omissions are usually dis-

covered, if at all, when a reader notices them and raises a question. Continuing qualitative review of a collection of hundreds of thousands of books becomes a practical impossibility.

But if the great books of the world were drawn together in one special collection, then readers could discover them effortlessly, and librarians could maintain a continuous survey of those books to make sure that each was available in sufficient copies, and in textually and typographically superior editions. How large might such a collection be? Genius is rare. Of the millions upon millions of books that have been published, the number of those that have withstood the test of time--the only certain measure of greatness--approximates two thousand. Add to those the five hundred or so tentative candidates from the last hundred years--works so recent that one cannot yet say they have failed the test of time--and you have a collection that fills only one side of a standard 24-foot stack unit. The estimate of 2,500 books, if in error, errs on the side of liberality. Robert Hutchins's "Great Books" series, for example, represents the work of less than a hundred authors, while the "Harvard Classics" compresses all into fifty volumes.

With 2,500 books chosen systematically from the standard bibliographical guides, one could be sure of including all authors of world stature. And with so small a collection one could take the considerable pains necessary to see that every author is represented in the best editions--editorially and esthetically-- that are available. Assume an average requirement of two copies of each work-- since the loan demand in such a collection will be predictably greater than the norm--and a collection of about 5,000 books is called for, representing fully "the best that has been thought and said in the world." The Harvard "Five-Foot Shelf" will become the Macalester Five-Hundred-Foot Shelf.

Would such a collection be actively used? That much can be guaranteed. For librarians like grocers know that the prominent display of any portion of their stock infallibly increases the demand for it. Place such a collection of books in an attractive area, as we propose to do, and a use rate several times greater than the usual invariably ensues. Students who would otherwise never read a word of Homer, or Sophocles, or Horace, or Tolstoy, are almost certain to do so under these circumstances. Under any other circumstances-- short of majoring in literature--they are almost certain not to do so, except on the lucky counsel of a well-read friend.

The documented fact of heavy, independent, voluntary student use of college libraries implies that students will eagerly acquire a liberal education on their own initiative, if given a convenient starting place. That is what college li- braries never give them. Instead of offering them somewhere to start, they offer everywhere, which is the same as nowhere in a collection of hundreds of thousands of books.

Now we can provide that starting place, with the special funds given by our generous friends.

We can never build at Macalester a library to rival in size those of the great universities. But we are about to do something better: make "the best that has been thought and said in the world" part of the everyday experience of students. Macalester cannot have an Astrodome. We can and soon will have an intellectual Parthenon.

Collection Statistics

During the year 9,368 volumes (or other units) were added to the collection bringing the total to 264,978 items, of which 252,171 are bound volumes of books and journals. That figure is more than double the median of all colleges having similar programs and enrollment.

Items Added 1974/75

Category	Volumes (or units)
Books	7,446
Bound periodicals and abstracts	1,217
Newspaper and periodical indexes	8
Microfilm reels	284
Microfiche	0
Records and tapes	800
Total:	9,755
Book withdrawals:	387
Net Increase:	9,368

Total Resources September 1, 1975

Category	Volumes (or units)
Books	223,836
Bound periodicals and abstracts	28,335
Newspaper and periodical indexes	367
Microfilm reels	4,449
Microfiche	2,410
Records and tapes	5,581
Total:	264,978

Subscriptions in Force September 1, 1975

Newspapers	44
Journals	897
Other serials	466

Technical Services: Cataloging

Statistics for the last six years are these:

	1969/70	1970/71	1971/72	1972/73	1973/74	1974/75
Volumes reclassed	1,908	25,923	26,778	24,891	4,303	255
Volumes cataloged	10,909	11,094	8,298	10,911	11,565	9,903
Volumes withdrawn	3,331	3,524	2,062	665	506	394
Total units processed	16,148	40,541	37,138	36,467	16,374	10,552

Circulation Department

Total recorded circulation for the year was 76,354, a decline of 5.5% from the previous year; enrollment decline over the same period was about 7%, indicating a marginal increase in per capita use of the library. It is worth repeating here what was documented in last year's Report: Per capita use of the Macalester Library is about double that of the sister colleges in the Twin Cities.

If the old maxim be true that the heart of a college is its library, then our circulatory measurements show the heart to be in strong and flourishing good health. How this can be when the Library's portion of the General and Educational budget has fallen from 5.7% in 1967/68, to 3.0% in 1975/76, is a mystery too elaborate to be unfolded here. But a reading of our four previous Annual Reports will fully illuminate the mystery, if he (or she) who runs will sit still long enough to read those voluminous documents.

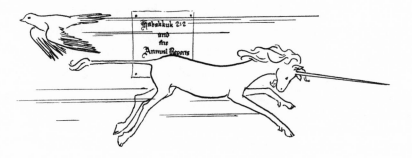

Habakkuk 2:2
and
the
Annual Reports

Circulation Statistics 1974/75

Category	Weyerhaeuser Students	Weyerhaeuser Faculty	Olin Students	Olin Faculty
Books (general)	38,127	3,423	787	252
FASTCAT	3,973	1,077	35	29
Curriculum Lab	619	53		
Juvenile	1,733	384		
Paperbacks & mysteries	120	43		
Government documents	78	0		
Phonodiscs	556	70		
Cassettes (general)	6,027*			
Cassettes (reserve)	598*			
Other Reserve Items	14,986*		237*	
Art Rentals		50		
Periodicals	2,606*		89	27
Storage	375*			
Totals:	69,798	5,100	1,148	308
Combined:	74,898		1,456	
Both libraries:	76,354			

In addition to the loans recorded above, the Reserve Desk made 2,910 loans of headsets for in-library use of cassette playback equipment. Use of the cassette collection was double that of the previous year. Individual cassettes circulated an average of six times per year, which is 30 times the demand rate for books in the general collection. Music tapes account for about 90% of total cassette loans. Literary texts on tape circulated an average of 1.5 times per year. Medieval, Renaissance, Baroque, and symphonic tapes are the most popular, folk and national music the least.

Recorded use of the FASTCAT collection has quadrupled over the past four years. The use rate of this browsing collection of new books (total loans in relation to volumes owned) is now five times that of the general collection. Among the faculty, use rate of FASTCATs has become thirteen times that of the general collections. Introduced at Macalester five years ago as a technique for making new books available for loan within 48 hours after receipt by the

---

*Student and faculty loans combined

Library, FASTCAT has proved to be an immensely attractive and pleasing creature,

not only at Macalester--where the species originated--but at the following li-

braries that have since adopted its numerous progeny:

> The University of Alberta (Canada)
> Brandon University (Canada)
> Red Deer College (Canada)
> The University of Windsor (Canada)
> Universidad del Valle de Guatemala
> Universidad de San Carlos de Guatemala
>   (where it is called "CAT-RAP," for Catalogacion Rapida)
> Manhattan College (N.Y.)
> Lake Forest College (Ill.)
> Wesleyan University (Conn.)
> Veterans Memorial Public Library (Bismarck, N.D.)
> Lansing Community College (Michigan)
> Field Museum of Natural History (Chicago)
> Temple University (Philadelphia)
> Bradley University (Ill.)
> Boise State College (Idaho)
> Medford Public Library (Mass.)
> University of Missouri (St. Louis)
> The Universities Center (Jackson, Miss.)
> Anderson College (Ind.)
> Mt. Pleasant Public Library (Mich.)
> Bir Zeit College (Israel)
> Duke University
> Corning (N.Y.) Community College
> College of St. Catherine
> College of St. Thomas
> Clinch Valley College (Va.)
> University of New South Wales
> Jamestown College (N.D.)
> Coker College (S.C.)
> University of South Carolina - Spartanburg
> Gordon College (Mass.)
> American Graduate School of International Management (Ariz.)
> Masconomet Regional High School (Mass.)
> McMaster University (Canada)
> Pacific University (Oregon)
> Washington State University
> Athabasca University (Canada)
> Kellogg Community College (Mich.)
> Piedmont Virginia Community College
> University of Alabama - Huntsville
> Los Angeles County Public Library System

Besides being enormously appealing to readers, FASTCAT has enabled us to

cut our cataloging costs by at least fifty percent.

In the last two years some 700 libraries across the country have joined the Ohio College Library Center (OCLC) computer-based cooperative cataloging network. Macalester has chosen not to join, because FASTCAT beats OCLC's computer silly. Costs run less than half the OCLC method, and books are made available for loan about ten times quicker. Why then have so many libraries signed up with OCLC? It is merely conjecture, but maybe they cannot tell a fast cat from a slow computer.

Even if we could find a more economical method of cataloging new books, it is doubtful we could ever abandon the FASTCAT collection, given its immense popularity among faculty, students, and library staff--who are spared the abiding frustrations that pervade most libraries, where the intense pressures for speedy cataloging of new books simply cannot be relieved by conventional cataloging practices.

An analysis of FASTCAT collection use, made October 5, 1975, appears on the following pages. Although the average demand rate on this collection is, as noted above, five times that of the general collection, more than half the books in FASTCAT are not borrowed even once during their first year on the shelf. Since the average demand on library books declines steadily with age (with the notable exception of books we call "classics"--and that is why they are classics: time cannot wither nor custom stale their attractiveness) it appears that much of our collection-building effort has been devoted to the gathering in of "alms for oblivion." Which is not necessarily a bad thing: for a comfortably wide margin of error is always required to avoid making a worse mistake, through failing to acquire promptly a high percentage of the new publications that will be needed. One may reasonably ask, though, if we do not err in granting perpetual tenure to those alms for oblivion, when the passage o

SUBJECT ANALYSIS OF FASTCAT USE 10/5/75

Volumes Borrowed at Least Once in 12 Months

Fastcat Classification	Vols. in Class	Vols. on Shelf 10/5/75	Vols. on Loan	% on Loan	Vols. on Shelf Borrowed at Least Once	Total Vols. Borrowed at Least Once	% Borrowed at Least Once	Average Shelf Age of Vols.	% Adjustment for 12 mos.	Adjusted % Borrowed at Least Once in 12 mos.
B Philosophy	141	95	46	32.6	27	73	51.7	11 mos.	+4.7	56.4
BF Psychology	172	120	52	30.0	61	113	65.7	10.5	+9.4	75.1
BL Religion	284	217	67	23.5	63	130	45.8	11.5	+2.0	47.8
D History	885	783	102	11.5	151	253	28.6	11.5	+1.3	29.9
G Geography	160	113	47	29.4	47	94	58.5	11.0	+5.3	63.8
GV Physical Education	94	72	22	23.5	39	61	64.8	8	+32.0	96.8
HB Economics	127	97	30	23.6	25	55	43.2	7.5	+26.0	69.2
HM Sociology	463	440	23	5.0	58	81	17.5	7.5	+0.8	18.3
J Political Science	503	451	52	10.3	86	138	27.5	11.5	+3.9	31.4
L Education	296	263	33	11.1	61	94	31.7	10.5	+4.5	36.2
M Music	97	79	18	39.2	20	38	59.8	12	0	59.8
N Art	62	61	1	1.6	23	24	38.7	9.5	+10.2	48.9
PA Classics	100	81	19	19.0	12	31	31.0	11	+2.8	33.8
PG Russian	140	139	1	2.1	8	9	7.8	12	0	7.8
PN Speech/Theatre	77	60	17	22.1	10	27	35.2	12.5	-1.4	33.8
PNA Journalism	21	15	6	28.5	3	9	42.7	8	+21.4	64.1
PQ French	115	92	23	20.0	16	39	33.8	10	+6.8	40.6
PQA Spanish	161	141	20	12.5	10	30	18.6	15	-3.7	14.9
PR English	889	780	109	12.4	103	212	23.9	12	0	23.9
PS Fiction, Poems, Plays	99	79	20	20.0	39	59	59.0	4	+180	100.0
PT German	160	154	6	3.7	4	10	6.2	16	-1.5	4.7
QA Mathematics	52	41	11	21.2	19	30	57.7	10.5	+8.2	65.9
QC Physics	41	31	10	24.4	14	24	58.7	10.0	+11.8	70.5
QD Chemistry	80	73	7	8.8	35	42	52.5	13	-4.2	48.3
QE Geology	69	59	10	14.5	5	15	21.7	12.5	-0.9	20.8
QH Biology	160	119	41	25.6	22	63	39.4	13.5	-4.4	35.0
Totals	5,448	4,655	793	14.5%	961	1,754	32.3%			

Median Figure in this column is 40.6%

ANALYSIS OF FASTCAT USE

Subjects Ranked By (Adjusted) Percent
Borrowed at Least Once in 12 mos.

Rank	1973/74	% Borrowed	Rank in 1974/75	1974/75	% Borrowed	Rank in 1973/74
1	Physical Education	100%	1	Physical Education	96.8%	1
2	French	100	2	Psychology	75.1	3
3	Psychology	93.8	3	Physics	70.5	16
4	Journalism	76.5	4	Economics	69.2	12
5	Mathematics	74.7	5	Mathematics	65.9	5
6	Sociology	72.0	6	Journalism	64.1	4
7	Classics	66.0	7	Geography	63.8	9
8	Philosophy	62.5	8	Music	59.8	11
9	Geography	62.0	9	Philosophy	56.4	8
10	Art	62.0	10	Art	48.9	10
11	Music	57.0	11	Chemistry	48.3	19
12	Economics	55.9	12	Religion	47.8	14
13	Biology	55.8	13	French	40.6	2
14	Religion	51.2	14	Education	36.2	17
15	Speech	46.5	15	Biology	35.0	13
16	Physics	45.2	16	Speech	33.8	15
17	Education	44.8	17	Classics	33.8	7
18	Political Science	40.2	18	Political Science	31.4	18
19	Chemistry	37.6	19	History	29.9	22
20	English	35.2	20	English	27.5*	20
21	German	30.4	21	Geology	20.8	23
22	History	30.1	22	Sociology	18.3	6
23	Geology	21.5	23	Spanish	14.9	24
24	Spanish	20.4	24	Russian	7.8	25
25	Russian	11.5	25	German	4.7	21

*Including PS

Note: Rank 13 is the median position both years.
Underlined subjects are those that ranked above the

time proves that that is what they are. Each year makes that question more
urgent, as surplus shelf space gradually shrinks to nothing.

Shelving Capacity of Libraries

A precise inventory of shelving was taken on August 24, 1973, and recorded
in the 1972/73 Annual Report. The estimated condition as of September 1975 is this:

Building	Shelf Ft.	Book Ft.	Load Factor
Weyerhaeuser	26,733	20,200	75.5%
Olin	1,479	1,500	101.0%
Storage	6,930	4,100	59.5%
Totals:	35,142	25,800	

The careful reader has correctly deduced that some Olin volumes are now
piling up on the floor. At this writing, criteria are being formulated for the
withdrawal of selected journal backruns to the Dining Commons storage collection.

Faced with the prospect of having no new library building in the immediate
future, we have made a close study of the total shelving possibilities and tentatively forecast a capacity to maintain a satisfactory operation with existing
facilities for at least another five years. This will require, however, the
transfer of an additional 30,000 low-use volumes to storage over that period, and
the purchase of some additional shelving--possibly as much as 5,000 linear feet,
at a cost not less than $3.00 per foot.

Reserves. Statistics for the past five years are the following:

Year	Books	Articles	Cassettes	Total in Collection	Total Loa
1970/71	1,391	605	-	1,996	20,162
1971/72	1,925	1,504	-	3,429	14,425
1972/73	2,337	1,533	-	3,870	12,374
1973/74	2,002	1,604	800 (est.)	3,718	17,815
1974/75	2,350	1,246	1,104	3,868	24,521

Note: Cassette figures include non-reserve music tapes which are circulated fr
the Reserve Desk, as well as those on reserve.

Periodicals.

Subscription statistics as of August 31 for each of the last four fiscal

years are:

	1971/72	1972/73	1973/74	1974/75
Subscriptions added (previous 12 months)	38	21	49	65
Subscriptions dropped	178	73	153	67
Subscriptions in force	1,055	1,003	899	897
Paid			748	749
Gift			151	148

During the year the staff bound 1,217 new journal volumes; added missing

issues to 137 previously bound volumes; and performed miscellaneous repairs to

148 others. Total cost to the College (including student help) for these bind

ing operations was about $2,500. A commercial binder would charge about $10,0

for the same work, and the volumes would have been unavailable to readers for

about two months longer than they are with the in-house operation.

Reference Department

Reference librarians experience in the most immediate way the "ten-thousa

things" whereof the Taoists make philosophical complaint. But librarians smil

as they go about their task of reducing them to the one: namely one body of
satisfied inquirers. Last year they presented some ten thousand questions
to our reference staff, and most of them were promptly answered. Questions
as to the origin of evil, or "where past seasons are, or who cleft the Devil's
foot," are as a matter of policy left unanswered--until after hours.

Besides attending to the ten thousand things, the staff also taught the
two courses that have been a regular offering of the Library in recent years:
"Methods of Research in Government Publications," and "Introduction to Bibliography." Both courses were presented in the fall and spring terms.

Another vital function of the Reference Department is the provision of
interloan services. Here is the record of activity over the last five years:

Items Delivered to Macalester Patrons

	Items Requested	Items Delivered	Success Rate
1970/71	5,780	3,399	58%
1971/72	4,900	3,442	68%
1972/73	3,950	3,041	77%
1973/74	4,050	3,335	82%
1974/75	4,144	3,287	80%

Items Lent to Other Libraries

	Items Requested	Items Delivered	Success Rate
1970/71	860	438	51%
1971/72	1,725	1,017	59%
1972/73	1,530	983	64%
1973/74	2,020	1,490	74%
1974/75	2,401	1,712	71%

In 1974/75 we satisfied 92% of our own patrons' requests for journal
articles, and 74% of those for books. Our CLIC network affords prompt and
convenient access to some three million different books, and more than 30,000
journal titles in the Twin Cities. Most requests are filled within 40 hours,
at no cost to the patron, whether student or faculty.

It is a matter of more than passing curiosity that, while we can satisfy 74 percent of the demand for books that must be obtained from other libraries, we could satisfy only 70 percent of last year's demand for books we own ourselves. Lest the latter result appear disgracefully bad, we note that various recent investigations disclose that the typical success rate among academic libraries is in the range of fifty to sixty percent. While we are not particularly pleased with our own relatively good showing of seventy percent, the situation is improving (as stated earlier in this Report) since we began the program of systematically duplicating high-demand titles.

Interloan service is not cheap. Available literature on the subject indicates that the average cost to libraries may be somewhere between three and fifteen dollars per item processed. We do not know what the cost is here, for much of it is borne by the Hill Library, which operates the CLIC union catalog and interloan referral service. Whatever the real cost may be, we can say conclusively that it is a good deal less than the millions of dollars we would have to spend each year if we were to acquire the collections that presently support our interloan services.

Loans of items to other libraries have more than quadrupled over the last five years, and the activity will continue to increase in 1975/76. Loans obtained for our patrons have remained essentially the same over the same period. But if one should inspect the records for 1969/70, or any year prior to that, he will discover that present levels of inbound interloans are about ten times what they were then. It appears that we reached saturation level for our own patrons' interloan needs in the first year (1970/71) that greatly expanded services were offered.

Audio-Visual Department

At the beginning of the year we hired as a technical assistant a man who was then completing his formal training as an AV technician at the Area 916 Vocational-Technical Institute, and he was assigned the formidable task of putting the entire equipment inventory in good working order. Within nine months the job was completed; and throughout the year, as substantially more equipment became available for longer-term loan, we were able to reduce the number of short-term repeat loans that previously had to be made in order to satisfy all demands on an insufficient supply of equipment. A paradoxical result of this service improvement is an apparent statistical decline in use of some types of equipment, following a reduction in repeat-loan requirements. A tabulation of AV loans and services appears on the following page. Besides these, the department performs numerous other services that are not conveniently quantifiable, but nonetheless comprise a significant part of its contribution to the academic program: among them are such things as consulting with faculty and staff regarding instructional design and other enterprises involving AV facilities; researching and locating films and other materials; and obtaining bids for equipment and materials to be purchased either for the department or other units of the College.

Major changes in the physical layout of the department were undertaken during the year to gain more useable space. Also, a large collection of rarely used audio tapes was transferred to storage, freeing up still more work space in the department. A service desk was set up in the main workroom to provide more convenient patron access to services and to control traffic flow in the department. A burglar alarm was installed to improve after-hours security, and no break-ins have occurred since then.

File and record-keeping procedures were reviewed, modified, and thereby much improved. As part of that effort, a comprehensive Operations and Procedures Manual was written (the first ever) for the department. Operations are now better controlled and documented than in the past, and procedures more consistent. The existence of the Manual also made smooth and easy a change in department heads at the beginning of the 1975/76 academic year.

Departmental operating efficiency is particularly difficult to maintain when fifty percent of the hours worked are contributed by a part-time student staff. That percentage will be even higher in 1975/76, from further reduction in regular staff positions. Most students never work in the department as many hours as would constitute a normal break-in period for employees of a service industry--say something on the order of a thousand hours. Nonetheless they must be, and are trained to provide a wide variety of services involving a wide array of equipment, and the record of service failures under these circumstances is surprisingly low, on the order of one in five hundred. Where there are prophecies, they shall fail; and where there is equipment it shall sometimes fail too. But where there are tongues to tell of such failure, it can be unfailingly prophesied that they shall never cease--nor do we ever cease listening attentively to them, in our continuing effort to improve on what already appears to be quite a satisfactory record of departmental performance.

AV Loans and Services

Equipment Loans	1972/73	1973/74	1974/75
Motion Picture Projectors	920	921	828
Slide Projectors	524	317	362
Filmstrip Projectors	160	59	70
Overhead Projectors	284	146	106
Opaque Projectors	147	101	76
Screens	263	129	120
Tape Recorders	1,143	571	545
Phonographs	150	80	188
Cameras	184	47	64
VTR Recording/PB	179	96	167
Public Address Systems	152	42	30
	4,015	2,509	2,556

Services			
Our Films Used	475	505	513
Film Rentals	305	319	187
Slides and b/w Prints	3,327	2,889	1,971
Rolls Film Sold	939	1,533	1,381
Tapes - Sold and Dubbed	1,121	1,080	1,117
Transparencies	856	494	695
Ditto Masters	1,869	3,530	2,638
Signs	470	380	113
	9,362	10,730	8,615

V. BUILDINGS

Planning for a new building has been indefinitely suspended for want of construction funds. Unpleasant as this outcome may be for all of us who were actively engaged or interested in the planning of a new building three years ago, it does have one agreeable aspect. Had a new building opened (as orig- inally planned) by September 1975, the cost of operating it (utilities and staff) would be at least a hundred thousand dollars per year more than our present costs. With the acquisitions budget cut by $36,000 in 1975/76, it is hard to see how we could afford more building when we were obliged to acquire fewer books.

As noted earlier in this Report, means have been discovered to shelve further acquisitions in existing facilities for at least another five years, al- though this will require stepped-up activity in transferring little-used mate- rials from both Weyerhaeuser and Olin to the Dining Commons storage area. At the same time we have been exploring ways to make Weyerhaeuser a more attractive building for students. One measure in progress at this writing is to provide a large, comfortable, carpeted reading room in Weyerhaeuser. The area chosen is the south end of the main floor, presently occupied by the juvenile collection and a number of small reading tables. The juvenile collection will be moved to the upstairs area adjacent to the Rare Book Room, and that floor will also be carpeted; and the Curriculum collection is being moved from that area to the Periodicals Room on the ground floor. After carpet is laid in the expanded main reading room, the fine old heavy oak tables scattered about the Library will be placed there, and by September of 1976 we also plan to have the nucleus collec- tion of Greats shelved in that room.

Although maintenance and custodial staff have been drastically reduced in recent years, Mr. Rognlie's men continue to give us prompt and expert help whenever it is needed. Mr. Bill Florek, who has been library custodian for many years, has long enjoyed the warm gratitude of the library staff for his good-natured determination to keep a high polish on an old building that everyone realizes is more than one man ought to be asked to keep up with. Not only does he somehow stay out front of an impossible task: he also stays out front long enough to keep our walks as free as may be of snow and ice; and I have often noted, with particular pleasure and appreciation (having a great fear of flying on ice) that our walks are always the clearest and the safest on campus.

VI. STAFF ACTIVITIES

Mrs. Archibald taught the course "Methods of Research in Government Publications" in the fall and spring terms, and served as secretary of the Government Documents Round Table of the Minnesota Library Association. She attended the ACM Library Conference in Chicago, and a meeting of ACM library directors at Carleton College. Besides her numerous supervisory duties in the Library, she coordinated library purchases from the Urban Affairs Grant, and made most of the decisions in acquiring the 1,400 added copies of high-demand titles in the course of the year.

Mrs. Salscheider completed three library science courses at the College of St. Catherine.

Dr. Dickinson taught the "Introduction to Bibliography" course in the fall and spring terms.

Mr. Vigeant was awarded the Audio-Video Technician diploma by the Area 916

Vocational-Technical Institute.

Mr. Gore served as a CLIC director and as a member of the Library Committee.
Under ACM sponsorship, he organized, promoted, and chaired a national
library conference in Chicago, April 17-18, 1975. Entitled "Touching Bottom
in the Bottomless Pit: ACM Conference on Space, Growth, and Performance Problems
of Academic Libraries," the meeting was attended by some 230 librarians, including a sizeable delegation from Canada, where academic libraries are also running
out of space. ACM sponsorship was provided with the understanding that the
conference would be fully self-supporting. It showed a profit. Proceedings of
the conference will be published by Greenwood Press in early 1976.

Mr. Gore published or presented the following in 1974/75:

"Let Them Eat Cake While Reading Catalog Cards: An Essay on the Availability
    Problem," Library Journal, Jan. 15, 1975, pp. 93-98.

"Zero Growth for the College Library," College Management, Aug./Sept. 1974,
    pp. 12-14. Reprinted in The Best of Library Literature 1974.

"Space and Performance Problems of Academic Libraries," a talk presented to the
    Minnesota Academic Library Directors meeting, St. Paul, Jan. 15, 1975.

"Farewell to Alexandria: A Theory of the No-Growth Library," paper presented
    to the Classics Colloquium, Macalester College, March 6, 1975; and to the
    Wisconsin Association of Academic Librarians, Milwaukee, April 3, 1975.

"The View from the Top of the Tower of Babel: Prospects for Academic Library
    Growth in the Near Future," paper presented as the annual University of
    Tennessee Library Lecture, Knoxville, May 13, 1975; and as the Ohio State
    University Library Lecture, May 29, 1975.

Review of Michael Buckland's Book Availability and the Library User, in Library
    Journal, June 15, 1975, p. 1196.

VII.   PROBLEMS PRESENT AND DISTANT

With the acquisitions budget for 1975/76 cut by 34 percent (from $104,500 to $68,500) there will be some difficulty in adjusting to such a sudden change in pace. Applying the brakes too fast usually sends something or somebody through the windshield. At this writing seven academic departments have already expended their year's allocation, and can place no more book orders until September. Other departments will soon share their predicament. Taking into account these current hardships, together with the fact that inflation shrinks further the value of a shrunken budget, and that the Library's portion of the total Educational and General budget of the College has dwindled from 5.7 to 3.0 percent over the last seven years--while demands on library resources remain demonstrably high--the Faculty Library Committee has recommended that the acquisitions budget for 1976/77 be no less than $100,000. Anything below that would require a degree of precision in book selection (from the hundreds of thousands of new books published annually) that is not, in our opinion, realistically attainable. Errors of judgment are inevitable, but the present budget allows for few or none to be made. When sudden heavy strains are placed on an inflexible cable, it is likely to break. Especially so if it is also a bit frayed, as our connection with the world of new books has recently become. Another year with an inflexible book budget may set us suddenly adrift.

Finding space for growing collections continues to be a problem in a library that was said to have reached design capacity in 1968. But as noted earlier in these pages, the problem appears not to be intractable, and satisfactory operations can be maintained with present facilities for at least another five years. After that, the College will either provide some new library building space, or accept the challenges and potential benefits of maintaining collections that remain constant in size, while their contents are periodically modified to meet the ever-changing needs of the library's patrons. If the latter choice is to be made, then thought should soon be given to computerizing our circulation and inventory control systems, to help us decide which ten thousand volumes should be removed to off-campus storage each year (beginning around 1981), to make way for the ten thousand new ones that will be coming in. To operate a computerized circulation system would cost about $15,000 a year more than the present system, but access to wanted publications (even in a no-growth library) should be substantially better than it presently is. To operate a new building of the size contemplated in our planning several years ago would cost about $100,000 more per year than we now spend, in addition to the cost of the $5,000,000 in required construction capital, which (conservatively) would come to $300,000 per year. Should any or all of these funds come to the College as gifts, the comparative situation would be partially or totally altered from the College's standpoint, though not from any general economic point of view. In utrumque paratus was Matthew Arnold's maxim on the question of man's immortality, and it is a good one for the College to apply to the question of a new library building: "Ready in either case." For if building funds have not been raised by the time they are needed, then it would be well if we had found means to maintain a satisfactory library operation without them.

Library staff salaries at Macalester have never been good. A succession of salary freezes during a period of steep inflation has yielded a situation today that is embarrassingly bad, particularly so as regards bi-weekly payroll staff. It is a melancholy thing to realize that thirteen people in the Library (and its AV Department) are now doing the work that five years ago was done by twenty-seven

and individually are being worse compensated now than they were then. No organization can thrive indefinitely with that kind of upside down scale of rewards.
We have learned pretty well to make bricks without straw, but nobody can make them
without clay, however ardent the desire may be. I devoutly wish that in 1976/77
the College may find means to provide suitable rewards to a library staff that
have made such large and distinguished contributions to the work of the College.
A better library staff than ours is hard to find; better-paid ones are numerous.

The Report ends here, but the work of the Library goes on and on. No one
is more sensible than I am of the fact that that work gets done not by policies
or procedures or even machines, but by people; and that the people who do the
work of this library not only do it diligently, but thoughtfully and amiably too.
That is why so much work gets done by so few people. The last word here is
properly theirs: a word of praise and thanks for the many days of faithful effort
they have put into the making of one more year's splendid work.

macalester college annual report of the library 1975·76
saint paul · minnesota·

MACALESTER COLLEGE

SAINT PAUL, MINNESOTA 55105

March 10, 1977

Dr. John Linnell
Vice President for Academic Affairs
Macalester College
St. Paul, MN 55105

Dear John:

Libraries are quiet places, and the people who work in them are thoug
to lead quiet, orderly working lives, securely removed from the fray and
confusion that plague other human endeavors. We wish it were so. But rea
any of our professional journals and you will discover there a spirit of
brawling contentiousness that makes ordinary scholarly debate sound like
the polite whisperings of pallbearers. Or ask a hotelkeeper why his heart
is so gladdened by the prospect of a librarians' convention, and he will t
you they run up a larger bar bill than a gathering of the Amalgamated Brot
hood of Boilermakers.

What is it that keeps librarians in flaming turmoil and parching thir
In a word, it is the astronomical dimensions of the bibliographical univer
they toil in, and the awful pace at which it grows: fifty million differe
books published since Gutenberg, and a half million new ones added to the
heap each year, whereof most libraries will own but a fraction of one perc
Yet any hour of the working day the questing scholar is likely to spring u
you with an urgent demand to be shown Dr. Puffendorff's recent Contributio
to the Bibliography of the Pleural Cavity of the Ibex, and glare at you in
stunned bewilderment upon learning the library doesn't own it. "But we ca
get it for you on interloan," you quickly offer. "How long does it take?"
the tense response. "Oh, a couple of days, maybe a week." "Can't wait. H
you no idea of the hectic progress in the ibex field today?"

Yes, we do, and in all the other fields too, and, with the fractional
resources at our command, considerable ingenuity is required to keep the
better part of our clientele from sinking in the slough of despond, or cli
ing the heights of indignation. The pages of this report on the library
staff's work in 1975/76 are offered as a celebration of their ingenuity, a
their success in carrying out a task which, mathematically regarded, looks
be impossible. I hope you will share my admiration and gratitude that so
have done so much with so little.

Sincerely,

Daniel Gore
Director

CONTENTS

I. INTRODUCTION

In libraries the size of Macalester's, you find as a rule that each
major function (acquisitions, cataloging, circulation, reference, etc.)
requires a separate department head to tend to it. And that is how it
was at Macalester in 1970, on the eve of hard times. When they came
and the library budget situation steadily worsened, we let attrition
steadily reduce staff numbers from 27 FTE positions (in 1970) to 13 positions today. Letting things like that happen sounds easy until you try it.

One result of that happening is that a person who might have supervised the work of one department in 1970 now has much more to look after.
Take Mrs. Pamela Cameron for example. Elsewhere she might be in charge
of an acquisitions department. Here she oversees acquisitions, cataloging, interlibrary loans, periodicals, children's literature, and the Olin
Science Library--and also does some reference work and teaches a bibliography course.

Mrs. Jean Archibald used to head the library's Reference Department.
Now, as Associate Director of the library, she has all the duties of a
general manager, continues to supervise the reference department, and also
offers each year a course in government documents bibliography. Mr. Wesley
Boomgaarden heads the Circulation Department and also acts as student personnel officer, recruiting and scheduling a hundred students each year for
library work. Reference work is also among his duties, along with administrative responsibility for the Reserve Desk. Mr. Buzz Vigeant came to our
AV Department as its technician, was promoted to head of the department, and
now that he is manager gives his technician a ride to work with him every
day, for he is they. Mrs. Rosemary Salscheider has worked in every department of the library except cataloging, and presently carries out duties in
four different areas.

Mrs. Dorothy Barnes's job title is Library Secretary, but it ought to
be Plenipotentiary, for she does all the things that nobody else can do,
and sees to it that everything that everybody else can and ought to do, gets
done.

It is an unusual organizational structure. Maybe it is not a structure

at all. Drawing an organization chart of it was impossible until I
learned where I figured in it from Schumacher's <u>Small is Beautiful: Economics as if People Mattered</u>. The chart, shown below, places the director
under the operating units, holding things loosely together in an arrangement
that constantly re-adjusts itself in relation to the breeze.

   The chief excellence of the design is that it works, and works well.
Or rather the people in it work well, for designs like directors are incapable of doing any work.

   "Now, what I want is, Facts," said Mr. Gradgrind at the beginning of
Dickens's <u>Hard Times</u>. At the end of ours I will give you one: the people
of this library provide services that in similar colleges cost twice the
money we draw from the Macalester treasury. They are bright, amiable
people, masters of their work and good-natured servants of their clientele,
and . . . . "Stick to facts, Sir!" Mr. Gradgrind exclaims. And I've tried
to do that throughout this chronicle, but the people do keep breaking in,
because without this very special group who do the work of the library,
there wouldn't be much here worth reporting. That's a fact.

II. STAFF

In July 1976, Mrs. Marymina Stenger left us to take a post at the
William Mitchell College of Law. Mrs. Stenger had been with the Macalester
Library for eight years, beginning her work here as a cataloger, and concluding it with a broad range of supervisory responsibilities, in cataloging, acquisitions, interlibrary loans, periodicals and other areas. She
it was who supervised the reclassification of 82,000 volumes from Dewey
to the Library of Congress system, a vast undertaking carried out successfully even while her processing staff was being drastically reduced. Although they will not know her name, scholars who use this library will
daily benefit from the fruit of all the work of re-organization that Mrs.
Stenger did for them.

Mrs. Pamela Cameron, who had been head of the Circulation Department
for one year, succeeded Mrs. Stenger. And Mr. Wesley Boomgaarden was promoted from evening supervisor (a post he had held for a year) to Head of
the Circulation Department. Mrs. Sally McGowan was appointed evening supervisor, coming to us from the Hamline University Library.

Mrs. Bernice Oliver, who had been with the library since 1962, retired
in November 1975. Always a good companion and diligent colleague, she is
affectionately remembered by all for her good work and bad jokes.

Staff rosters appear below. Some of these appointments are less than
full time. For the library,the FTE complement is 11 positions, and for AV
it is 1 3/4. The fall of 1970 roster showed 24 FTE positions in the library, and there were 3 1/4 FTE positions in AV when that department was
assigned administratively to the library in 1971. Staff positions are fewer
than we would like, but all we have been allowed to have. New programs and

services can be offered only if existing ones are dropped, but none can

be since all inessential activities were long since stripped away.

Staff Rosters, Fall 1976

Library   AV Department

Daniel Gore   Duane Vigeant
Jean Archibald   Jean Jackson
Dorothy Barnes
Wesley Boomgaarden
Pamela Cameron
Regina Crouse
Corinne Kellar
Sally McGowan
Lois Nelson
Ruth Newcomb
Rosemary Salscheider
Dorothy Ward

Student Staff

Students continue to account for about half the hours worked in the

library: a proportion several times greater than the typical. There are

reasons for that extraordinary apportionment. Since students are after

all what our work is all about, their heavy participation in it keeps the

rest of us from feeling alienated from the results of our labor: for the

results are right there in the middle of it. Teaching young people to

work in fruitful cooperation with others is no less vital than teaching

them chemistry or Shakespeare. Learning to work that way is for college

students the indispensable rite of passage between adolescence and the re-

sponsibilities of adult life. The library is unusually well situated to

administer that rite, and we choose to do it as fully as may be.

Student hours worked in 1975/76 came to 19,728 for the library, plus

5,075 for its AV Department. Totals over a six-year period are:

Hours of Student Work

	Library	AV Department
1970/71	29,387 hours	No data
1971/72	22,622	6,685 hours
1972/73	22,245	7,118
1973/74	22,029	5,115
1974/75	18,985	5,455
1975/76	19,728	5,075

In the course of a year nearly ten percent of all students at Macalester will work for us. And at any one time probably a fourth of the students on campus will be present or past library workers. With that kind of participation in our work, students cannot and do not regard the library as an indifferent, uncaring, bureaucratic preserve. The library is not just made for them. It is made by them too, and we all prosper under that arrangement.

Recruiting large numbers of students each year for library assignments is a complicated and difficult task for the College's Personnel Department. Assignments must be made right at the outset of each semester, so the library will be properly staffed during all 101 hours it is open each week. Ms. Tanis Yonkers of the Personnel Department understands and appreciates the special urgency of our needs, and meets them with amazing, gratifying success.

III.   The 1975/76 Budget

Library (excluding AV)

The sum budgeted was $195,956; the net expenditure was $194,321.

Neither figure includes student help, which came to about $43,000. The

six-year record of expenditures (from College funds only) is as follows:

	Salaries	Acquisitions	Operations (Net)	Total Spent	Total Budgeted
1970/71	$149,638	$101,158	$13,463	$264,259	$292,500
1971/72	127,826	105,579	9,402	242,807	255,000
1972/73	121,137	123,163	8,400	252,700	253,000
1973/74	126,829	113,238	8,072	248,139	251,900
1974/75	124,572	94,773	5,599	224,944	242,030
1975/76	111,505	65,218	17,598	194,321	195,956
1976/77					225,347

Since 1970, college library budgets nationwide have increased about 50%.

If Macalester had followed national trends, our budget for 1976/77 would be

$440,000, or nearly double what in fact it is. Funding for the library is

about one-half the norm for first-rank colleges of similar size, a circum-

stance that may please some and alarm others. Certainly it is not an oc-

casion for complacency. With funding at such a relatively low level, it

would be a good thing for everyone periodically to consider what might be

done if the library had more money, then decide what ought to be done and

see if the money can be found to do it. Present budgets offer little scope

for improvements or expansion of library services.

Still they do happen, piecemeal and through unorthodox measures. In

1975/76 the library received $16,957 in income from various sources, of

which $7,000 was mandated to the College treasury. The balance was used to carpet various public areas of the building (for the first time in its 35 year life), to remedy some deficiencies in the design of the budget, and to restore funding to a restricted gift account which in illo tempore (the high and palmy days of yore) simply vanished from the records.

Library Budget 1975/76

Actual Expenditures (College Funds Only)

Salaries and Wages		$111,505
Acquisitions and Binding		65,218
Books	$41,502	
Periodicals	22,350	
Binding	1,366	
Other (Net; expenses less usable income)		17,598

Expenses

Supplies	$4,400
Telephone	146
Postage	509
Printing	727
Travel	45
Equipment Purchase	7,724
Equipment Repair	400
Photocopying	7,805
CLIC	2,042
Interloans	650
Restore Word Library Account	3,107
Total	$27,555

Income	Actual	Usable
Fines and fees	$9,022	$4,022
Photocopying	6,349	4,349
Other	1,586	1,586
Totals	$16,957	$9,957

Total expenditures:	$194,321
Budgeted Total:	$195,956

AV Department Budget

The net sum budgeted was $21,514: $16,014 for salaries and $4,400 for net operating expenses. The net sum expended was $20,077: $15,782 for salaries and $4,295 for net expenses. Income in the amount of $11,357 was credited against gross expenses. Much of that income is generated through the sale of AV equipment and supplies to students and faculty, the department acting as broker to obtain substantial discounts for Macalester people.

Significant additions during 1974/75 to the department's equipment inventory are the following:

Video camera	$850
Video mixers, etc.	1,931
16 mm projector	500
Cassette recorders (6)	240
Headsets (4)	90
Dry mount press	750
Type fonts	400
Adding machine	110
	$4,571

IV.   DEPARTMENTAL ACTIVITIES

Technical Services: Acquisitions

Total College expenditure on acquisitions (including binding) was
$65,218. An additional $3,918 was expended from a federal grant, $2,928
from an Urban Studies grant, and $6,987 from a private gift (of $15,000)
for the development of the Greats Collection. Value of books given to
the library and added to the collections is estimated at $2,100. The
total dollar value of acquisitions in 1975/76 comes to $81,151.

Value of acquisitions for each of the last six years is:

1970/71	1971/72	1972/73	1973/74	1974/75	1975/76
$108,658	$130,388	$134,469	$131,120	$104,588	$81,151

The steep reduction in acquisitions funding compelled the Faculty Library
Committee to re-assess departmental allocation patterns of previous years,
and develop a formula that would distribute scarce funds on the basis of
actual need, insofar as that could be measured. The formula was based primarily on two easily measured factors: departmental enrollment patterns,
and comparative rates of non-use of new books (FASTCATs) among subject
fields. While no one claimed the formula was perfect, neither did anyone
profess to have a better one, and the general effect appears to have been
satisfactory. Allocation percentages by department were as follows:

Anthropology	2.4%	English	7.3%	Mathematics	3.2%	Religion	2.0%
Art	2.6	French	2.4	Music	2.5	Russian	0.9
Biology	5.5	Geography	2.9	Philosophy	2.9	Sociology	3.4
Chemistry	5.5	Geology	1.6	Phy. Ed.	0.8	Spanish	1.4
Classics	1.2	German	1.9	Physics	2.7	Speech	1.4
Economics	4.9	History	7.3	Pol. Sci	5.8	Library	18.7
Education	2.2	Journalism	0.7	Psychology	5.8		

Actual expenditures by department are listed on the following page. Actual
distributions, for a variety of reasons, never exactly match allocation percentages.

Book and Periodical Expenditures 1975/76.

DIVISION	Expenditure by Division Books	Periodicals	Total
Social Sciences			
Geography	$1,509.21	$ 523.47	$2,032.68
Political Science	2,864.06	1,389.57	4,253.63
Psychology	2,465.33	2,217.47	4,682.80
Sociology & Anthropology	3,377.40	832.89	4,210.29
Totals	$10,216.00	$4,963.40	$15,179.40
Business and Economics	$1,448.87	$1,550.66	$2,999.53
Education	$1,326.84	$408.86	$1,735.70
Fine Arts			
Art	$894.33	$512.01	$1,406.34
Journalism	326.81	119.60	446.41
Music	1,433.47	108.32	1,541.79
Speech	374.60	288.03	662.63
Totals	$3,029.21	$1,027.96	$4,057.17
Humanities			
Classics	$815.33	$147.80	$963.13
English	5,258.22	762.76	6,020.98
Foreign Languages			
French	1,075.24	215.05	1,290.29
German	1,287.52	389.55	1,677.07
Russian	429.01	235.77	664.78
Spanish	327.44	168.74	496.18
History	4,569.12	241.99	4,811.11
Philosophy	1,305.65	596.64	1,902.29
Religion	1,380.71	244.13	1,624.84
Totals	$16,448.24	$3,002.43	$19,450.67
Physical Education	$443.84	$79.04	$522.88
Science & Mathematics			
Biology	$1,255.99	$2,570.21	$3,826.20
Chemistry	1,278.47	1,831.08	3,109.55
Geology	449.27	736.11	1,185.38
Mathematics	662.30	1,520.14	2,182.44
Physics	517.38	1,108.38	1,625.76
Totals	$4,163.41	$7,765.92	$11,929.33
Library & Miscellaneous	$8,343.25	$3,552.70	$11,895.95
Grand Totals	$45,419.66	$22,350.97	$67,770.63

Duplication Program

Begun in 1973/74 to improve the availability rate of books in high demand, the program was continued systematically in 1975/76. An analysis of copies acquired by major subject groupings appears below. (The figures for 1973/74 represent only about six months' activity, since the program was started up in mid-year.) It appears from these data that we are fast approaching the saturation point for provision of high-demand copies, and no more than several hundred added copies may need to be acquired each year hereafter.

Subject	1973/74	1974/75	1975/76
Philosophy	66	62	20
Psychology	64	84	59
Eastern religions, myth	38	30	15
Christianity	12	16	3
Civilization	3	7	
History	95	109	44
Geography	4	4	3
Anthropology	6	14	5
Sports	–	6	3
Economics	17	40	17
Sociology	84	123	51
Politics	26	49	14
Law	7	13	4
Education	23	20	17
Music	10	15	11
Art	19	48	17
Linguisitics	4	12	4
Classics	21	7	2
Misc. Languages	7	8	6
Russian literature	11	9	6
Speech, theatre, criticism	26	28	10
French literature	30	38	13
English literature	100	83	37
American literature	166	104	56
German literature	12	27	12
Misc. novels	20	19	11
Sciences	17	60	27
Photography	10	28	4
Children's books		3	1
FASTCATs		48	25
	898 vols.	1,114 vols.	497 vols.

Gifts and Grants

The Greats Collection, described in last year's Annual Report (pp. 14-18), is being formed with a gift of $15,000 made to the Library by two anonymous patrons of the liberal arts. A nucleus collection of about a thousand volumes was acquired in the summer of 1976. When complete the collection will number something in excess of two thousand volumes. The initial selections were made by library staff in consultation with the patrons of the Collection, who welcome additional recommendations for its continuing enlargement. The Greats Collection is placed in wooden bookcases in the south wing reading room, which has been carpeted and handsomely furnished as a special inducement for young readers to study in the presence of the world's great authors. Fine reading editions are being sought for each author represented, a tedious task in an era when many publishers have lost all concern for books as beautiful artifacts. As time and opportunity permit, certain copies will be replaced by better editions. Donations from private collectors of fine editions would be especially welcome.

During 1975/76 the library received the final allotment of $2,928 from the Urban Affairs Advisory Committee of the Associated Colleges of the Twin Cities. (A similar sum was expended in 1974/75.) About $1,500 of this grant was used to purchase five films recommended by the Sociology and Geography departments, and the remainder of the allotment was devoted to improving the library's collection of books and maps dealing with urban affairs. Several very expensive and desirable atlases were acquired through this fund.

An HEW grant of $3918 was applied to the general purchase of books in all subject areas.

Collection Statistics

During the year 7,143 volumes (or other units) were added, and 2,212 volumes of outdated editions and unused duplicates were withdrawn. Net increase was thus 4,931 volumes, bringing the total collection size to 269,909 items. This is about double the number generally found at similar colleges. It is also half or less what you will find in the libraries of Amherst, Bowdoin, Smith, Swarthmore, Trinity, Vassar, Wellesley, and Wesleyan. We do not suffer so much from that adverse comparison now as we might have in past decades, because people are coming to realize that what bulks largest in a large library is not wisdom.

"I have taken all learning to be my province," said Sir Francis Bacon; caught a bad cold late in life through the zealousness of his researches and died shortly afterwards, the first martyr to his own Experimental Method. "At the end of March, 1626, being near Highgate on a snowy day," states the Dictionary of National Biography, "he left his coach to collect snow with which he meant to stuff a fowl in order to observe the effect of cold on the preservation of its flesh. In so doing he caught a chill;" the end of the tale is already told. Librarians, though more modest in utterance than Sir Francis, have in fact staked out for themselves a province vastly larger than his, and in some ways more interesting too. For we have taken not only all learning to be our province, but all ignorance too, and many other things besides, such as folly, beauty, falsehood, outrage, malice, the whole panorama of cosmic disorder and confusion that eventually finds its way to the shelves of a library. Like Sir Francis at the latter end of his researches, librarians--and those who support their labors-- are finding their province getting chilly too, as its continuing expansion brings continually smaller benefits.

We offer it as an axiom that the accumulation of recorded error proceeds at about the pace at which we discover new knowledge, and that the
size of our libraries testifies as much to the magnitude of our ignorance
as of our learning. We do not wish it otherwise. Man is a creature so
readily disposed to erect imposing monuments commemorative of his imagined
grandeur, he needs large libraries to remind him of his real and imposing
ignorance. The question is, How large? As the library grows, its proportion of durable knowledge and wisdom shrinks--a dilemma that prompts second
thoughts when we celebrate the stupendous size of our libraries.

While we cannot gauge the intrinsic worth of the library's holdings--
there are books in it we have not yet read--we can offer the following
count of what is in the library, or was when the counting was done:

Category	Volumes (or units) Added 1975/76	Total Resources Sept. 1, 1976
Books	5,201	226,825
Bound Periodicals and Abstracts	1,425	29,760
Newspaper and Periodical Indexes	9	376
Microfilm Reels	177	4,626
Microfiche		2,410
Records and Tapes	331	5,912
Total:	7,143	269,909
Book Withdrawals:	2,212	
Net Increase:	4,931	

Subscriptions in Force September 1, 1976

Newspapers	44
Periodicals	819
Other Serials	225
	1,088

Technical Services: Cataloging

Cataloging statistics usually mean nothing at all to anyone except catalogers--and those who pay for their services, who regularly express perplexity and dismay when they learn that in academic libraries the cost of cataloging a book usually runs ten dollars or more. At Macalester the figure is around two dollars, which makes a magnificent difference in the annual operating costs of the library.

Everyone understands the frustrating effect of prolonged delays in getting new books cataloged, delays that typically average three to six months. New books are usually cataloged in a few days at Macalester. The speed and economy of the process here are partly a result of system design, and very much a result of the excellent work that has been done day by day, for many years now, by our sole cataloger, Mrs. Ruth Newcomb, her assistant Mrs. Lois Nelson, and the students who work with them. While their work is easily summarized in numbers, the numbers tell nothing of its effects, which bring large benefits to everyone who uses this library.

Cataloging Statistics, 1975/76

Books or other items cataloged:	8,356
Revised or reclassed:	347
Withdrawn from collections:	2,212
Total:	10,915

Circulation Department

Total recorded loans for the year were 76,844, apparently the same as the previous year. Actually there was a drop of about 3,600 loans. In spring of 1976 we began counting and recording (for the first time) items that returned from loan without having first been formally borrowed. Between then and August, 3,622 uncharged books returned to the library, indi-

cating that about one book in seven leaves the library informally. Presumably these are fairly long term loans, which subvert our systematic
efforts to make wanted books readily available. Informal loans of that
magnitude also point to an uncomfortable vulnerability to theft, which
probably increased at summer's end when the library at St. Thomas installed
electronic exit controls, leaving us the only library in the neighborhood
without them. (St. Catherine's made an installation several years ago.)
Taking those things into account we recommended to the College that electronic exit control equipment be installed, and at this writing it has
been in place about a week.

Why circulation fell five percent from the previous year is not
easily explained. Categories in which there were decreases are General
Loans (8.8%), FASTCATs (8.4%), Curriculum Lab (25.5%), and Periodicals
(35%). Offsetting these were significant increases in Reserves (25%), and
Olin (33%). John D. Rockefeller's classic prediction of stock market
activity fits precisely the phenomenon of library circulation: It will
fluctuate. So will the accuracy of record-keeping, and at the five percent level one cannot be sure of observing a change in reality or in accuracy of records.

There is no doubt, however, that Macalester students make vigorous
use of their library. Per-capita use rates are about double those in the
other CLIC libraries, and the library is regularly a scene of intense
scholarly activity.

People who borrow library books (myself among them) do not much like
to return them. Were the case otherwise--or were there not often another
borrower waiting for a wanted book to be returned--we could spare ourselves

the enormous effort of persuading the tardy borrower to get that book
back. Some 13,000 notices were mailed out last year to induce the return of overdue books. As a further inducement, fines totalling $9,000
were assessed, a large plump sum that falls short of covering the considerable expense involved in prompting the dilatory scholar to do his duty.
The system works well enough, but we would as soon be rid of it as taxes
if we could.

At the Reserve Desk, music and spoken-word cassettes continue to be
actively used, the combined year's loans being 4,367. Music cassettes
circulate an average of six times per year; spoken-word, twice a year.
(Books in the general collection circulate at the rate of once each six
years.) The Reserve Desk also lends headphones to people who want to use
the library's listening equipment. There have been about ten thousand such
loans since the service began several years ago, and only one set of headphones has been lost. We are reporting that fact to Guinness's.

Running a reserve operation is a more complicated matter than it may
appear. Each year thousands of items are placed on reserve, while thousands
of others are removed, and alacrity is ever the watchword, so books and articles and tapes will be available early each semester when the lineup of
questing students begins. Faculty cooperation has been excellent, and indispensable to the cause of swiftness in the periodic revision of holdings.
Mrs. Corinne Kellar, for some years now the supervisor of the Reserve Desk,
presides over that turbulent scene with unflappable calm, lending out twice
ten-thousand pieces of College property every year, and getting the same
number back too. Much more than books and articles and cassettes are on
reserve at the Reserve Desk: patience and energy and ability are there too,
but the statistics don't show that at all.

You, gentle reader--and all our other gentle readers--probably have
no very accurate notion of what it is like working at a library's public
service desk and dealing with the miscellaneous ungentle readers who
drop in on us. Edmund Pearson's newspaper column "The Librarian,"
though written sixty years ago, gives a remarkably exact portrayal of how
things are even in our tranquil era:

A Man. "Would you mind telling me why there should be a statue of
Benjamin Franklin in front of this library?"
    Miss A. (the desk attendant) "I do not know for sure, but Franklin
was interested in libraries in Philadelphia, was he not?"
    The Man. "Yes, yes, in Philadelphia, of course. But what has that got
to do with us? Why should he have a statue here? Come, why should he?"
    Miss A. "Well, he was a great American, was he not; ambassador to
France, and all that . . .?"
    The Man. "Just what has that got to do with this library?"

(Miss A. is still in doubt whether The Man knows the answer to his rid-
dle, and is merely trying it on her, or whether he is a genuine seeker of
information. She was not what could be called directly responsible for the
placing of the Franklin statue in front of the library--in fact she was not
consulted about the matter at all. But her present inquisitor seems determined to make her justify its existence.)

    The Man. "Just why should there be a statue of Franklin in front of
this library--that's all I want to know!" (His bearing would seem to add--
"and I intend to stand right in this spot until I find out.")
    Miss A. (smiling) "I guess I have told you all the reasons I have to
account for its being there."
    The Man. "Reasons? You haven't given any good reasons!"
    Miss A. "They're all I have. The statue was presented to the library
by a former resident, I think, and the trustees accepted it."
    The Man. "But why Franklin--tell me that, please!" (as if to say,
"I dare you to do it!")
    Miss A. "I have already told you all I know about it." (She is find-
ing the process of charging books and attending to wants of other readers
somewhat difficult during this cross-examination. But The Man is quite
unwearied.)
    The Man. "Why shouldn't it have been Washington, or anyone else?"
    Miss A. "I really do not know, sir. The trustees accepted it, and
they probably could tell you about it."
    The Man (in great contempt) "The trustees!" (He makes a noise like
the opening of a soda-water bottle to express his opinion of the trustees,
and then tries to engage Miss B. in conversation on the subject of the
offending statue. She sees him coming, however, and hurries to the other
end of the desk, where she seeks to placate a near-sighted and very irritable clergyman. The clergyman, it appears, has taken home the wrong book.)

Ms. Dorothy Ward and Ms. Sally McGowan of our circulation staff are
equally diplomatic in dealing with the hard cases who come along, and
manage to get a lot of useful work done in between too. But it is not
what you would call a quiet life.

Shelving Capacity of the Libraries

An inventory of shelving was taken in August 1973 and recorded in the 1972/73 Annual Report. No shelving has been added at least since 1970, but one mile of books has been. This creates a problem, not insoluble, as there is still room in Weyerhaeuser and storage to hang another half-mile of shelving, holding another 20,000 books.

The estimated shelving situation as of September 1976 is this:

Building	Shelf Ft.	Book Ft.	Load Factor
Weyerhaeuser	26,733	20,600	77%
Olin	1,479	1,350	91%
Storage	6,930	4,500	65%
	35,142	26,400	

Assuming that the net growth of collections has levelled off at five or six thousand volumes per year, the additional shelving will enable the library to accommodate continuing acquisitions perhaps through 1982. Around that year the College must then either provide more building capacity or begin removing volumes from on-campus facilities at the same rate new ones are acquired.

The Olin shelving crunch was relieved somewhat by removing to storage certain journal volumes, following criteria recommended by the Olin science departments. Additional removals will probably be required in academic year 1977/78, as the collection continues to grow.

Periodicals

Subscription statistics as of August 31 for each of the last five fiscal years are:

	1971/72	1972/73	1973/74	1974/75	1975/76
Subscriptions added (previous 12 months)	38	21	49	65	23
Subscriptions dropped	178	73	153	67	92
Subscriptions in force	1,055	1,003	899	897	828
Paid			748	749	682
Gift			151	148	146

During the year the staff bound 1,245 new journal volumes; added missing issues to 96 previously bound volumes; and performed miscellaneous repairs to 131 others. Total cost to the College (including student help) for these binding operations was about $2,500. A commercial binder would charge about $10,000 for the same work, and the volumes would have been unavailable to readers for about two months longer than they are with the inhouse operation. Unlovely to look at, our home-bound volumes are functionally superior to commercial bindings which, when they wear out, cannot ordinarily be replaced, because a good bit of the inner margin was shaved off in the binding process. The bindings we use can be replaced any number of times because no material is shaved away. This becomes a major concern when journal volumes are repeatedly placed on a photocopier screen and the bindings damaged in the process.

Reference Department

This department is unusual in having no regular staff. Seven years ago there were three full-time professional positions. Today there are none. Reference assistance and interloan service are provided by assigning staff from other departments part-time, and employing student assistants. The arrangement is less than ideal, but works. A regularly assigned reference librarian could help faculty develop bibliographical instruction as part of their course offerings--a need that was cited in last year's North Central accreditation review.

Library staff regularly offer two courses in the use of libraries, "Introduction to Bibliography," taught by Mrs. Pamela Cameron, and "Methods of Research in Government Publications." The latter course, developed by Mrs. Jean Archibald, appears to be unique in undergraduate curricula. It has proved enduringly attractive to social sciences students, and is consistently well enrolled. Among other things students are required to write an extensive research paper using government documents as source material. I have read some of these papers and am vividly impressed by the breadth and solidity of the research work students are doing under Mrs. Archibald's supervision. These papers demonstrate convincingly what a vast improvement results when students are systematically taught how to carry out bibliographical research, instead of being merely told to do it.

In addition to course offerings and reference service, staff conduct numerous building tours at the beginning of the school year and offer special sessions of bibliographical instruction for those classes whose professors request it. None of these things is reducible to statistics. Judgment and observation are the sole measures, and jointly they confirm that we have a strong and effective reference program though we have no reference staff.

Interlibrary Loan Services

Some students asked me the other day if the sizeable number of loans we obtain from other libraries does not signal some strong weaknesses in our own collections? The question is plausible but the answer is no, with an explanation. The several thousand items we borrow from other libraries each year are in fact drawn from a total pool of about four million books. If we owned all of them (which a capital outlay of a hundred million dollars would allow us to do) then our interloan demands would fall to zero, or nearly so. Interloan is clearly the more economic strategy to follow, so long as the material is not likely to be wanted again and again. If it is then we buy it, if it is still in print.

In 1975/76 our patrons asked for 3,743 items on interloan, half of them books and the other half journal articles. Of these we were able to deliver 3,126, for a batting average of 84%. From other libraries we received requests for 3,085 items and delivered 2,172, or 70%. Just a decade ago such levels of interloan activity were unheard of--and unimaginable--in college libraries, which typically would receive no more than a few hundred interloans (all for the faculty), and deliver much fewer than that to other libraries. Inter-loan--rather than continual staggering increases in collection size--has now gained wide acceptance as the only practical way of coping with a bibliographical universe consisting of tens of millions of books (to which a half million new ones are added each year) and several hundred thousand journals currently in publication.

The existence of a swift and reliable interloan service enables us to make some rough approximations of overall library effectiveness. When people have come to know, as they generally do at Macalester, that items not available here can usually be obtained for them elsewhwere in a few days, then one may (with some reservations) assume that virtually everything that is strongly desired, but not available locally, will be asked for on interloan. Adding the year's interloan requests of 3,743 to the 76,844 loans made from our own collections indicates a total of 80,587 items that were wanted badly enough for people to search for them in the library and then ask for them on interloan if they weren't found. Of those 80,587 strongly wanted items, 79,970, or 99%, were actually provided: 3,126 through interloan, and 76,844 from our own collections.

No, we don't believe for a minute that the library is meeting 99% of its clientele's desires. No institution functions at anywhere near that level of human satisfaction. But of those desires that are strong enough that the patron will come to the library and even make a special request, if need be, to have them filled, virtually all are satisfied.

Library effectiveness can only be measured in terms of what is agreed upon as a reasonable kind of service provision. If one believes a library should provide home delivery of everything that is wanted, then our effectiveness is right at zero. If one believes that everything that is wanted should be immediately available to the person who seeks it in the library, whether the desire be casual or profound, durable or transient, then our effectiveness is probably around the seventy percent level. That is a hard thing to measure. But if one agrees that the proper measure is the effectiveness in delivering what is strongly and durably desired, then it appears we are doing very well indeed.

Macalester and CLIC

CLIC is well known on campus as the miraculous source of our heavily used interloan service. But few people have any knowledge of how and why it came into being, how it is funded, or what its future prospects may be. CLIC has reached a stage of development when significant changes will shortly occur in its mode of operations and in its sources of funding. Everyone assumes or hopes the changes will be beneficial, but this will not be known for some time. The changes are being initiated by the Hill Library, which has been the principal support for the consortium's inter- loan services. Since these changes may have significant impact on those who use the interloan service at Macalester, as well as the college bud- get, I will review here briefly the history of our involvement with CLIC, and outline the prospects for the near future.

CLIC (Cooperating Libraries in Consortium) is a group of eight Twin Cities libraries legally incorporated in 1969. The member libraries are those of Augsburg College, The College of St. Catherine, The College of St. Thomas, Bethel College, Concordia College, Hamline University, and Macalester College; and the Jerome J. Hill Reference Library, a private li- brary located in downtown St. Paul. As stated in its Articles of Incorpor- ation, the purpose of the Consortium is

> (1) To serve as a means and entity for the accomplishment of joint or cooperating efforts by its members. (2) To provide an entity which can receive, use, and dispense potentially avail- able funds which will support and encourage programs operated by cooperating libraries and librarians. (3) To improve through these efforts both individual and combined library resources and services.

The principal activity of CLIC since its incorporation has been the provision of interloan services to its members. Other forms of cooperation

have been explored from time to time (e.g. cooperative collection development) and significant sums of grant money have been obtained for joint
purchase of special resource materials, but the raison d'etre for the
Consortium has up to this time been the interloan program.

In 1969 the Hill Library Board engaged a consultant, Mr. Herman Henkle,
to study the Hill Library's services and recommend new programs for the Library to undertake. On January 20, 1970 the Board acted "to commit its
physical facilities and administrative organization to serve as headquarters
for the cooperative program of academic libraries" and to "devote its service resources to serving as the central reference services and switching
center for this group of libraries and their respective constituents."
The consultant's "Special Report to the Board of Trustees" of June 1, 1970
states that in effect "the potential of this decision was to establish the
James Jerome Hill Reference Library as the operating service center for a
true network of academic libraries, beginning with the CLIC group of libraries but expanding to embrace any other college or university libraries
that might become affiliated with the Consortium."

The consultant envisioned an elaborate program of central services
(interloan, acquisitions, processing, reference, storage), including the
possible relocation of the Hill Library on the University's St. Paul campus,
where it might additionally serve as the center of a computerized library
network serving a number of libraries around the state. But the interloan
program for the CLIC libraries is the one activity among those he recommended that ultimately became a reality.

A central union catalog, merging in one alphabet the holdings records
of all CLIC libraries, was necessary to the proper functioning of the pro-

posed interloan network, and on the recommendation of the consultant a
union catalog (in card format) was created at the Hill Library. The cost
of the union catalog was about $50,000, all of it borne by Hill. It be-
came operational in mid-1971, and the Hill Library also provided (as it
still does) from its own operating funds a staff to maintain the catalog
and to provide complete referral service for all interloan requests arising within CLIC. The exact cost of these services is known only by the
Hill Library, but is thought to run more than $50,000 per year.

The worth of the interloan program to the CLIC libraries and their
patrons is well attested by the magnitude of deliveries made. In fiscal
75/76 23,000 items were delivered, of which about half were books and the
other half photocopies of journal articles. Using national average cost
figures of six dollars for a library to send one item on interloan to
another library, the approximate monetary value of the interloan service
comes to about $140,000 per year. Direct costs to the CLIC libraries
(excluding Hill) are about $15,000 annually, comprising the annual member-
ship fees of about $2,000 that each library contributes to the operation
of the Consortium. Staff costs contributed by each library have never
been isolated, but probably amount to at least one FTE staff for each library. Without the Hill subsidy, it is clear that each library would have
to contribute a good deal more to support the direct costs of the program,
in addition to the indirect staff costs they presently bear.

CLIC and MINITEX

MINITEX is a state-wide interloan service located at the University
library and funded by direct appropriations from the legislature. Begun
in 1969 as a pilot project to provide interloans to selected academic

libraries outside the Twin Cities, it became in 1971 a regularly funded service to all Minnesota academic libraries and certain other public and special libraries as well. Participating libraries pay none of the direct operating costs of MINITEX, since they are paid by the state.

Why did CLIC libraries not obtain full MINITEX services when they became available to all academic libraries in 1971, and thus escape all of the direct costs of operating their own network? Briefly the answer is that the CLIC network, under Hill Library sponsorship and subsidy, was just becoming fully operational at the time (1971) when MINITEX services were being expanded to include all academic libraries in the state, and there was no compelling economic reason to shift to MINITEX since Hill was subsidizing the major expenses of the operation. Moreover, Hill Library had already invested substantially more than $50,000 in staff and other costs to begin the CLIC union catalog operation--an investment that would have been largely wasted had the CLIC libraries taken on the MINITEX service directly. Finally, MINITEX delivery would be somewhat slower (probably by several days) than delivery by CLIC courier.

MINITEX service is nonetheless partially provided to CLIC libraries at present. Loans that cannot be provided from CLIC resources are forwarded from the Hill referral center to MINITEX, and in the last fiscal year 6,350 loans were thus made to CLIC by MINITEX. At the same time CLIC provided to MINITEX a total of 5,032 items, for which no reimbursement was made, except for photocopy costs of ten cents per page. The monetary value of loans made by CLIC to MINITEX (using MINITEX's own operating cost of $2.00 per item) is thus about $10,000 per year. And since CLIC provides to its own libraries some 18,000 items per year that in the absence of CLIC would presumably be provided by MINITEX, it is reasonable to say that CLIC

relieves the MINITEX fiscal burden by about $36,000 per year, in addition
to providing to MINITEX deliveries worth about $10,000 per year, as noted
above.

The Computer-produced Microfilm Union Catalog

In 1974, on its own initiative, the Hill Library sought and obtained
funds from the Northwest Area Foundation to develop a computer-produced
microfilm union catalog of CLIC libraries' holdings. The project was endorsed by the CLIC directors with the understanding that the microfilm
union catalog (a copy of which could be placed in each CLIC library as a
possible substitute for its own card catalog) would be accepted only after
a trial use had proved it to be a satisfactory alternative not only to the
present union catalog on cards, but also to the card catalog in each of the
member libraries.

The potential advantages of the microfilm catalog are substantial, if
it lives up to expectations. It will enable a reader at any CLIC library
to determine what books are held in all CLIC libraries. It will permit the
economical revision of catalog records when the location status of a book
is changed--for example, when a book is transferred to on-campus storage,
or, looking into the future, if it should be removed to a cooperative storage
facility off campus. And if it proves to be an acceptable substitute to
each library's locally maintained card catalog, then the cost to each library of producing the microfilm union catalog may eventually be no more
than the present cost of producing its local card catalog.

A pilot version of the microfilm catalog became available for testing
in CLIC libraries in January 1977. A decision to accept or reject the new
format must be made within the ensuing twelve months.

If the catalog project fails, the CLIC board has been advised by the Hill Library director that Hill at that time might cease to operate the union card catalog and withdraw all its special support of the interloan operation. The CLIC Board has, however, received no indication from the Hill Library Board of any intention to withdraw its support from the program it advocated and sponsored beginning in 1969. But if that were done, CLIC would then have to consider the following options, and act very swiftly to prevent any interruption in an interloan service that has become a vital and indispensable part of each college's academic program:

(1) Assume the full operating costs of the union catalog, and the referral and delivery services. The additional cost to each library on an even-share basis would be around $8,000 per year, on top of the current average membership assessment of about $2,000. Each library would thus pay about $10,000 a year for interloan services that all other academic libraries in the state obtain free from MINITEX.

(2) Apply to MINITEX for full interloan service.

(3) Seek special state subsidies for CLIC interloan service, in lieu of full MINITEX service: an option that might involve unacceptable delays and interruption in service.

If however a decision is reached by the CLIC Board to accept the microfilm catalog at the conclusion of the test period, certain other

economic consequences must be faced. Total annual additional cost of producing the microfilm catalog is estimated to be around $50,000, or about
$6,000 to each library on an even-share basis. Shifting from a card to a
microfilm catalog may enable a library to eliminate one staff position in
its processing department, thus releasing sufficient salary money to cover
the outside production costs of the microfilm catalog. But that may not
be the case.

Further, if the microfilm catalog be accepted, the Hill Library director
has indicated that Hill will even so withdraw some of its present support
from the interloan referral and delivery service, though how much has not
been said. Again, CLIC has received no communication on this matter from
the Hill Library Board, which inaugurated the service and, at that time
communicated its intentions quite promptly and fully to the CLIC colleges.

Assuming the worst possible case for contingency planning purposes,
Hill might withdraw all support for interloan delivery and referral services, leaving the CLIC libraries to fund them completely. The cost might
run around $20,000 per year, or roughly $3,000 per library. Each library
might then expect to bear a total additional expense of $9,000 in the
first year of the microfilm union catalog's operation ($6,000 for catalog
production, $3,000 for interloan services) but less in subsequent years if,
as noted above, the microfilm catalog yielded some reduction in staff costs
at the local library.

The present outlook is neither bright nor gloomy, only dim. In another
twelve months the situation will be much better focused and the range of
available choices much better defined. All that can be confidently predicted at this writing is that the method of providing interloan services may
change in 1978.

Audio-Visual Department

Under the genial supervision of Mr. Buzz Vigeant, who came to us as a wizard technician in 1974 and then miraculously metamorphosed into a manager, this department has flourished like a green bay tree. Through many years of frequent changes in department heads, the saving element of continuity in the department has been Mrs. Jean Jackson, who has been its secretary since 1964, but actually functioning as its assistant manager. Present staffing, though scant in numbers, provides an excellent combination of technical, managerial, and operational skills and experience, and the department's services have been thereby much improved.

Statistics show equipment use up 10% and production services up a whopping 50% from the previous year. Our video tape system was improved through the modification of existing equipment and purchase of a new video camera. This allowed us to service a mass-media course for the Speech Department in addition to providing normal video services.

We offered for the first time a passport photo service, which was well received. The department's darkroom provided most of the processing work for Spotlite, the campus pictorial directory. Staff also provided major support (both equipment and training) for a Super 8 film course, and for a photo-journalism course.

Comparative data on college audio-visual services do not exist, so it is hard to gauge the relative standing of one's own program. Although one commonly finds far more extensive AV programs in the public schools than we have here, I have found in all the other colleges I visit much less attention given to AV than we give it at Macalester. Our situation seems to lie about mid-way between two extremes, satisfying at least the ancient

Greek counsel "Nothing in excess," however it may be viewed by conflict-

ing pedagogical factions.

AV Loans and Services

Equipment Loans	1972/73	1973/74	1974/75	1975/76
Motion Picture Projectors	920	921	828	916
Slide Projectors	524	317	362	425
Filmstrip Projectors	160	59	70	50
Overhead Projectors	284	146	106	107
Opaque Projectors	147	101	76	40
Screens	263	129	120	131
Tape Recorders	1,143	571	545	571
Phonographs	150	80	188	114
Cameras	184	47	64	94
VTR Recording/PB	179	96	167	178
Public Address Systems	152	42	30	90
	4,015	2,509	2,556	2,805

Services

	1972/73	1973/74	1974/75	1975/76
Our Films Used	475	505	513	532
Film Rentals	305	319	187	297
Slides and b/w Prints	3,327	2,889	1,971	2,849
Rolls Film Sold	939	1,533	1,381	1,149
Tapes - Sold and Dubbed	1,121	1,080	1,117	1,137
Transparencies	856	494	695	509
Ditto Masters	1,869	3,530	2,638	3,058
Signs	470	380	113	547
Civilisation bookings				104
"Art of U.S." slides				2,370
Tapes recorded				443
	9,362	10,730	8,615	12,995

V. BUILDINGS

Since a new building remains at best some years away, we sought and
found some modest special funding to begin a piecemeal program of making
Weyerhaeuser a more comfortable, attractive, and quiet place to study in.
During the summer carpet was laid in part of the south wing, the lobby,
and a second floor area to which the children's collection was removed.
A room opening off the lobby was vacated by the Acquisitions staff, thus
freeing up about 700 square feet of prime building space for public use.
That room was also carpeted, and was destined to become the new (and probably permanent) location of the Reserve Desk, as well as the microfilm
collections. As more areas are carpeted, the building will gain a special
aura of comfort and civility that has been long and earnestly desired. The
quietest libraries are always those with carpeted reading rooms; the more
we have the quieter and more appealing this aging building will become.

Moving the children's collection upstairs to a carpeted area allows
children and others to talk and cavort at will, leaving older students in
the main reading room (from which it was removed) undisturbed by the un-
inhibited frolics of their juniors. Adjacent to the new location is a
large seminar room (recently carpeted) where, among other uses, courses
in children's literature can be most conveniently offered.

In the spring of 1976, students asked the Faculty Library Committee
to designate for student use (unassigned) at least four of the second-floor
studies, all of which had been assigned, ab origine, for faculty use only.
The Committee complied, the faculty cooperated, and the studies have been
actively used since they first became available to students. With enrollment down by a fourth from the 2,100 students Macalester had in 1970, and

with the provision of both more and better study accommodations, the
Weyerhaeuser Library, though seven years older than it was then, is now
a much better place for students to work in. Their general and keen
appreciation of that fact is manifest to our staff who work in close
daily association with students.

Last night there was a heavy snow, and the only walks entirely cleared
by noon were those around the Library. Mr. Bill Florek, our custodian for
many years, is undaunted by Minnesota snowfall, but maintains that machines
are and holds them in high disdain for their slow progress against the snow.
The observable facts justify his position. What is more, though scientists
always fail in their attempts to make a perpetual motion machine, Mr.
Florek has achieved perpetual motion in himself, to which the high polish
he keeps on this large old building bears full and gratifying witness.

Mr. Jim Rognlie's maintenance crew always give us good service, and
good naturedly too, and we are grateful for those things, especially considering how few people he has to look after so many buildings. If things
don't always get done exactly when we want them, we understand about that
too. We need extra time ourselves to deliver hard-to-get books, and sometimes we can't deliver at all. Mr. Rognlie's men always do.

VI. STAFF ACTIVITIES

Mrs. Jean Archibald taught the course "Methods of Research in Government Publications" in the fall and spring semesters. She chaired a panel
discussion on government documents at a meeting of the Minnesota Library
Association on November 14, 1975, and attended a U. S. Bureau of the Census
workshop in Mankato, March 18-19, 1976. She participated in the institute

"The Mythic Image: Mythology, Folklore, and Libraries" in Minneapolis on April 1-2.

Mrs. Pamela Cameron taught the course "Introduction to Bibliography" in the spring semester. She attended the "Children's Book Showcase" at St. Catherine's in April, and a reference workshop at St. Thomas's in June.

Mr. Gore served as a director of CLIC and was named president for fiscal 1976/77. He spent three fine spring days in Atlanta as Visiting Scholar at the Georgia Universities Center, presenting papers and consulting with the librarians of Georgia Tech, Emory, the University of Georgia, and Atlanta University. He also spent a lot of time in 1975/76 doing nothing at all but recovering from back surgery. The Library lost not an inch of ground in the process, since the staff are all mature, able people who know perfectly well what needs doing, and get it done too regardless of who may be on the binnacle list from time to time.

Items published or presented by Mr. Gore during the year are these:

"The Destruction of the Tower of Babel," Catholic Library World, Vol. 47, (Sept., 1975), 52-53.

"The View from the Tower of Babel," Library Journal, Sept. 15, 1975, pp. 1599-1605.

"Zero Growth: When Is NOT-Enough Enough? A Symposium," Journal of Academic Librarianship, Vol. 1, No. 5 (Nov. 1975), 4-11.

Farewell to Alexandria: Solutions to Space, Growth, and Performance Problems of Libraries, ed. Daniel Gore. Westport, Conn.: Greenwood Press, 1976. 180 pp.

"Farewell to Alexandria: The Theory of the No-Growth, High-Performance Library," in Farewell to Alexandria (Greenwood Press, 1976), pp. 164-180.
"Going Out of Bibliographical Control: A theory of Library Organization Based on Human Principles," paper presented to the General Session of the Louisiana Library Association Annual Conference, Lafayette, La., March 31, 1976; and to the faculty of Knox College, Galesburg, Ill., April 22, 1976.

"Some Things Your Boss Never Told You About Library Management," paper
presented to the Academic Section of the Louisiana Library
Association, Lafayette, La., April 1, 1976; to the Emory University
Graduate Library School, April 6, 1976; to the University of Georgia
(Athens) Library Staff, April 8, 1976; and to the General Session of
the 11th Annual Community College Learning Resources Conference,
Belleville, Ill., April 20, 1976. 16 pp.

Mrs. Rosemary Salscheider attended the "Annual Book Program" at the

University of Minnesota, October 21, 1975.

Mr. Buzz Vigeant attended a video workshop in Hibbing, a video hard-

ware conference in St. Cloud, and toured the video and language labs of

Winona State College.

VII. PROBLEMS NEAR AND FAR

Funds for 3,000 linear feet of additional shelving have been requested

for fiscal 1977/78. That is about all the stack areas can accommodate.

When all shelves are maximally loaded, probably around 1982, one of several

solutions to the problem of continued growth should by that time have been

carried out:

Construction of a new building;

Addition to the present building;

Conversion of stack areas to compact shelving capable of holding

    twice the present collection;

Maintaining collection size at constant volume through systematic

    withdrawal of long unused volumes.

Since the proper exercise of any of these options will require serious

study, wide debate, and (for all but the last option) provision of substan-

tial capital funding, the planning effort should begin soon and a decision

should be taken by the end of fiscal 1977/78 as to which of the several courses open to it the College will follow.

Since Weyerhaeuser will continue to be used for at least another five
years, further modest refurbishments can greatly enhance its study areas.
Carpeting the south wing has solved the noise problem there. That large
area is now quiet as a tomb in Egypt before the Egyptologists arrived.
But we have thereby achieved a congestion problem. The two other large
study rooms (Reference and Periodicals) have become so comparatively un-
attractive, lacking carpets, everyone avoids them, preferring the carpeted
congestion of the south wing. The Reference and Periodical rooms should
be carpeted soon to produce more balanced use of the building.

Libraries have been experimenting with computerized circulation systems
for at least a decade. Erratic and very costly to operate in the experimental years, these systems are presently being commercially marketed by
several vendors, and costs and performance are both guaranteed, the latter
high and the former, well, modest. But still more costly than our existing
microfilm system. Computerized systems can however perform a number of
vital inventory control functions that a manual system cannot, such as identifying automatically high-demand titles that should be duplicated, and unused titles that should be sent to storage or elsewhere. They can also produce useful data regarding the distribution of demand across subject areas,
as a guide for current acquisitions practice. A CLIC task force is presently exploring the desirability of installing a computerized circulation
system that will interconnect all eight member libraries. Should they recommend favorably, the potential benefits should induce Macalester to participate. If the recommendation is unfavorable for a consortium-wide system,
then Macalester should proceed with its own local system as soon as the fund-

ing is available.

While the distinctly low level of funding for the library has not yet caused problems of much consequence, increases at least on the order of inflationary rates will have to be routinely made hereafter to maintain the present level and quality of service. Any expansion or significant improvements in the library program will require support beyond the inflation increment.

Libraries of course always have problems. In libraries that have not yet departed from traditional practices, the problems have attained distress status. Macalester, having broken with tradition seven years ago, today has a library relatively free of problems, and those that remain serve the useful purpose of keeping our imagination fresh and lively.

(Calligraphy and illustrations by
Judith Anne Duncan)

Index

Compiled by library science students at California State University, Fullerton, under the supervision of Michael and Doris Sadoski.

ABOUT THE AUTHOR

Daniel Gore is Library Director at Macalester College in St. Paul, Minnesota. His previous library experiences were at Western Michigan University, McMurry College, University of North Carolina at Asheville, New York Public Library, and Duke University. Among his earlier publications are *Farewell to Alexandria* (Greenwood Press, 1976).